Range Wars

RANGE WARS

THE ENVIRONMENTAL CONTEST
FOR WHITE SANDS MISSILE RANGE

Ryan H. Edgington

UNIVERSITY OF NEBRASKA PRESS
LINCOLN AND LONDON

Portions of this book have previously appeared in
"The Safari of the Southwest: Hunting, Science,
and the African Oryx on White Sands Missile
Range, New Mexico, 1969–2006," *Western Histori-
cal Quarterly* 40 (Winter 2009): 469–91 (copyright
by the Western History Association; reprinted
by permission); "Fragmented Histories: Science,
Environment, and Monument Building at the Trinity
Site, 1945–1995," in *Militarized Landscapes: From
Gettysburg to Salisbury Plain*, edited by Chris Pearson,
Peter Coates, and Tim Cole (London: Continuum,
2010), 189–207; and "An 'All-Seeing-Flying-Eye': V-2
Rockets and the Promises of Earth Photography,"
History and Technology 28 (September 2012): 363–71.

Library of Congress Cataloging-in-Publication Data
Edgington, Ryan H.
Range wars: the environmental contest for White
Sands Missile Range / Ryan H. Edgington.
pages   cm
Includes bibliographical references and index.
ISBN 978-0-8032-3844-2 (hardback: alk. paper)
ISBN 978-0-8032-5535-7 (paperback: alk. paper)
ISBN 978-0-8032-5562-3 (PDF)
ISBN 978-0-8032-5563-0 (ePub)
ISBN 978-0-8032-5564-7 (mobi) 1. White Sands Mis-
sile Range (N.M.)—Environmental conditions.
2. White Sands Missile Range (N.M.)—History.
3. Land use—Environmental aspects—New
Mexico—White Sands Missile Range—History.
4. Land use—Political aspects—New Mexico—
White Sands Missile Range—History. 5. Social
conflict—New Mexico—White Sands Missile
Range—History. 6. Nuclear weapons—Testing—
Environmental aspects—New Mexico—White
Sands Missile Range—History. 7. Landscape
protection—New Mexico—White Sands Missile
Range—History. 8. Environmental policy—United
States—History. 9. United States—Military
policy. 10. Militarism—Environmental
aspects—West (U.S.)—History. I. Title.
GE155.N6E34 2014
304.209789'6—dc23   2013048673

Set in Chaparral by Renni Johnson.
Designed by N. Putens.

For Angelica

Contents

List of Illustrations   ix

Acknowledgments   xi

Introduction   1

1 Seeds of Discontent   15

2 Atomic Attractions   53

3 Boundaries   83

4 A Consumer's Landscape   118

5 Range Wars   144

6 Natural Security States   171

Conclusion   199

Notes   205

Bibliography   237

Index   257

Illustrations

FIGURES

1 Proposed Bombing Range map   39

2 Trinity explosion, 1945   60

3 Trinity crater, 1945   61

4 Members of the Manhattan
   Engineer District in protective
   clothing   63

5 Rada cows, 1945   65

6 Trinity monument   79

7 "V-2 Rocket-Eye View from
   60 Miles Up," 1948   88

8 Felipe Chavez-Garcia holding
   a piece of a downed Pershing
   missile, 1967   107

9 An oryx on White Sands
   Missile Range   120

10 Oryx trophy, Tesuque,
New Mexico   129

11 Dave McDonald with a
member of the White Sands
Missile Range Public Affairs
Office, n.d.   145

12 Mexican gray wolf   172

13 Minor Scale explosion,
White Sands Missile Range,
June 1985   202

MAPS

1 White Sands Missile Range
and Greater New Mexico   4

2 The White Sands Region,
ca. 1946   28

3 The Reach of White Sands
Missile Range   104

Acknowledgments

I have spent more than nine years researching and writing this book. I am indebted to many colleagues, friends, and family members. If for no other reason the process of writing is rewarding because of the people you meet and work with along the way. I have had the opportunity of sharing this project with advisers and colleagues who commented on just a chapter or read the manuscript in its entirety. *Range Wars* started as a dissertation at Temple University, but it first began as an idea. I owe a huge debt of gratitude to the late historians Timothy Moy and Ferenc Szasz for their guidance while I was both an undergraduate and graduate student at the University of New Mexico.

Once in Philadelphia, I had the opportunity to work with other talented historians. Richard Immerman and Beth Bailey offered thoughtful comments on placing my story within the context of the Cold War. David Farber, who took me under his wing as an undergraduate, has long taught me to think like a good historian. His comments on this project (and his friendship) proved invaluable. Louis Warren offered kind criticism on how to make my dissertation a good environmental history of the American West. Finally, I cannot thank Drew Isenberg enough for his advice as I worked through research, writing, and, in the process, becoming a historian. My successes are a testament to the enthusiastic support he gives to all of his graduate students.

Over the years I have given conference papers and have talked to colleagues informally about my book project. Several of them deserve recognition: Gretchen Heefner, Lincoln Bramwell, Andy Kirk, Sam Truett, Nicolaas Mink, Neil Prendergast, Erik Loomis, Jeff Roche, Adam Sowards, Kate Scott, Abby Perkiss, Matt Johnson, Peter Coates, Chris Pearson, Tim Cole, David Havlik, Bob Deal, J. C. Mutchler, Leisl Carr Childers, Mike Childers, Catherine McNicol Stock, Richard Tucker, Dave Nesheim, Eric Otremba, Jamie Monson, Eric Carter, and Chris Wells. I would also like to thank students and faculty in the history departments at the University of New Mexico and the University of Wisconsin–Stevens Point and the participants of the Imagining Cold War Environments conference at Temple University. My conversations with Matt Bokovoy at the University of Nebraska Press have made me think and rethink how I write history. I thank him for his commitment to this book. Thank you to Jane Curran for her thoughtful comments and generous time through the copyediting process. I would also like to thank three anonymous readers who spent their valuable time critiquing the manuscript.

My students at Temple University, Haverford College, the College of Wooster, Central Michigan University, and Macalester College also deserve a shout out. Not only did they lead me to consider studying the past in new and interesting ways, but they also endured countless stories about White Sands and my love for New Mexico.

I am also indebted to several people tied to the missile range. Interviews were not always easy to come by, but those people who did talk to me gave powerful insight into life at White Sands. I would like to thank Jim Eckles, Patrick Morrow, Tom Waddell, Mike Hyatt, and Denny Gentry. Jim also offered sources and images when I could not find them. Archivists are the unsung heroes of the writing process. I would like to extend my gratitude to the staff and faculty of the Rio Grande Historical Collection, the Center for Southwest Research, the Fray Angélico Chávez History Library, the Joseph R. Skeen Library, the Nevada Test Site Library and Archives, the New Mexico State Records Center and Archives, White Sands National Monument, the National Park Service

Southwest Office, the New Mexico Farm and Ranch Heritage Museum, and the Rocky Mountain Region of the National Archives. Finally thanks to Doyle Piland and the staff of the White Sands Missile Range Museum and Archives for sharing not only documents and stories but also in offering half a sandwich here and there for an unprepared academic.

It would be remiss not to mention the personal and financial support of my family. My mother, Kathleen, my father, Ron, stepfather, Jeff, and grandmother, Alice, helped along the way. Charlie, Josie, Albina, Lita, Hilary, Heather, Melanie, Jackie, Calgary, and the rest of the Maez/Quintana/Ruiz posse offered financial support, New Mexican food, and much-needed distractions from work. Nick and Sue Pino allowed me to sleep in their closet while doing research in Santa Fe. Lucy Bloom and Hurleigh Pablo became my companions in general revelry around the Pino household. Thank you also to Jason Ward, Orly Cordova, Rocky Norton, Jonas Melvin, Shannon Mullen, John Bermel, Rachel Chandler, Luke Mclean, and Ted and Jacey Lucas.

Most importantly, this book is for Angelica Maez Edgington, who made the nearly two-thousand-mile move to Philadelphia when I started PhD work. Since then we have been on what seems like an unending and at times wearisome adventure across the Rust Belt. I owe her the world for her love, emotional support, and frequent trips to pubs from New York City to Minneapolis.

This book was completed with generous financial support from the Charles Redd Center for Western Studies at Brigham Young University, the New Mexico Office of the State Historian, and the Center for the Humanities at Temple University.

Range Wars

INTRODUCTION

In March 2008 the U.S. Fish and Wildlife Service named the massive White Sands Missile Range in south-central New Mexico the recipient of the 2007 Military Conservation Partner Award. Director H. Dale Hall explained: "As the Fish and Wildlife Service's former Regional Director in the Southwest, I learned first hand the depth and breadth of the installation's commitment to native species. Their dedicated people have always been willing to work with partners, and their ability to deliver conservation on the ground and their enthusiasm in sharing what they have learned with others has truly benefited the wildlife resources they manage." The now more than sixty-year-old missile range does deserve recognition. It played a critical role in the protection of the endangered northern aplomado falcon. It manages about 95 percent of the White Sands pupfish in rivers and streams across the region. White Sands has also worked with bat conservationists in the protection of the species on regional military reserves and remains a key partner in protecting the endangered desert bighorn sheep.[1]

By 1980 White Sands had conducted more than sixty thousand weapons tests. Wildlife conservationists have found a most unexpected value in a place the average environmentalist might deem a military wasteland. Some even consider the military reservation a de facto wildlife preserve. In 2006 Corry Westbrook, legislative representative for the National Wildlife Federation, argued that while seemingly unusual places for wildlife regeneration, weapons testing facilities, military bases, and research laboratories, including White Sands Missile Range, Los Alamos National Laboratories, and Kirtland Air Force Base in Albuquerque, have acted to protect and conserve both endangered and abundant wildlife species in New Mexico. As Westbrook believes, "they've actually done a really good job, some of the stuff they've done is pretty amazing."[2]

By removing domestic livestock, eliminating the barbed wire fences that demarcated private property prior to World War II, and keeping poachers away from wild game, White Sands has transformed a rural landscape once dominated by small ranches and an extensive cattle business into an unexpected haven for wildlife. However, neither the Department of Defense nor the Department of Energy (and its predecessor the Atomic Energy Commission) entered into protecting wild game of their own accord. Environmentalists and the Fish and Wildlife Service have used the National Environmental Policy Act (1969) and the Endangered Species Act (1973) to compel the military to play a greater role in conserving the lands that it occupies.

The recent use of militarized landscapes for wildlife protection is not just a story about New Mexico. Military installations across the United States have recently played a role in the protection and revival of many species, including the red wolf, loggerhead sea turtles, and the desert tortoise (all endangered). In the West, China Lake Naval Weapons Center, Edwards Air Force Base, and the now-defunct Rocky Mountain Arsenal, among others, are either directly involved in the protection of wildlife or have new lives as wildlife preserves in the post–Cold War West.[3]

The history of global military sites as conservation landscapes is a burgeoning subfield of geography and environmental history. Yet most scholars have told a story of negative environmental and cultural change as result of militarization during and after World War II. That trend is understandable. Scholars have deemed the militarized American West the "Ugly West" and the story of a "tainted desert." For Mike Davis, it is in part the story of a "dead west." Often measured by nuclear landscapes, and especially the Nevada Test Site, military-scientific sites are reduced to irredeemable wastelands cratered by weapons testing, a historical trend that shapes public understandings of militarized landscapes. The specter of the bomb has masked a more complicated environmental history of the militarization. In limiting analysis of places like White Sands Missile Range to merely ruined places, scholars have largely ignored the more complex and entangled environmental histories of the national security state not only in the West but also across the rest of North America.[4]

This is the history of how White Sands Missile Range came into being, how weapons testing altered the region's environment, how the human community challenged its existence, and how and why it became a site of wildlife experimentation and regeneration even as it continued to conduct missile testing on an almost daily basis.

It is important first to define militarized landscapes. I follow the historian Edmund Russell's suggestion that they run on a continuum. He argues:

> Rather than using "military" and "civilian" as terms that cleave the world in two, we should think of them as terms anchoring endpoints of a continuum. On the highly civilianized end are places people have sculpted as part of a conscious rejection of war, such as a Quaker meeting house. On the highly militarized end are places dominated by armed forces to the exclusion of civilians, such as a high-security missile silo. In between lie landscapes that, to varying degrees, are both militarized and civilianized. Essential to understanding these is historical memory, since the balance between militarization and civilianization has fluctuated over time.[5]

This means that militarized landscapes are not only fixed war zones and battlefields. They can also be small or large sites of weapons testing, refugee zones, prisoner of war camps, missile silos, and even scientific laboratories. Militarized landscapes are fluid rather than fixed in place. They have histories before they were militarized and long after the war has ended. Those same militarized landscapes can appear briefly or exist for long periods of time. They are often well-known heritage sites documented by historians but can also be places with hidden histories.

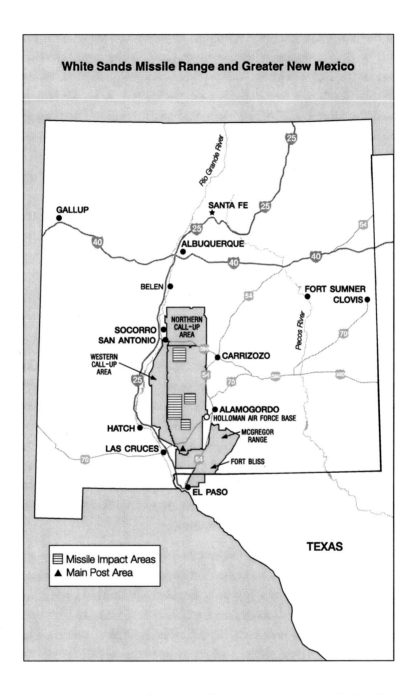

MAP 1. White Sands Missile Range and Greater New Mexico. Author's collection.

The environmental histories of militarized landscapes rarely follow a similar or expected trajectory.

While perhaps best known as the home to the Trinity Site, White Sands Missile Range is a Department of Defense facility that acts as a "large-scale" site of weapons experimentation. It is utilized by the U.S. Army, Navy, Air Force, National Aeronautics and Space Administration, and other private entities that contract with the Department of Defense and other agencies. After 1945 the missile range tested both missiles and space technology. Under the auspices of the U.S. Army Test and Evaluation Command, weapons tested include surface-to-air, surface-to-surface, air-to-air, and air-to-surface weaponry. Other programs included gun system analysis, laser programs, and atmospheric studies. At the Lyndon B. Johnson Space Center White Sands Test Facility, NASA tests a number of space-related technologies. As one observer has suggested, White Sands Missile Range is one of the largest "black spaces" on the map. It is a massive militarized landscape with deep ties to military preparedness, but many do not know the missile range exists, and even fewer understand its mission.[6]

The Main Post at the southern end of the missile range acts as central headquarters. The area includes launch complexes, administrative offices, personnel housing, industrial buildings, and basic human services. The South Range Launch Complex provides for ground-to-air and ground-to-ground missile tests. Located south of Highway 70 (which cuts southwest to southeast across the southern end of the range), the South Range Land Use Area includes Condron Airfield, used for a number of launch tests, the Nuclear Effects Laboratory, which offers a mock nuclear environment, and areas that house ordnance and missile engines. Within the Land Use Area north of U.S. Highway 70 there exist a series of ordnance disposal sites and the Small Missile Range, which acts as support for missile tests. The Central Range and Northern Range Land Use Centers (which house the Stallion Range Center) offer further support for missile tests. Missiles do not simply impact anywhere on the range. Large areas of White Sands act as buffer zones. Several impact areas, including the Yonder, Oscura, and Red Rio, are reserved for missile tests. While many begin on the range, other launches have happened from the Green River Missile Complex in Utah or from Fort Wingate, New Mexico. The missile range also has a Large Blast Thermal Simulator and climate chambers to mimic different environmental conditions. White Sands has a "landlocked" naval vessel. The navy likes the site because testing missiles at sea causes obvious issues with the recovery of data.[7]

The missile range inhabits an arid region of New Mexico known for its searing summer heat, bitter winter nights, and lack of annual precipitation. It occupies the aptly dubbed Jornada del Muerto (Walk of the Dead), a stretch of unforgiving desert that Spanish explorers and settlers traveling between Mexico City and northern New Mexico came to know all too well. Established as White Sands Proving Ground at the end of World War II, the missile range is 3,200 square miles in size and measures larger than Rhode Island and Delaware combined. With two call-up areas to the north and west (civilian areas that the missile range can evacuate for certain tests), it is near the size of Connecticut. Jim Eckles, former public affairs officer for White Sands, suggested one need only imagine evacuating Connecticut's more than 3.5 million residents to understand just how big the missile range actually is. White Sands is the largest contiguous overland military facility in the Western Hemisphere (Woomera Test Range in South Australia is the largest in the Western world). Most impacts happen on the basin floor, where missiles are easier to retrieve. In some of the higher elevations of White Sands, deer, mountain lions, and other wildlife may go months, if not years, without feeling a human presence. The missile range is not the only military facility in the region. Holloman Air Force Base (HAFB) lies at its northeastern boundary just north of the gypsum dunes on White Sands National Monument, and Fort Bliss abuts its southern edge. Collectively the region inhabits most of south-central New Mexico and the lands north of El Paso, Texas.[8]

A place largely overlooked in Cold War historiography, White Sands was the site of the first nuclear explosion, an origin of ecosystem science, the birthplace of the American space program, and the primary site for testing U.S. missile capabilities. The history of White Sands reveals that Cold War–era militarized landscapes were not contained places, but instead sites of cultural and environmental contestation. This is in part a history of the troubling impact of weapons testing on a western landscape. However, in placing White Sands at the methodological crossroads between environmental history, the history of the American West and U.S.-Mexico borderlands, and the history of science and technology, I reconsider the history of the Cold War and militarized West by suggesting that we cannot narrow militarized landscapes to sites only destroyed by weapons testing.

The environmental history of the missile range exemplifies the uneasy relationship between westerners and the national security state after World War II. Local communities, state and federal agencies, and politicians transformed the meaning of and uses for a desert landscape militarized after World War II. In the process they challenged the authority of the national security state to dictate the environmental value of White Sands without dispute. Collectively they remade the missile range into a place of competing environmental narratives etched not only from the far-reaching intellectual, economic, and environmental changes wrought by the Cold War, but also from regional history and traditions. They found their own needs and desires in White Sands. In turn the national security officials charged with overseeing the missile range were forced to amend the range's primary mission as a weapons testing facility as they wrestled with the political and environmental transformation of the region after World War II. White Sands was a hybrid landscape.

White Sands was not unique. From the Hanford plutonium production facility in Washington to the Rocky Mountain Arsenal near Denver, the militarization of rural western communities opened once private landscapes to a new public discourse on nature, culture, and the federal presence in the region. This was a revolutionary transformation in land-use in the North American West—a revolution shaped by the defense industry. In clearing south-central New Mexico of its ubiquitous cattle herds and creating a vast open space, the Cold War military-scientific apparatus allowed local, regional, and national communities to know nature in ways that transcended weapons testing. While historians of the post–World War II era have located the military-industrial apparatus and new consumer economy in the urban and suburban landscapes of the West, places like White Sands were not simply hinterlands in the battle global against communism. Military bases, testing facilities, and private military contractors dotted the rural and urban West, creating a new social landscape and federally mandated economy.[9]

Like the national park system (which was also large federal landscapes, withdrawn from local control and from the path of economic development, and managed by a government bureaucracy), the formation of militarized landscapes created conflicts in many rural places. Reflecting the historical tension between local uses of western environments and federal natural resource management in the region, the postwar experience in south-central New Mexico reveals how a diverse group of actors refused to acquiesce to state-based ideas of unmitigated national security and environmental containment during the Cold War.[10]

It was not only wildlife conservationists and environmentalists who created new-fangled land-use ideals for White Sands. Ranchers tied the missile range to their vanishing rural lifestyle. Nuclear scientists used it as a place to nurture the theories of ecosystem ecology. State game and fish personnel, the National Park Service, and state and federal political figures recognized the environments on the missile range as vital to outdoors tourism specifically and the state economy generally. The missile range was ultimately forced to negotiate its primary mission as a weapons-testing facility with the political transformation of the postwar West.

To fully understand what effect postwar militarization had on the region, historians must redefine the boundaries that separated military sites from the surrounding cultural and environmental landscape. Only by crossing those boundaries can historians of the post–World War II West know the cultural and environmental history of a complex national security state that emerged in the West. The War Department and later the Department of Defense administered White Sands under the auspices of the army, but the military did not go unchallenged. Instead, negotiation, resistance, and ultimately the human imagination marked the history of a militarized landscape.

The War Department and then the Department of Defense sought to inscribe security and containment upon the desert landscape. But, as with all militarized landscapes, those plans rarely worked out in the ways that the state desired. New Mexicans exploited for their own purposes and profit a large federal landscape ostensibly legible and secured. However, rather than a site of fixity, the missile range was reinvented in ways that challenged the singular mission of weapons testing. The missile range's history is hardly as rigid as its boundaries might suggest. As the anthropologist Edward Casey suggests, "places not only *are*, they *happen*." Just as missiles would have an effect on places beyond White Sands, so too would local, regional, and national communities leave their mark on the missile range.[11]

Coupled with the growth of mass consumerism, a monolithic Cold War culture defined by fallout shelters, doomsday movies, and nuclear anxieties shaped an American discourse on global communism, the military-industrial state, and Cold War citizenship in the postwar years. Historians have often looked to Berlin, Germany, Cuba, the Korean Peninsula, the Ia Drang Valley in Vietnam, the halls of the Pentagon, suburbia, and college campuses as places to study that dissonant encounter with national-security states. Beginning during World War II it was the West that became bastion of the American military-scientific mechanism. From the mid-1950s through the early 1980s, the Pacific and Mountain West procured the greatest amount of federal defense dollars. Between 1945 and 1960, $150 billion in military federal expenditures spread across the region. While not the only pull to the West, that money continued the significant regional demographic change that began during World War II. California alone held 40 percent of aerospace monies, and one in ten Californians relied on the federal government for a salary. Between 1950 and 1970 the population of Nevada jumped from nearly 160,000 to more than 488,000, an increase of more than 200 percent. During those years California's population grew from about 10.5 million to almost 20 million, an expansion by 88 percent. By 1970 New Mexico had become a major center for weapons research and development, and its population had grown from about 600,000 to more than one million over the prior twenty years. The state was home to Los Alamos National Laboratories (LANL), Sandia National Laboratories (SNL), Kirtland Air Force Base (KAFB), Cannon Air Force Base (CAFB), as well as Holloman, Fort Bliss, and White Sands.[12]

As the historian Patricia Nelson Limerick explains, "certainly, no location on the planet is remote enough to escape the troubling issues of nuclear power. But the American West has been particularly close to the power of the atom, in ways that followed directly the established themes of Western history." Landscapes once seen as isolated wastelands became optimum sites for scientific inquiry into the greatest of new weapons technologies. The West was home to some of the most important research and development laboratories, nuclear testing sites, and waste disposal facilities in the United States. They include the Nevada Test Site and the Yucca Mountain nuclear waste site in Nevada, the Hanford plutonium production site in Washington, and LANL, SNL, the Trinity Site, and the Waste Isolation Pilot Plant in New Mexico (WIPP). Colorado, Nevada, and New Mexico also saw operations as part of the "peaceful" deployment of nuclear weapons under Project Plowshare (namely for natural gas exploration). Utah, Colorado, and New Mexico (including areas on the Navajo Nation) were also locations of a uranium mining industry that scarred the landscape and created community health problems.[13]

To ignore the central importance of nuclear weapons in the postwar West is foolhardy at best. Scholars cannot lose sight of the troubling environmental legacy that surrounds nuclear weapons testing. But we must avoid what the historian Richard White has called the "just so story" in environmental history. Scholars must not assume that militarization (a complex and ultimately incongruent process) inherently leads only to environmental ruin. We will continue to study the Atomic West. However, from Edwards Air Force Base in California to the

Dugway Proving Ground in Utah the analysis of nonnuclear militarized landscapes demonstrates that the region's relationship to military power remains more complex than we can explain just through nuclear testing. While never wholly separate from the Atomic West, army bases and air force and navy staging facilities offer fertile ground for complicating the culture of military power in the postwar West. Moreover, such an approach requires examining the dealings of not only the Department of Defense and Atomic Energy Commission but also private defense contractors including Lockheed Martin, Boeing, Honeywell, and Halliburton (all of whom have played a role in the national defense industry in the region). Perhaps most importantly, a better picture of the Cold War West emerges from an exploration of how everyday citizens from the surrounding social and cultural landscape reacted to the immense presence of the military in the region after World War II.

Ultimately this book is about New Mexico, known by its motto as the "Land of Enchantment." Tourist literature and popular media have characterized the state as a landscape of Indian arts and culture, high desert vistas, Spanish heritage, and outdoors recreation. None of this is wholly false, but it is not a complete picture either. Popular readings of the state cast it as not very urban, although by 1970 two-thirds of the state's population lived in cities. New Mexico thus is a seemingly agrarian place, but not of industrial farms. This despite recent complaints about pollution generated from the thirty thousand cows on eleven farms in a region known as "dairy row" between Las Cruces and El Paso. Mountains abound, but the eastern plains are rarely mentioned. New Mexico is where hippies go to die. Mabel Dodge Luhan, Georgia O'Keeffe, and Dennis Hopper perfect the image of New Mexico as artist and bohemian paradise.[14]

But pull back the utopian curtains, and reality hits you in the face. Scholars, writers, and activists, including Rudolfo Anaya, John Nichols, William DeBuys, V. B. Price, Jake Kosek, and Joseph Masco, have pointed out that under the land of enchantment lay property dispossession, cultural exploitation, and environmental destruction. The history of White Sands Missile Range offers a unique landscape to explore the ways in which militarization made New Mexico a place of, to use the words of DeBuys, "enchantment and exploitation."[15]

The following pages use the history of one militarized landscape to uncover how everyday peoples comprehended and confronted the creation of a new kind of state-controlled natural environment. In 1960 the urban planner Kevin Lynch postulated that humans create an "environmental image" by identifying a place and making sense of its spatial relationship to surrounding landscapes. They then attach meaning to those places, a process that is critical in how cities are both understood and experienced. Lynch explains that the environmental image "is a product of both immediate sensation and of the memory of past experience, and it is used to interpret information to guide action. The need to recognize and pattern our surroundings is so crucial, and has such long roots in the past, that this image has wide practical and emotional importance to the individual." I use a similar theoretical approach in rural south-central New Mexico. No singular environmental ideal dominated the White Sands region, and not all interpretations were concerned specifically with nature. Yet large militarized landscapes (a geographical concept generally unique to the post-1940 era) challenged how everyday peoples understood their relationships with the nonhuman natural world.[16]

I have used the idea of contestation to define the history of the White Sands region. However, I do not merely mean protest of the military's presence in New Mexico. Instead, each chapter investigates competing perceptions of the missile range as local, regional, and national landscape and how those views challenged the basic understanding of White Sands as a closed military site. Several themes run throughout the history of the military-scientific apparatus in south-central New Mexico. The first was the myth of the rural West as the rightful domain of ranchers and farmers. Indeed local landowners, whose brethren had occupied the area since the mid-nineteenth century, cast White Sands as part of a rooted regional livestock economy even as the Department of War and Department of Defense confiscated their lands. Ranchers rarely recognized that a lack of environmental stewardship in the region during the prior hundred years played a role in the environmental collapse of the desert grasslands by the 1930s. Nor did they recognize that the military had a presence in the region since the Mexican-American war. Militarization of south-central New Mexico during and after World War II would in part develop out of both trends.

A second theme is the place of science in shaping the militarized landscape. Nuclear science, aerospace technology, and missile experimentation were central to the missile range's existence and held a critical place in rationalizing the construction of the testing facility. Science and military power went hand in hand. At the same time, wildlife management officials from within the New Mexico state government and scientists tied to broader environmental movements created unexpected ideas about the value of the secured desert environment as site of animal experimentation. By the 1980s White Sands would become the domain of exotic game and a potential site for protecting endangered wolf species. As a result White Sands became a most unexpected partner in both environmental tourism and wildlife protection.

The political turn of the 1960s acts as a third crucial theme. Environmentalists wielded power over military sites in the wake of the environmental legislation of the late 1960s and early 1970s. The legal and direct action tactics of the era inspired local communities (although with very different political motivations) to challenge the right of the Department of Defense to occupy south-central New Mexico. This was especially true for ranchers whose argument for fundamental property rights reflected that of the Sagebrush Rebellion and Wise Use movement of the Reagan era. They were bound to the missile range through prolonged property lease and grazing permit suspension agreements signed during and just after World War II. Dispossessed of their property, ranchers believed that they were the rightful owners of lands used to create the missile range.

The final theme is the unexpected nature of militarization. The following pages offer a new way of thinking about state power, local environmental knowledge, and access to landscapes deemed off limits to the very citizens they are supposed to benefit. The story of environmental declension as a result of weapons testing weaves its way through the sixty-year history of White Sands. Missiles cratered the desert landscape, White Sands tested depleted uranium, and rockets and missiles often missed their target on the missile range. As they helped to recover rocket debris and radioactive materials strewn across the U.S.-Mexico borderlands, both rural westerners and Mexicans became de facto citizens of the American Cold War national security state despite living hundreds of miles away from White Sands.

Yet missiles did not merely explode. A myriad of factions remade White Sands to fit their political ideologies, economic needs, and environmental ethics. For environmental historians the environmental history of a militarized Cold War New Mexico offers a persuasive case for knowing nature in unexpected places and in unexpected ways. It encourages us to avoid the "just so story" in doing environmental history. For historians of the American West and U.S.-Mexico borderlands it encourages thinking about the region's Cold War environmental history as not only atomic but also as an entangled web of military sites that tied the rural to the urban, the desert to the Pacific Ocean, terra firma to outer space, and the nuclear to the nonnuclear. More generally, peoples did not simply acquiesce to the Cold War cult of secrecy and security. In fact they transformed it. They were not always successful in shaping their vision for lands held by the national security state. But when they were, the political and environmental consequences were profound for everyone invested in the missile range. The contestation of White Sands emerged from a cacophony of individual, organizational, and political voices seeking to fulfill the desires they found in a massive militarized desert landscape. From those desires emerge a more complex environmental history of the Cold War American West.[17]

1

SEEDS OF DISCONTENT

On October 5, 1942, a letter reached the former under secretary of the interior and soon-to-be governor of New Mexico John J. Dempsey. Rumors of an airfield, gunnery ranges, and a proving ground circulated among residents of south-central New Mexico. As World War II raged in Europe, North Africa, and across the Pacific Ocean, the growing presence of military surveyors in south-central New Mexico was a dead giveaway. R. G. Walker, chairman of the Otero County Board of Commissioners, told Dempsey that despite the state of war "we do not believe that it is necessary to take from Otero County the taxable values that will be involved in the divorcement of this southern part of the county."[1]

Walker thought residents would "give up everything" for the war effort, but taking taxable lands that the county relied on for revenue went too far. He explained that ranching was vital to the regional economy, and that vast tracts of federal land more suitable for military use, namely the Mescalero Apache Reservation and Lincoln National Forest, existed in the region. Rangelands in south-central New Mexico could best support the war effort by producing meat.[2]

Local ranchers showed as much enthusiasm for the military's plan as Walker. In September 1943 an anonymous editorial in Carlsbad's *Daily-Current Argus* argued that the "seizure of some 1,800 sections of land in southeastern Otero County by the War Department for a gunnery range would produce unwarranted hardship and an enormous waste of cattle range that it is inconceivable to believe the Department will countenance it when it has learned the facts." Ranchers and their families were "working 12 to 14 hours a day to produce the essential food for the armed forces and civilian personnel." While the military listened, they rarely offered the relief that ranchers sought.[3]

Ranch owners and their supporters protested the potential taking of their homes and economic livelihoods rather than concede to the militarization of New Mexico. The militarized landscapes of south-central New Mexico emerged as contested places from the arrival of World War II–era military surveyors. Walker's objection to the confiscation of private lands and suggestion of alternative military sites reveal the often overlooked discontent among many westerners during World War II. The protest of wartime military presence in New Mexico emerged as part of a longer process where local communities tried to make sense of their everyday economic livelihoods in a region dominated by federally sponsored grazing lands, forests, and national parks. Those conflicts expanded to the taking of private property and interests in state and federal rangelands for large military sites. The military had withdrawn 3.5 million acres of public lands administered by the Grazing Service across ten western states by the end of 1942.[4]

The militarization of south-central New Mexico during and after World War II stood as a major episode in the origins of a New West. The writer Tom Vanderbilt argues "the desert was the perfect home for the Cold War; not simply for its sheer size and ostensible emptiness, but because the desert has paradoxically come to signify the future of America." World War II realized that vision. In the 1940s and 1950s the militarized deserts of California, Nevada, Colorado, and New Mexico became the backbone of superpower America. The deserts were no longer seen as promised lands able to fulfill Jeffersonian democracy, and the military removed them from public use for military testing and scientific inquiry during the worldwide struggle against fascism and communism.[5]

The bases, munitions factories, and proving grounds created conflicts between westerners and Washington DC not unlike those that arose with the creation of the national parks and forests. Militarized sites existed as part of a long legacy of land-use quarrels that spanned from the Mexican-American War to the 1990s. The Department of War and later the Department of Defense cast militarization as necessary for the greater public good. Since the 1840s, Hispanos, Indians, and Anglos squatted on federal lands not yet open to settlement. They resisted the Forest Service and National Park Service by ignoring laws that limited cutting timber, grazing livestock, and hunting wildlife. In places like Glacier National Park, Indians continued to lay claim to landscapes they relied on for subsistence. In northern New Mexico residents dispossessed of lands deeded under Spanish land grants challenged the presence of agents tasked with overseeing public lands.[6]

In similar fashion New Mexicans wrestled with the creation of large federal landscapes created in the post-1940 era. The struggle against military designs for south-central New Mexico between 1943 and 1958 planted the seeds of discontent among a cross-section of the region's rural and eventually displaced population. Like the Wise Use movement that emerged in the rural West some forty years later, ranchers at White Sands argued for the fundamental American right to private property. The roots of that conflict ran deep.[7]

With White Sands Proving Ground and its several military antecedents ranchers faced a private property lease and grazing permit suspension system. Under the arrangement the Department of War paid ranchers on a year-to-year basis for the temporary use of private property during the war. The military also agreed to pay ranchers for idle grazing permits on state lands. During World War II Congress amended the Taylor Grazing Act to include a proviso (section 315q) where ranchers would also receive payment for dormant federal grazing leases, which were a new wrinkle in an already contentious land tenure system. While property buyouts remained an option for the military once Congress appropriated funds, lease and suspension agreements remained the best form of property use at a time of war. With the growth of White Sands Proving Ground during the early 1950s, parties renegotiated contracts for another twenty years.

Ranchers leased their property to the military. Many property holders believed that they remained rightful owners of militarized lands both private and public. This belief, which would propel protest at White Sands in the 1970s and 1980s, reflected a deeper notion within the livestock industry. Namely ranchers, like the federal government, understood their relationship to the public domain through the lens of private property. As the historian Karen Merrill argues, "By World War I, ranchers saw their use of those lands through their private real estate; that private real estate, in turn, served as the institutional foundation for their access to public lands; those public lands were owned by a government, whose ownership was understood to be like that of an individual." However, in the political realm the federal government and ranchers held two very different notions of what property meant. The agreements at White Sands transformed the displaced livestock community into the missile range and kept alive the pastoral past in the region. In the 1970s and 1980s those messy agreements created prolonged conflict over notions of ownership and compensation.[8]

Despite military land-use needs created by World War II and the early Cold War, the urgency of the war cannot alone explain the taking of south-central New Mexico for airfields, gunnery ranges, and eventually the massive missile range. Nor can it alone explain the concurrent protests from local residents. The military did not choose rural New Mexico for bombing and gunnery ranges by mere serendipity.

At the end of the Mexican-American War, American military land surveyors found a desert grassland environment untrammeled by large numbers of European livestock. During the seventeenth and eighteenth centuries Spanish colonists rarely crossed the arid center of New Mexico preferring to stay closer to permanent settlements along the Rio Grande River. Potential conflict with Apaches and Comanches and the searing daytime temperatures created a no-man's-land. After 1700 the Mescalero Apaches held large horse herds and other livestock. They hunted wildlife in the region's mountains. What Anglos saw when they arrived were desert grasslands dominated by largely mobile societies.

At the end of the Mexican-American War the military established forts in an effort to stave off raids on new settlements by Apache and Comanche bands. With the military presence came settlers, permanent homesteads, and massive herds of cattle. In turn there emerged a new and powerful land-use ethic with devastating environmental consequences. Cattle came by the hundreds of thousands. In less than one hundred years a once semi-fertile grassland environment collapsed as a result of extensive grazing and the continuous droughts that characterized the late nineteenth- and early twentieth-century New Mexico climate. These fell within the longer "climate shocks" that corresponded to El Niño and La Niña disturbances during the period from 1880 to 1902. In the place of grasses emerged an environment dominated by creosote bush, mesquite, and sand. Enclosure would forever alter the ecosystem of south-central New Mexico.[9]

By the 1930s the region experienced the dust bowl conditions that crippled the Great Plains. The Department of Interior used the 1934 Taylor Grazing Act under the auspices of the newly created Division of Grazing (1934) and later the Grazing Service (1939) and the Bureau of Land Management (1946) to reduce the environmental pressure on eighty million acres of depleted rangelands across the West. The total amount of federal lands in south-central New Mexico taken by the military during and after World War II amounted to 1,415,547 acres or almost 63 percent of the total lands incorporated into the proving ground. The profound amount of public domain was a key reason why the War Department chose the landscape for testing sites.[10]

Into an already marginal economy with a new wartime land-use ethic came the age of rapid military-scientific development. Major General Gladeon Marcus Barnes and his team from the Office of the Chief of Ordnance, Research and Development designated the region perfect for White Sands Proving Ground in 1945. Since the Spanish colonized the region, travelers had seen south-central New Mexico as a waterless wasteland. It was the Jornada del Muerto ("Route" or "March" of the Dead Man) to colonists along the Camino Real both because of its aridity and an Indian presence. In relation to lands in

Europe, eastern North America, and even along the Rio Grande, the area was indeed arid.[11]

In confiscating the region for White Sands, the military pointed to its climate and landscape as desirable. The wartime emergency necessitated a need for vast and largely empty landscapes to carry out military testing. The basin was flat, had low vegetation density, and had sparse cloud cover that made the area perfect for missile and rocket testing. Surrounding mountains harbored good lookout points. The area also had good transportation routes and the militarized infrastructure (namely Fort Bliss and the Alamogordo Army Air Field) to support the proving ground's mission.

Ranchers remained. The property lease and permit suspension agreements left the displaced ranchers in the unusual position as peculiar landlords to the military even though they did not technically own grazing lands. Even after Manhattan Engineer District scientists exploded the first nuclear weapon at the Alamogordo Bombing and Gunnery Range in July 1945 and as German and American scientists tested the first V-2 rockets at Fort Bliss and White Sands the following year, ranchers contested the taking of their property, a conflict that continued into the Clinton era.

Militarization came in two waves. Beginning in 1942 and lasting until 1945 the War Department created a number of smaller temporary facilities. The second wave came with the July 1945 establishment of White Sands Proving Ground. Until 1958 the military created more permanent sites (including Holloman Air Force Base and the McGregor Range) that incorporated lands militarized before and during the war and property acquired from other federal agencies and private titleholders. Ranchers protested throughout but rarely succeeded in retaining their lands. They failed to understand the connections between the already federalized landscape under the Grazing Service, militarization in the mid-nineteenth century, and the rise of military sites during and after the war. The seeds of discontent were sown not only during World War II but also in the history of the livestock economy. We must begin with the project to make south-central New Mexico a cattle kingdom to understand militarization in New Mexico.

In his 1963 book *Tularosa: Last of the Frontier West* the historian C. L. Sonnichsen paints a picture of south-central New Mexico as inhospitable and "tough country." He explains, "in all the sun-scorched and sand blasted reaches of the Southwest there is no grimmer region." On the Tularosa Basin only the resilient and "rugged" have survived the desert's uninviting conditions. "The Tularosa Country," he describes, "is a parched desert where everything, from cactus to cowman, carries a weapon of some sort, and the only creatures who sleep with both eyes closed are dead." For Sonnichsen south-central New Mexico was a place where only the toughest of species, including snakes, prickly pear cactus, yucca plants, tarantula spiders, and cowboys could thrive.[12]

Sonnichsen's characterization is not complete hyperbole. Several mountain ranges—the San Andres along the west, the Oscura to the north and east, the Organ and San Augustín south and west, the Jarilla at the southeastern edge, the Sacramento along the east, and Guadalupe at the southeastern end—hem in the Tularosa Basin. To the west of the San Andres (often referred to as the San Andreas) lay the Jornada Basin, known by Spanish colonists as part of the Jornada del Muerto. Between December and January temperatures hover at freezing and can dip to as low as negative six degrees Fahrenheit. Between June and August daytime temperatures average over ninety degrees Fahrenheit but can easily reach above the century mark.[13]

Annual precipitation is scanty. While some fresh groundwater exists at depths of one thousand feet, water near the surface remains highly brackish. During the region's monsoon season (from late June to early September) it experiences more than thirty days of rainfall, making it susceptible to flash flooding. However, the basin receives only about ten inches total annual precipitation. In the winter it snows, and some small accumulation is not uncommon even on the desert floor. Higher elevations of the Sacramento and San Andres can get from twelve to thirty inches of precipitation each year. Stream flows from the Sacramento Mountains deposit small amounts of water into the Tularosa Basin, and those ribbons of water rarely offset the lack of annual precipitation. Humidity remains extremely low, leaving the desert floor parched. In 1956 the area went 123 consecutive days without measurable precipitation, attesting to its extreme environment.[14]

Desert grasslands surrounded by pockets of Chihuahuan desert scrub, plains-mesa sand scrub, plains-mesa grasslands, and montane scrub make up the vegetation on this large northern section of the expansive Chihuahuan Desert. Shrubs, including honey mesquite and soaptree yucca, among other species of the shrub genera, are widespread in the region. Creosote bush exists plentifully in Chihuahuan desert scrub areas at the southern end of the Tularosa Basin and at the edges of the San Andres Mountains. Sand sagebrush characterizes the plains-mesa sand scrub of the west-central area of the basin. To the north and on the eastern slope of the Oscura Mountains, montane scrub areas include eleven distinct desert shrub species.[15]

The gypsum dunes of White Sands National Monument and the alkali flats on its western edge comprise a large section of the present-day center of White Sands Missile Range. The remnants of the ancient Lake Otero (which at one time engulfed between 1,600 and 1,800 square miles) are visible in the intermittent Lake Otero and the surrounding saline fen and alkali flats. Rain and other hydraulic forces, which deposited gypsum in the ancient lake bed over thousands of years, led to the creation of the dunes. As water slowly receded, the gypsum remained, where it experienced a series of eolion episodes that gave the dunes their ever-changing and flowing form. Where the dunes meet desert grasslands myriad species thrive, including soaptree yucca, soft-orange globe mallow, and squaw bush sumac. Between the dunes several plant species, including rabbit bush, alkali sacaton, and soaptree yucca, survive only until the wind-altered dunes overcome them.[16]

The higher elevations of the San Andres, Organ, and Oscura mountain ranges contain some coniferous and mixed woodlands. At higher elevations some pinyon pines and junipers exist, but elsewhere desert shrubs and creosote bush dominate. Desert grassland and Chihuahuan desert scrub generally dominate lower elevations. The Sacramento Mountains, which include the Lincoln National Forest, have areas of montane conif-erous forest at higher elevations including species from the Douglas fir family. At lower elevations coniferous and mixed woodlands character-ized by pinyon pines and junipers are common.[17]

Wildlife abounds in the region. Coyotes, gray foxes, kit foxes, bobcats, and mountain lions make up the family of carnivorous mammals that live in the area. Native ungulates, including mule deer, pronghorn, the endangered desert bighorn sheep, and elk mix with exotic African oryx introduced in 1969 by the New Mexico Department of Game and Fish (dis-cussed in chapter 4). Birds and raptors include the black-throated sparrow, mourning dove, golden eagle, American kestrel, and quail, among other species. Reptiles are plentiful, including bull snakes, western diamond-back rattlesnakes, and the roundtail horned lizard. Countless beetles, butterflies, spiders, ants, bees, and wasps, among thousands of other arthropods, also call south-central New Mexico home. This is not merely "desert" but a patchwork of ecosystems with a unique natural history.[18]

What the region looks like today differs vastly from what European settlers found some 450 years earlier. South-central New Mexico's natural history stretches some 500 million years. Humans would not become a part of that history until 10,000 BCE. Settlement of the region began with the recession of glaciers, warmer temperatures, and greater pre-cipitation. The earliest inhabitants of the greater Southwest would have found a region with significant precipitation, large lakes, and verdant grasslands that supported a number of megafauna species, including horses, camels, mammoths, bison, and giant sloths. The peoples of the Clovis traditions first utilized the region's vast natural resources but remained highly nomadic. Most megafauna slowly disappeared from the area due to pressure from hunting and as a result of the warmer climatic conditions between 8000 BCE and 5000 BCE, which led to a contraction of the region's grasslands. In turn indigenous communi-ties increasingly supplemented hunting of bison and antelopes with normalized seasonal gathering practices.[19]

Sometime after 6000 BCE peoples of the Chihuahuan Tradition (as well as peoples from the Cochise and Oshara Traditions) continued to follow the seasonal hunting and gathering patterns of their ancestors in south-central New Mexico. By 900 BCE they had adopted stone tools, built some architectural structures, and increasingly relied on crops including beans and corn. Approximately 200 BCE, the Mogollon came to dominate most of present-day New Mexico before disappearing around 1400. The Jornada Mogollon would have inhabited areas from present-day Lincoln County, New Mexico, in the north to the region of Mexico south of El Paso. Like their brethren in other parts of region, the Jornada most likely arose from the ancient peoples of the area. More sedentary than their ancestors (they relied first on pits-style houses and later pueblo-style structures), the Mogollon maintained trade networks with the Hohokam peoples to the west and Anasazi to the north.[20]

Today the Mescalero Apaches are most identified with south-central New Mexico. Like other Apaches whose dialects fall under the Athapaskan phylum (the Navajos have similar linguistic roots as well), the Mescaleros were part of a larger migration from the western subarctic during a warming period some 1,500 to 2,000 years ago. By 1500 CE Athapaskan peoples would have lived at the edges of the modern-day American Southwest. An autonomous and egalitarian people, Apaches often settled into small groups despite their broader connections through kinship, language, and shared culture. The Apaches remained mobile hunters and gatherers up to contact with the Spanish. They interacted with the Pueblo peoples along the Rio Grande and exchanged goods with their ancient Navajo relatives to the northwest.[21]

Francisco Vásquez de Coronado's expedition into present-day New Mexico opened a new age for Indians. Beginning in the 1540s the introduction of diseases disrupted Native family organization, economic patterns, and spiritual ways across the present-day U.S.-Mexico borderlands. The growing European presence necessitated adaptation. From trade to warfare, the horse revolutionized the region as new kinship networks emerged and the range of trade systems expanded. Spanish and Indian groups formed alliances, traded, warred, and intermarried. While the sedentary Pueblo peoples of New Mexico suffered from both forced-labor systems and challenges to traditional religious ways (which led to revolts in 1680 and 1696), the Apaches, Comanches, Kiowas, and others used their newfound mobility to confront Spanish colonization and compete among one another for control of the region. Through the mid-eighteenth century the Comanches in the southern Great Plains and Apaches across the greater Southwest borderlands continued to contend with one another, as well as other Indians, the Spanish, and later both Mexicans and Americans for control of the region.[22]

As early as 1581, Spanish explorers traveling the north-south route from Mexico City interacted with Apaches, but into the early nineteenth century the Tularosa Basin remained outside of Spanish control. While some Apache bands, such as the Sierra Blanca, attempted to avoid the Spanish, Mescaleros and Western Apaches resisted encroachment on their lands through the Mexican-American War. Most migrants found traveling the Camino Real to the west of the San Andres Mountains a treacherous task not only because of sweltering temperatures and a lack of potable water but also because of the potential violent encounters with different Apache groups. By the 1770s the few Spanish settlers in the Rio Grande Valley of New Mexico found themselves hemmed in by Mescaleros to the south and southeast, Mimbreños and Gileños to the west, and Comanches to the east. The isolated villages of the Mesilla Valley along the Rio Grande, including Doña Ana established in 1839, experienced repeated Indian raids. This practice was fueled in part by the importance of the horse. Up to the American Civil War indigenous peoples continued both trading with and laying plunder to settlements in New Mexico.[23]

Americans made south-central New Mexico into a cattle kingdom in the mid-nineteenth century. First the United States had to displace the Mescaleros. The Mexican-American War ushered in the long history of American military control in south-central New Mexico. The army surveyed the region and protected Anglo migrants from Indian raids. The U.S. and the Spanish military quarreled with the Apaches during the war. As the war ended, raids on traveling American parties led to increased concerns about safety in southern New Mexico.

As a result by the 1850s white speculators and settlers called for an even greater American military presence in south-central New Mexico and southwestern Texas. Between 1849 and 1865 the military erected several forts, including Camp Doña Ana (1849), Fort Fillmore (1852), Magoffinsville (1854), Fort Stanton (1855), and Fort Sumner (1862), Fort Selden (1865), among others. The increased military force after 1860 allowed for the emergence of two towns along present-day U.S. 54: Tularosa in 1861 (first abandoned, it was resettled in 1863) and La Luz in 1862. The chaos of the first two years of the Civil War, including skirmishes at San Augustín Pass (July 1861), Valverde (February 1862), Peralta (April 1862), and Glorieta Pass (March 1862), amplified raiding by Apaches and other Indian groups. It was not only the small Anglo population affected by the Civil War in New Mexico. The towns of Las Cruces, founded in 1850 by Mexican families just to the American side of the border with Mexico, and La Mesilla, founded the same year just to the southwest on the Mexican side of the border (later incorporated as part of the Gadsden Purchase), were also consumed by the chaos of the war.[24]

By the end of the war the Mescaleros faced increased pressures from Union general James Carleton and the "California Column" as they took control of the Department of New Mexico. In 1862 Carleton ordered Colonel Kit Carson to force nearly four hundred Mescaleros to the Bosque Redondo near Fort Sumner. The U.S. military waged a similar campaign against the Navajos, whose horrific "long walk" to the Bosque Redondo is well known. In the fall of 1865 the Mescaleros, who had quarreled with the Navajos while also facing dire economic and environmental conditions, left the Bosque Reservation and headed toward their homelands. Recognizing removal had failed, President Ulysses S. Grant used an executive order in 1873 to establish the Mescalero Apache reservation first near Fort Stanton. Ten years later it was moved to the present-day location in the Sacramento and White Mountains.[25]

Surveys of the regional landscape accompanied the militarization of New Mexico. General Stephen Kearny sent Lieutenant James W. Abert with aide from Lieutenant William G. Peck to survey sections of the territory and its population in 1846. At the end of the war Colonel John James Abert (father of James W. Abert) of the Corps of Topographical Engineers sent Lieutenant General William H. Emory to explore the region with the hopes of surveying the area. Both Emory and Abert came within as little as one day's ride of the Tularosa Basin. In the spring of 1849 Captain Samuel G. French learned of the salt flats east of the present-day San Andres Mountains (near the present-day White Sands National Monument) and took notes on perceptions of the area and its Indian residents from people in El Paso. During the same year Captain Randolph Marcy made the first significant trek into the southern Tularosa Basin as part of an expedition to determine the best routes from Fort Smith, Arkansas, to California. He passed over San Augustín Pass (now U.S. 70) at the southern edge of the Organ Mountains and southeast toward the Sierra Hueco Mountains. In September Lieutenant W. F. Smith as part of the Marcy expedition made the first significant foray into the areas near the sand dunes.[26]

The reports that came out of the earliest surveys of south-central New Mexico revealed the environment of lands that would soon open to American settlers. Grass cover existed on the desert floor and most likely dominated the region's lower elevations. Yet even though some would claim that as late as the 1890s grasses "stood belly high to a horse," military reports from the 1850s suggested less than impressive rangelands. In 1853 and 1854 military surveyors in search of railroad routes explained lands along the Rio Grande near Doña Ana as "the richest and best timbered in the region," but outside the realm of state control. Along the Jornada del Muerto, on the other hand, "water is very scarce, there is no wood, and the grass is indifferent." To settle the Jornada would require supplying water to the area and therefore "would render necessary the maintenance of a strong military force for the defence of the route over it."[27]

As Indian displacement played out, the railroad spurred a population explosion as lines across the region tied southern New Mexico to eastern markets. The Atchison, Topeka, and Santa Fe north-south line through New Mexico (completed in 1873) and the Southern Pacific

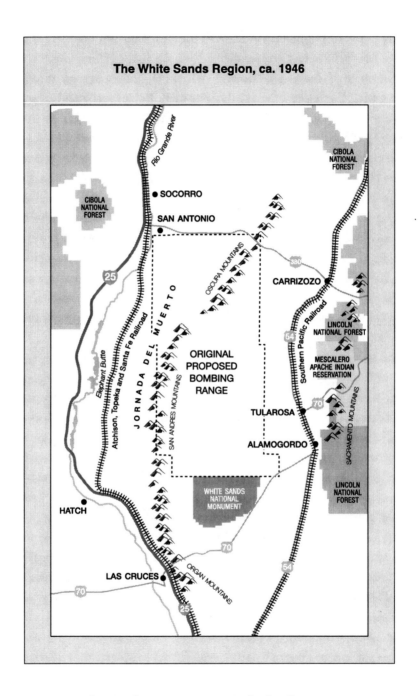

MAP 2. The White Sands Region, ca. 1946. Author's collection.

(completed in 1883) across the southern edge of the state brought settlers to south-central New Mexico. In the summer of 1898 the El Paso and Northeastern Railroad ran its first engine from El Paso through Alamogordo (a town conveniently established during the same year) and north to Capitan, New Mexico. The arrival of the Northeastern alone brought four thousand claims on public domain lands from potential homesteaders.[28]

Like many places across the West, a small mining boom was one of the earliest reasons for settlement on the Tularosa Basin. But mining had a brief history as the precious minerals sought by speculators never materialized in large quantities. The Organ Mountains held veins of silver, copper, and gold. However, of the thousands of claims filed by prospectors and speculators, few tendered a significant monetary return. Miners had greater success in the Jarilla Mountains, where they discovered lead, iron, and copper deposits. The increased presence of the railroad and newly built smelters in El Paso lead to an influx of speculators and small-scale mining ventures. With the discovery of gold at White Oaks (northeast of Carrizozo) in 1849, miners made away with $3 million during the community's short boom. With the discovery of copper deposits at the turn of the century, Estey City (on the present-day missile range) developed into a bustling but short-lived town. Located near the Oscura Mountains, Estey had a boarding house, office building, blacksmith, and housing for employees, among other improvements. Despite its volatile weather and lack of water resources, the Tularosa Basin briefly emerged as an outpost for Americans seeking to strike it rich.[29]

Ultimately mining would not define the region's long-term economy. By 1900 a growing livestock industry dominated much of the business on the Tularosa Basin. Into the 1920s the desert grazing commons remained largely unregulated by any state or federal government agency. To remain economically viable, livestock owners had to understand the limits of the region's environment. As early as the mid-1860s ranchers started to migrate to south-central New Mexico from points east. Cattlemen followed the Goodnight-Loving (named for cattle barons Charles

Goodnight and Oliver Loving) Trail out of Texas east toward Carlsbad and then north to Fort Sumner. Others later followed the Chisum Trail (named for the cattle baron John Chisum) from Roswell, New Mexico, into the Lower Rio Grande Valley. Of twenty-four of the earliest cattlemen on the Tularosa Basin, only one was of Hispanic descent. The rest were Anglo and came from Alabama, Missouri, North Carolina, Ohio, New York, Canada, and most importantly Texas. They set their cattle to the open range. By the end of the Civil War requests for meat led to an expansion of the cattle industry. Tularosa beef fed Indians at the Bosque Redondo reservation and soldiers at Fort Stanton. From its birth the New Mexico cattle industry was bound to the military.[30]

As both land speculators and homesteaders settled the region between the 1870s and early 1900s, they found themselves battling for a finite amount of potable water in the mad dash to harness the precarious water resources of the desert environment. In 1883 severe drought and bitter cold temperatures crippled the cattle industry in the American Southwest. The arid conditions had the duel impact of bringing overstocked Texas cattle to arid rangelands in New Mexico and altering the open range of previous years. In the aftermath ranchers enclosed the grazing commons, set to capturing subsurface water sources, and increasingly focused on breeding large cattle for the market.[31]

As time wore on, several large landholders came to govern south-central New Mexico. Among them was Oliver Lee, who reflected the culture of the large property owners in post-1880 south-central New Mexico (best known for cattle rustling in the region and suspected role in the death of lawyer and politician Albert Jennings Fountain). In 1885 Lee migrated from Taylor County, Texas, to settle on the Tularosa Basin. At just twenty-one years of age he was a young entrepreneur. After acquiring land at the foot of the Sacramento Mountains, Lee founded the Sacramento Cattle Company with several compatriots. For the sake of feeding and watering their stock, the company's owners understood the importance in appropriating scant water resources before anyone else could. To extend their land holdings they built an irrigation ditch to water alfalfa and acquired water tanks at a site called the Grapevine

Horse Camp. While the company broke-up in 1889, Lee continued to expand his property throughout the period.[32]

Like Lee, other ranchers sought the best grazing lands and sources of water to maintain profitable livestock numbers. As Lee's speculative activities reveal, water defined the economy and politics of the region, and his landscape improvements reflected the realities of rangelands in desert environments. The most common of all improvements included irrigation canals, reservoirs, wells, and earthen stock tanks used to catch rainwater. In 1907 Lee constructed an additional pipeline that ran from the Sacramento River to a portion of his land in the Basin.

The lack of water incited competition and speculation across the Basin. Many settlers who had come to the region in the years after the completion of the Northeastern Railroad were less likely to acquire rights to water. Several geological studies revealed the problems with water resources in south-central New Mexico. In 1910 the geologists O. E. Meinzer and R. F. Hare had suggested that, "vast tracts of arable land, potentially capable of producing crops of great value, are at present lying practically idle." There simply was no water for agricultural endeavors. As a result most small farmers sought to use dry farming methods, which failed to produce significant returns on investments in arid lands. Meinzer and Hare recognized that large portions of the water table held moderate to large amounts of dissolved solids, including salt. Depending on the level of salinity, waters could prove poisonous to humans, animals, and crops. After 1900 farmers and ranchers (whose economies intimately intertwined through the production of desert-resilient sorghum for feeding cattle) could not expect to harvest significant subsurface freshwater, which earlier settlers had taken. Moreover, meager precipitation offered little solace for regional farmers and ranchers without prior legal rights to freshwater deposits. Between the years 1901 and 1911, yearly averages for Alamogordo leveled at a mere 10.59 inches. In 1927 W. Carlos Powell and C. G. Staley of the New Mexico State Engineer Office concluded that shallow water sources produced from several alluvial fans along streams and rivers that emptied into the Tularosa Basin also did not offer significant sources for large agricultural development. Neither the quantity nor the quality of water existed.[33]

Late nineteenth- and early twentieth-century surveyors often used the word *prairie* to describe the region. Unlike the Jornada del Muerto, there remains more than anecdotal evidence to suspect that at one time good desert grasses covered the region. Using 1858 land surveys completed on the future Jornada Experimental Range and Chihuahuan Desert Range Research Center, ecologists have recently explored the transformation of southern New Mexico's desert landscape. During 1858 very good to fair grass covered 98 percent of the Jornada Experimental Range. Surveyors considered about 70 percent of those grasses as good and 9 percent as very good. Studies done at the Chihuahuan Desert Range Research Center showed that in 1858 very good to fair grasses covered 67 percent of the desert floor.[34]

According to a 1915 survey (more than thirty-five years after Anglo settlement of the region), mesquite made up only 26 percent of what is today the Jornada Experimental Range. By 1998 mesquite dominated 59 percent of the range. In areas where it had existed as a subdominant species, mesquite covered as much as 84 percent of the desert floor. Similarly, creosote bush and tarbush expanded by 20 percent between the 1915 and 1998 studies. In 1915 black grama grass had declined to about 19 percent on the Jornada Experimental Range. By 1998 it made up only 1.2 percent. In other words, the study revealed that between 1915 and 1938, "shrubs had made large increases in area at the time of the surveys."[35]

Mesquite and creosote bush are native to the region but were not always the prevailing species. Their rapid expansion during the second half of the nineteenth century and early twentieth century raise questions about the relationships between nature and changing land use in the region. No matter what surveyors said they found, the grasses were only good under certain conditions. It remains widely accepted that desertification resulted from the vegetation changes caused in part by extensive grazing that began during the mid-nineteenth century. With the resilient shrubs came the sandy soils common in the region today. While a perpetually arid place, south-central New Mexico of the 1850s looked markedly different from the one the military would found in the 1940s.[36]

Why did the desert grasslands recede? First, as military surveyors suggested in the 1850s, the region held little subsurface water and lacked annual precipitation. Second, ranchers overgrazed their livestock. While some ranchers ran sheep, the Tularosa Basin was cattle country. Numbers for Otero County reveal the growth of the industry. By 1890 figures suggested that as many as eighty-five thousand cattle foraged between the town of Three Rivers and the Dog Canyon area in the Sacramento Mountains alone. Finally, drought was common in an already parched desert. Between the 1870 and 1940, the ranchers that enclosed the region settled on an unforgiving and unpredictable desert landscape. They also failed to understand the limits of the range. Between 1892 and 1930, only two years saw statewide averages of more than 20 inches of precipitation. One dry spell after another crippled the region. As previously mentioned the 1883 drought completely altered how ranchers utilized the grazing commons as they battled for receding grasses and finite water. As more cattle populated the landscape between 1888 and 1900, widespread drought again hit most of New Mexico. As a newspaper report suggested in 1889, "due to a lack of rainfall and shortage of grass in the fall of 1888, the cattle came through the winter and losses were slight." Nevertheless, cattlemen sent their stock to Kansas and Indian Territory "to fatten and then put them on the market in the summer."[37]

The drought of 1900 stood out for many residents. Bob Martin, one of the first Anglo settlers in the region, relayed to reporter Dave Cushman that in the last decade of the nineteenth century some areas had grasses "boot high" and in others "stirrup high." Yet after that and without warning "cattle commenced dying like flies." Numbers of cattle fluctuated with drought and the economy. A 1900 census report tallied 10,400 cattle in Otero County. Yet by 1910 cattle numbers reached more than 38,000 head and remained relatively unchanged for the next ten years.[38]

In 1922 drought again hit the region just as Otero County's cattle numbers leveled off at 36,000. New Mexico's agricultural economy did not fare well. The Extension Service explained, "the outlook is none too bright for the livestock and farming interests in the state." The year-long post–World War I recession helped to destabilize an economy that for a brief period grew to meet the need for meat during the war. In 1925 A. J. Walker and J. L. Lantow, working for the Agricultural Experiment Station of the New Mexico College of Agriculture and Mechanical Arts (now New Mexico State University), suggested that in parts of southern New Mexico "the forage covering is sparse or entirely absent, requiring large tracts upon which to run an economical sized unit." The pastoral experiment forever altered relationships between ranchers and state and federal governments. The desert grasslands of the pre-1850s no longer existed, and creosote bush, mesquite, and other shrubs dominated south-central New Mexico's lower elevations. Resilient to the stresses of arid environments, shrubs simply outcompeted grasses. The relationship between extensive grazing, drought conditions, and a lack of fresh subsurface water spelled disaster for the region's onetime grassland environment.[39]

By 1930 dry conditions similar to those of the Great Plains struck parts of eastern and central New Mexico. During the same year conditions reached such alarm that the Agricultural Experiment Station compiled a brochure that explained how to find emergency feed for livestock. Their report encouraged the use of several desert plants including saltbush, sagebrush, and cut yucca as supplemental forage. Residents later remembered the often-destitute conditions that occurred during periods of drought. Natalia Lucero Di Matteo recalled that during one stretch with little precipitation "cattle were like flies; they were dying." The cattle climbed into the water tanks to consume any water they could find. Her father resorted to killing calves that the family could no longer support. After her father had shot them, Di Matteo's brother hit them on the head with a hatchet to "make sure they were all dead."[40]

In 1930 the Jornada Experimental Range received 5.73 inches of rain for the year, a departure of 5 inches from the 10-inch annual average. Cattle numbers in Otero County dropped to 23,844 during the same year, a decline of 12,840 head over the prior ten years. Inopportune national and global fiscal conditions wreaked havoc on desert grasslands. But the effects of overgrazing coupled with constant drought had the consequence of making an already dire economic situation even worse.[41]

Government officials and residents recognized the problems created by the economic and environmental disaster of the Great Depression. A rancher later explained that the Tularosa Basin was "as bare as a rat's tail." Les Beatty, county extension agent for Otero County, explained that "had there been intelligent using of these grazing lands starting a couple of decades ago, the vegetative cover would have been sufficient to protect the grass roots over a long drouth period [sic]." The Depression also came to the region. Holm Bursum III recalled that "nobody had any money to speak of." If a family needed a new windmill, or anything else for that matter, "you bartered for it, you traded something for it."[42]

Like elsewhere in the rural West, the New Mexico state government responded to the calamitous conditions by appealing to the federal government. New Mexico governor Richard C. Dillon telegrammed Secretary of Agriculture Arthur M. Hyde with a request to reduce freight prices for areas of the state under drought conditions. The governor's appeal included Otero, Dona Ana, and Lincoln Counties. Federal intervention transformed land use in the region. The Division of Grazing established under the 1934 Taylor Grazing Act and placed under the Department of Interior entered the western ranching economy to alleviate the conditions created by drought and overgrazing. In 1946 the Bureau of Land Management replaced the Grazing Service.[43]

Western ranchers had faced the range policies of the federal government since the early nineteenth century and had responded by organizing into powerful cattle growers associations. In 1914 New Mexicans organized the New Mexico Cattle Growers Association. Yet by 1934, more than ever before, the success of the onetime cattle kingdom hinged on widespread federal conservation practices. Through the use of livestock permits and the establishment of grazing districts, the Division of Grazing acted as a stopgap measure in the continued depletion of grasslands. The federal government sought to prop up the livestock economy by encouraging conservation of already crippled western rangelands.[44]

While a contentious piece of legislation, the Taylor Grazing Act affirmed that large swaths of the arid West remained in the domain of the livestock industry. Under the Taylor Grazing Act ranchers filed licenses for grazing privileges and paid appropriate fees based upon the accepted number of cattle, horses, and sheep allowed by the Division of Grazing. For example, in 1936 the Division of Grazing granted Socorro-based Holm Bursum and Company (a decidedly large endeavor) a license for 1,000 cattle, 125 horses, and 10,000 sheep with 54 percent of the stock on public domain. During World War II federally managed lands would become an asset to the War Department.[45]

As the authors of a recent ecological study of the region suggest, "there can be little doubt that heavy grazing in the latter part of the nineteenth and early twentieth centuries helped trigger the encroachment of shrubs." However, south-central New Mexico was arid before the cattle came. The pastoral experiment simply revealed the harsh realities of life on the Tularosa Basin and surrounding area. Environmental change was swift. From the dual problems of overgrazing and drought came creosote bush, mesquite, sand, and the Division of Grazing. And the military had its eyes on the region before the United States had even entered World War II. The failure of the pastoral experiment would contribute to the militarization of the region.[46]

NEW RANGELANDS

As ranchers dealt with the new rules established by the Taylor Grazing Act, they could not have foreseen the militarization of their community. But World War II brought new demands for military weapons testing and personnel training on western lands. This was the first wave of militarization. Nearly all 189 military public land orders or executive orders issued between June 1942 and August 1945 had an effect on Department of Interior lands in the West. New Mexico was not alone. Arizona, South Dakota, Washington, Wyoming, Idaho, Nevada, Utah, and other western states were home to gunnery and bombing ranges, aircraft pilot schools, ordnance storage depots, landing fields, naval bases, and other military sites. The Second War Powers Act affirmed the legal right of the military to take lands for war purposes. It permitted the secretary of war to introduce condemnation proceedings for acquisition of land, to purchase land, and to accept donations of land. The act stipulated that any property taken by condemnation would exist under temporary use status. However, it did not state that the Department of War would automatically return those lands with the end of hostilities.[47]

As the military buildup transformed the region, people seeking work came in droves. As the historian Gerald D. Nash explains "no other single influence on the region—not the Mexican War, not the Civil War, not World War I, nor even the Great Depression—brought such great and cataclysmic changes to the West." The North American West experienced significant economic boosts behind war-related expenditures. California companies alone received more than $1.5 million in contracts for the construction of war facilities and more than $14 million in contracts for war supplies. New Mexico received more than $100,000 in contracts for military facilities alone. Between 1940 and 1950, the population of the Mountain West increased by 22.3 percent. New Mexico grew by 18 percent. During the same period Las Cruces's population grew by 47 percent, and Alamogordo's increased by 71 percent. Military use of western lands concomitantly expanded. Of the seventy-three public land orders and executive orders related to military land withdrawals issued during 1942 alone, six happened in New Mexico.[48]

Even before the United States formally entered the war, the U.S. Army Air Force saw in sparsely settled south-central New Mexico potential sites for military preparation. In April 1941 the Army Air Force established the Alamogordo Army Air Field (later Holloman Air Force Base) as a training site for the British Royal Air Force strained by wartime conditions at home. Pearl Harbor necessitated an expansion of activities by American military personnel at the site. The War Department immediately directed ranchers to vacate their lands. On January 20, 1942, President Franklin Delano Roosevelt signed Executive Order 9029, which withdrew public lands in New Mexico for eventual use as a bombing and gunnery range. The military informed landowners that they would have to leave their homes to make way for the 1,243,000-acre Alamogordo Bombing and Gunnery Range. The Grazing Service knew of the plan and complied with plans to transmit public lands from the Department of Interior. Under the order the War Department was to consult with the Department of Interior in choosing a site. It also stipulated that "the lands reserved by this order shall be returned to the administration of the Department of Interior when they are no longer needed for the purpose for which they are reserved." Similar agreements would shape land use negotiations with private ranchers.[49]

South-central New Mexico was abuzz with military activity as war preparedness ramped up in the months after the Japanese attack on Pearl Harbor. In May 1942 the federal government had initiated lease proceedings against 291 landholders (which included mine claimants) whose property fell within the proposed Alamogordo Bombing and Gunnery Range. The plan called for a five-year easement. Private property amounted to a mere 3 percent with another 1 percent acquired in fee simple. The federal government held an astounding 75 percent of the land, and the state of New Mexico 21 percent. Ranchers would receive payment on their property and rights to grazing permits. Those who refused to leave faced forceful ejection by the U.S. Marshals Service.[50]

In early January 1943 Secretary of War Henry Stimson explained to newly elected governor John Dempsey that the War Department would "suspend the exercise of Federal and State grazing privileges by leasing privately owned property within the area, rather than by buying out the fee title to the privately owned lands and terminating the grazing privileges or rights." While complicated on paper, the Department of Interior's control of most of south-central New Mexico made military use of lands less complicated than the process of outright purchase of lands from ranchers. In fact, there remains little evidence to suggest that in 1943 the military believed it would need the land beyond the end of the war. Essentially, ranchers faced leases renewable only for the foreseeable future.[51]

Under those agreements they received payment from the federal government for the use of titled property and interest in grazing leases

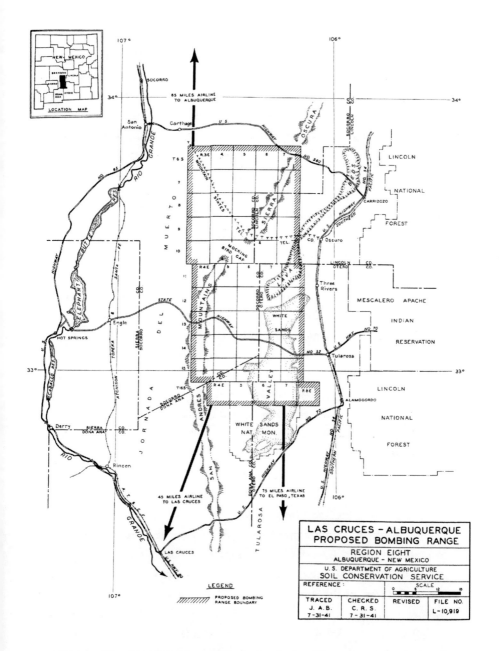

1. Proposed Bombing Range map with the San Andres Mountains to the west and U.S. 54 and U.S. 70 to the east. Soil Conservation Service, USDA, ca. 1946. Courtesy of the National Archives and Records Administration–Rocky Mountain Region.

on state lands. Congress amended the Taylor Grazing Act to deal with leases on federal lands. Added in 1942 to relieve those who held federal grazing permits suspended by the military, section 315q states: "Persons holding grazing permits or licenses and persons whose grazing permits or licenses have been or will be cancelled because of such use shall be paid out of the funds appropriated or allocated for such project such amounts as the head of the department or agency so using the lands *shall determine to be fair and reasonable for the losses suffered* by such persons as a result of the use of such lands for war or national defense purposes" (emphasis added).[52]

Ranchers fervently questioned plans for military use of rangelands. In an October 1942 letter to Secretary of War Henry Stimson, Alamogordo mayor E. D. McKinley, the Alamogordo Chamber of Commerce, and the Otero County Board of Commissioners protested the proposed Guadalupe Aerial Gunnery Range in the Guadalupe Mountains at the southern end of the county. Noting that the livestock community in New Mexico had shown a "complete willingness" to cooperate with the war effort, they strongly opposed the military installation. The letter explained that the gunnery range "would embrace a tract of land south and east of Alamogordo thirty miles in depth and sixty miles in length, all of it carved out of the best cattle range in the State of New Mexico." Moreover drought-stricken lands in eastern New Mexico, northwestern Texas, and southwestern Oklahoma owned by the federal government remained available and "wholly unsuited for the production of food." Thus, they were ideal military sites.[53]

Some ranchers argued that they willingly gave up their lands to support the war effort. The son of a rancher who lost lands to the Alamogordo Army Air Field later explained, "At the time that they took it, everybody felt that it was for the country's good." The New Mexico Cattle Growers Association passed a resolution stating that it would use its services to help Governor John E. Miles (who served through the end of 1942) "in such a way as he may direct in the present emergency." Yet many more residents revealed consternation with the process of militarization across south-central New Mexico. In 1943 Alton Jones, an Otero

County rancher, explained that it would be a hardship to move cattle from the region because it was "impossible to find range for sale or lease anywhere in the Southwest due to drought conditions."[54]

The same year the Alamogordo Chamber of Commerce encouraged their counterparts in El Paso to join in opposition to the proposed gunnery range in the Guadalupe Mountains. In a letter they explained, "the establishment of this Range will seriously and adversely affect Alamogordo and Otero County and we think, deprive El Paso business houses of a great deal of business which they have heretofore enjoyed from this area." They believed the "best livestock grazing area in Otero County" could maintain fifty thousand head of cattle. They explained further in their plea to the businessmen of El Paso to take up the cause: "we are convinced that the establishment of this Range in this County will require a sacrifice on the part of our citizens far beyond the necessity of or value to the war effort."[55]

Rancher A. B. Cox, one of thirty-eight ranchers who faced eviction, suggested that moving such a large number of cattle under the wartime economic situation amounted to "a hardship on every ranch operator." Cox believed "it would ruin every rancher in the area." An anonymous editorial in the *Albuquerque Journal* argued "it is to be hoped—and expected—that the War Department will find its way clear to abandon the notion of taking up the 1800 sections of range land to transform it to a gunnery range." After all, the families in the region spent most of their days producing food for the war effort, and the region had ceded 1.5 million acres for the Alamogordo Bombing and Gunnery Range.[56]

Protest in south-central New Mexico was not unique in the wartime West. For example, in the months after Pearl Harbor the Wendover Bombing Range in Utah (1941) and Tonopah Bombing Range in Nevada (1942) met similar opposition from local communities. At Wendover, ranchers lobbied the Grazing Service to challenge the size of the military installation. This led the Army Air Corps to acrimoniously protest to local business officials that the bombing range was "materially reduced due to concerted action of sheep grazers through the Grazing Service of the Department of the Interior." At Tonopah mine claimants and private landholders who felt forced into "take it or leave it" buyout arrangements resisted forceful removal. Some even refused to vacate their property.[57]

The McCarran Senate Committee on Public Lands and Surveys (led by Nevada senator Patrick McCarran, who had mitigated the conflicts between ranchers and the military in his home state) and the entire New Mexico congressional delegation backed the opposition to proposed bombing and gunnery ranges in New Mexico. Moreover they opposed the military's promise of opening rangelands to ranchers two days out of every week. Rancher A. B. Cox said the co-use agreement was "not practical and would ruin every rancher in the area." Livestock owners asked Governor Dempsey to lobby President Roosevelt for reconsideration of the plan. In a September 1943 newspaper interview Dempsey sided with the ranchers, calling the Guadalupe Mountain test site "the most awful thing I've ever heard of." When army activities intensified during the fall, local residents complained that military personnel had started brush fires and stray bullets nearly missed residents near the site. The ranchers of south-central New Mexico used their powerful lobby to push back at the military. By 1945 they would fight a losing battle to stay on their property.[58]

LINES IN THE SAND

In 1944 designs for a larger proving ground intensified within the Office of the Chief of Ordnance, Research and Development Service. Led by Major General Gladeon Marcus Barnes, a team of military personnel sought a place with good year-round weather conditions and little cloud cover. They also sought a site near major transportation routes including railroads. The team located potential areas in Nevada, Texas, and Utah but eventually suggested the Tularosa Basin. Signed in February 1945, Real Estate Directive 4279 established the military's need for the land. Known as ORDCIT (Ordnance–California Institute of Technology, the original name for the site that would become White Sands Missile Range), the area included parts of Fort Bliss and the Alamogordo Bombing and Gunnery Range. With ORDCIT operations already underway a month earlier, on July 9, 1945, Army Service Forces Circular 268 established a testing project under the Office of the Chief of Ordnance in the Department of the Army. On July 12, 1945, Adjutant General Otto Johnson signed a letter formally establishing White Sands Proving Ground.[59]

Why did Barnes and his colleagues in the Office of the Chief of Ordnance choose this area of New Mexico? They pointed to several factors. First, the army needed large expanses to test and easily recover projectiles. The landscape had to include widespread level lands. The operations would necessitate proximity to proper transportation networks (namely railroads, highways, and air strips, but transportation lanes could not cross the proving ground). U.S. Highway 70 offered a corridor to major transportation hubs. The presence of Fort Bliss to the south of the proposed site and the Alamogordo Army Air Field to the northeast offered the necessary military infrastructure to support missile testing. Nearby cities, namely Las Cruces, would afford off-duty personnel places to spend their downtime. The environment itself offered good reasons for establishing the proving ground. The San Andres and Sacramento Mountains offered perfect sites for monitoring missile tests. The more than three hundred days of annual sunshine would make it easier to follow rocket flights. A lack of dense vegetation on the landscape made missile recovery easier.[60]

The military also noted the Grazing Service's hold on most lands in the region. Prior to protest from ranchers, the War Department and the Department of Agriculture intended to work together to acquire lands in fee title. The relationship between the two federal agencies had benefits that did not exist in talks with ranchers. Yet, the process of transferring land to the War Department and the construction of co-use agreements with other state and federal entities did not occur overnight. At the start of World War II, the War Department had acquired large swaths of south-central New Mexico. The total area amounted to near 1,696,500 total acres cut from rangelands and private property. Through previous agreements the proving ground acquired lands from the Alamogordo Bombing Range (1,242,000 acres), the Dona Ana Target Range (8,500 acres), Castner Target Range (8,500 acres), and Fort Bliss Antiaircraft Firing Range (400,000 acres). With the military's hold on remaining private lands and a stake in grazing permits, only ranchers stood in the way of the militarization of an entire region.[61]

The military presence in the region continued to expand as tensions between the United States and Soviet Union mounted during the early Cold War. In 1948 the Department of the Army (who would administer testing at the proving ground) began the process of suspending co-use land agreements negotiated with private parties (namely ranchers grazing on military lands). Lease and suspension agreements remained the primary mode of land transfer. The same year, the federal government designated U.S. 70 a military highway and thus subject to intermittent closure during missile and rocket tests. The National Park Service for White Sands National Monument and the Department of Interior for the Jornada Experimental Range signed agreements that stipulated the occasional evacuation of their lands during tests. The mission of the Jornada, which was established in 1912 and was now located near the southwestern section of the proving ground, was to explore and promote sustainable rangeland use. As with the national monument, the rise of the military state encumbered programs on the Jornada.[62]

That same year the military terminated all co-use agreements with private interests. The following year the army and air force issued a joint military acquisition directive that formally suspended the co-use agreements. The military also announced to the media its plans to make a three-thousand-square-mile proving ground. While "hesitant about disclosing details," unnamed military officials did suggest that they had completed land surveys across the American West in making decisions about where they would locate military reserves. The relative success of V-2 and other rocket tests in 1945 and 1946 prompted the call for a larger proving ground in south-central New Mexico (see chapter 3).[63]

Signed in 1952, Public Land Order 833 withdrew nearly all the public and private lands (including mineral interests) in south-central New Mexico. Public and nonpublic lands taken amounted to 2,394,384 square miles. In 1958 the proving ground was renamed White Sands Missile Range, and the army made a final tally of lands taken ten years earlier. The numbers varied from the original. Lands leased from the state of New

Mexico amounted to 364,526.87 acres. Lands leased and transferred from other federal agencies came to 1,453,278.34 acres. Special use agreements with White Sands National Monument and the Jornada Experimental Range added 159,058.54 acres. Property acquired from state, federal, and patent holders in fee simple included 167,974.70 acres. The air force owned outright 2,996.79 acres. Finally, lands leased from patent holders added an additional 78,829.65 acres to the total. Minus tracts (11,214.82 acres) "disposed of as not required," the total came to 2,215,450.07. The order included a stipulation that "when the lands described herein are no longer needed for the purpose for which they are reserved they shall be returned to the administration of the Department of Interior, the Department of Agriculture, and any other federal agency according to their respective interests of record." Of course ranchers had an interest in federal grazing lands because of their suspended grazing permits.[64]

How big were the ranches taken by the military? A preliminary 1951 acquisition tract register for Holloman Air Force Base Bombing and Gunnery Range suggests the total acreage ran the gamut. It is important to note here that in the 1958 tally of lands taken to create White Sands, Air Force accountability was 1,243,518.12 acres and army (ORDCIT) accountability was 2,215,450.07. The Department of the Army would eventually manage the missile range. The Holloman register broke down each landowner by patented, federal, and state acreages. William and Ann Walters held 160 patented acres and interests in 1,736.84 federal and 640 state acres. Ross and Dave McDonald held 640 patented acres and interests in 22,535.87 federal and 4,468.34 state acres. Red Canyon Sheep Company held 2,960 patented acres and interests in 13,947.13 federal and 2,680 state acres. Dick Gilliland had 200 patented acres and interests in 18,502.61 federal and 2,240 state acres. In all more than 55 families and partnerships were listed in the record.[65]

The War Department had started the process of lease and suspension agreements prior to the passage of Public Land Order 833. In the long process of militarization the ORDCIT project had implanted in the community of displaced ranchers the idea of a potential return to their lands. Replacing agreements arranged between 1942 and 1951, the twenty-year contracts with private ranchers included several stipulations. Under lease agreements private landowners continued to receive payment for property. Through suspension agreements they received payment for state-leased grazing lands and federal grazing permits either deferred for the duration of the lease or terminated altogether. Importantly, permit holders received compensation as required under section 315q of the Taylor Grazing Act. When lease and suspension agreements came up in 1970 and new negotiations commenced, the military decided to no longer pay on the suspension of federal grazing interests, a major reason for the conflicts between ranchers and the federal government in the following decades (see chapter 5).[66]

Other military reserves in the region (including some that would cede lands to the proving ground) followed similar patterns of land acquisition. The Alamogordo Army Air Field (renamed Holloman Air Force Base in 1948) signed leases with ranchers similar to those on the proving ground. Doña Ana Target Range included 75 percent public lands, 20 percent state lands, and a mere 5 percent actually owned by private interests. Until 1946 when the military acquired the federal funds to purchase the land outright, co-use agreements allowed for both the military and ranchers to use the land. Established in 1948, the McGregor Guided Missile Range (key in guided missile programs established at White Sands) went through a long process of expansion in the mid-1950s that led to a series of deals for the purchase of ranch lands. The military acquired most private property outright by 1954. As condemnation suits played out in the 1970s, the purchase of lands at the Doña Ana Target Range and McGregor Guided Missile Range would emerge as a key point of contention for White Sands ranchers forced into the drawn-out lease and suspension agreements.[67]

But even as the military-scientific apparatus took hold of the region after 1945, ranchers protested the actions of the military. Road closures became a major issue as plans for the proving ground went forward. In a telegram dated April 21, 1945, Doña Ana County Commissioners relayed to Governor Dempsey that "Doña Ana county residents are greatly disturbed over possibility of closing highway seventy between Las Cruces and Alamogordo because of condemnation proceedings for bombing range in that area." The Las Cruces Lions Club sent a similar telegram to the governor while the State Highway Office opposed "the securing of additional acreage for the bombing or target range near Alamogordo, which would interfere with the normal use of U.S. Highway 70."[68]

Beyond disruption to travel routes, ranchers also leveled protest against land valuation methods, whether as part of lease and suspension agreements or as part of the federal taking of property. At the Doña Ana Target Range most families readily evacuated their land, but payment did not come immediately. The Beasley family raised concerns about manipulation of their contract in 1948, which they claimed stipulated that capital from the salvaging of fences and other structures would not be subtracted from the total land payment until after they vacated. Local officials argued that payment would not come until the family paid the government for those materials salvaged. In a letter to John Cobb (the federal agent dealing with land transactions) Mrs. Beasely exclaimed that she had "notified Dept. of Justice in Washington of this illegal transaction which you instructed your man to put over and since I see that your Dept continues to act in a dirty manner, I notify you and have notified the Dept of Justice that I will shoot to kill the next Army representative who enters my home."[69] Ten years later Tom Bell of El Paso, Texas, claimed that compared to other ranchers who lost land to McGregor Range, the Army Corps of Engineers had not evaluated his ranch properly. In a letter to Senator Dennis Chavez he explained that the check for $51,000 he had received for his lands was "an unjust settlement in accordance to the amounts paid to others for their property to be used by the United States Army for the same purpose." Whether or not he ever received the adjustment sought is not known.[70]

For those who had lost property to White Sands, questions arose not to the inevitability of military use of the land, but if the military might reconsider the already contentious co-use land agreements. On August 2, 1948, the Department of Interior initiated hearings to be held in Las Cruces on the expansion of the proving ground to its present size. The release reminded readers that the federal government had withdrawn

1,250,000 acres of public land for the bombing range and had requested an additional 2 million acres. It also emphasized suspension on any mining claims or grazing interests therein. The assistant director of the newly formed Bureau of Land Management and General John L. Homer of the Department of the Army at Fort Bliss met with interested citizens. The discussion that came out of those hearings is telling.[71]

Ranchers believed there remained a chance that they could use military lands for grazing, despite opposition to the military's proposal for a two-day-a-week land-use system. By the end of 1948 those hopes began to fade. On New Year's Eve G. W. Evans, president of the New Mexico Cattle Growers Association, wrote to his members that contrary to recent news out of Washington DC, the association had "made a thorough check of the matter and can find no basis for this report." Yet Evans also said the Department of the Army "had made no attempt whatever" to talk with any ranchers. The Department of Interior informed ranchers that nothing was final without a workable co-use agreement. Yet by January 1949 E. R. Smith, regional administrator for New Mexico, suggested to Roscoe E. Bell, associate director of the Bureau of Land Management, that "liberalization of the military's present attitude on co-use" was necessary for any sort of compromise between an increasingly angry ranching contingent and the Department of the Army. One month later, the New Mexico Cattle Growers Association informed its members that "the Army Department has completely backed-up on their previous offer to work out a fair co-use program on the bombing range." The Department of the Army believed ranchers roaming the rangelands would interfere with the mission of the proving ground.[72]

In the wake of the 1948 hearings ranchers in southern New Mexico revealed their frustration in what they heard at the Las Cruces meeting. The Southeastern New Mexico Cattle Growers Association had sent a representative to hear about the military designs for rangelands and the end of co-use agreements. The association sent a lengthy response to Secretary of Interior Julius A. Krug wherein they raised protests: "The proposed extension of The White Sands Bombing Range in Districts 4 and 5 has created a feeling of acute uneasiness in that area, that what virtually amounts to confiscation of private property by Federal authority. Our neighborly and friendly interest prompts us to inquire further into a matter involving property rights of citizens and the validity of existing permits covering use of the Public Lands." Moreover, the letter continued, "While this particular group is engaged in an effort to defend their homes and fortunes against an invasion of Federal authority, it would appear ill advised that disinterested persons should attempt interference. We are, however, concerned with an attitude which does not recognize property rights and in the exercise of administrative authority over the Public Lands in effect denies the validity and sanctity of a contract entered into in good faith under the conditions of a 10 year term permit."[73]

Following much debate about leases on public lands, Bell had asked Thomas Young of the Department of the Army's Legislative and Liaison Division to clarify how compensation would work for displaced ranchers, to reconsider co-use agreements (even on a part-time basis), and to think about the value of ranchers in military testing (namely that they could play a role in searching out missiles). The military's response was far from conciliatory. In a separate correspondence during the same month Smith reaffirmed to Bell that little chance remained for co-use land agreements. Smith explained that at the 1948 hearings the military had drawn the lines in the sand. Any further meeting with grazing interests was pointless. Smith explained "these most recent proposals represent little advance beyond Army's thinking at Las Cruces hearing and would prove equally unacceptable to ranchers whose opposition has been maintained at white heat up to present."[74]

Ranchers, along with individuals holding mining interests on the proposed proving ground, disapproved of the plan. Attorney J. O. Seth, who represented the New Mexico Cattle Growers Association, argued that the association would "oppose every way we can" the taking of the lands for the sole purpose of military testing. He explained further, "the cattlemen are opposed to the move, not only because they would lose their ranches, but because it would wreck the economy of southern New Mexico." While Seth understood why missile and rocket testing was important to the nation, he pressed that the military had already asked "for too much from one area." Either way most felt the two-day-a-week co-use agreements would not allow for a profit.[75]

The ranchers had other reasons to complain. A number of property owners with lands within Alamogordo Bombing and Gunnery Range invited their friends with land on the proposed northern extension to White Sands Proving Ground to visit their former homes in January 1949. What they found unnerved them. Rancher Riss Bishop relayed reactions to Krug. He explained that "the Army had moved windmills from some ranches to others, also storage tanks, destroyed spreader dams, cut one earth dam, and tore up houses and barns, moved houses, burned one house, and all the improvements were in very bad shape." Bishop felt that a co-use agreement would not work when the military had destroyed improvements. He explained, "we can understand how the ranchers in the Old Bombing Range feel, working all their lives fixing up a ranch and then have the army take it, tear it up and get practically nothing our of it [sic]."[76]

Why did the federal government purchase the lands to create Doña Ana Target Range and McGregor Guided Missile Range, as well as other regional military facilities, but failed to do so at White Sands? As mentioned earlier, the War Department, the Department of Agriculture, and the Soil Conservation Service intended to work toward taking lands in fee title to make the proving ground. Yet opposition from ranchers altered their plans. A 1952 report stated "as a result of resistance of the ranchers to the method of acquisition, the directive was then amended to provide for the acquisition of an estate tantamount to a use term for years, in lieu of the fee title." Lease and suspension agreements removed most of south-central New Mexico from public access by February 1952. In the process the Department of the Army tied ranchers to the proving ground. Yet the proving ground remained rangelands for many ranchers, despite a lack of access to their private property or grazing lands.[77]

The most well-known resistance to the militarization of south-central New Mexico came from rancher John Prather on the McGregor Range south of the proving ground (now a part of Fort Bliss). In a story eerily similar to the one told in Edward Abbey's novel *Fire on the Mountain* (1962) and reminiscent of parts of Cormac McCarthy's book *Cities of the Plain* (1998), in 1956 Prather refused to sell the family's property in the expansion of the McGregor Range. As a result the Department of Justice initiated condemnation proceedings on his land. Despite a March 1, 1957, deadline to vacate, Prather refused to leave. When U.S. marshals attempted to evict him, twenty-five armed and ready friends planned to defend the Prather ranch. Under pressure caused by negative media coverage the army agreed to let Prather stay on his property and graze on portions of the McGregor Range under a co-use agreement. While offered more than $100,000 for his property in 1959, Prather refused to cash the check and remained on his land until his death six years later.[78]

State officials also showed outrage at the land seizures. Senator Dennis Chavez blamed "the indifference of officialdom in New Mexico" for the conflict at McGregor Range in 1957. Reflecting the deep-seated tensions between New Mexico and Texas, Chavez suggested that had New Mexico's congressional delegation stood up to the powerful Texas delegation, perhaps the military site would have been in some West Texas wasteland. From politicians to local ranchers, New Mexicans balked at the taking of property by the federal government.[79]

Yet not all residents saw the arrival of the U.S. Army and Air Force as a bad thing. Las Cruces mayor Mike Apodoca expressed concern about rumors of a reduction in size and even the closure of White Sands Proving Ground in 1954. In a letter to Senator Chavez he explained, "you know that the rapid development of our community in recent years has been directly related to the activities of the Proving Ground, and the extent of planning for future expansion is dependent upon its continued operations." The region had seen substantial economic growth because of White Sands Proving Ground, Holloman Air Force Base, and other military sites. Between 1950 and 1960 Las Cruces experienced a 138 percent population growth and Alamogordo jumped by 220 percent. According to the missile range's information office, during the 1960–61 fiscal year White Sands Missile Range and the Air Force Missile

Development Center at Holloman Air Force Base added $200 million in total capital to the Las Cruces, Alamogordo, and El Paso areas. The seventeen thousand employees at the missile range and air force base contributed $100 million in salary alone to the regional economy.[80]

However, even as the military-scientific land regime invaded the region, the displaced livestock community remained. Two patterns of land use, one tied to the agrarian past and the other to the exigencies of a global cold war, collided during World War II. The Cold War led to an expansion of military presence in the region after 1945 through a property lease and grazing permit suspension program that sowed the seeds of discontent among the displaced White Sands ranchers.

With the ecological decline of the desert grasslands and continuous drought came federal conservation efforts that placed some one-half million acres of land into the hands of the Department of Interior. Ranchers in part shaped military interest in the region. In the sixty-years prior to the war, the largely Anglo migrant population had brought extensive grazing practices to an already arid place. The Grazing Service and later the Bureau of Land Management sought to prop up the livestock community of south-central New Mexico through federal management of the grazing commons. However, with the pressures of World War II and the military's perceptions of deserts as perfect for weapons testing, south-central New Mexico became a part of the new rural West where America's military might was forged. Those designs for the desert never went uncontested.

Manhattan Project scientists convened on the Alamogordo Bombing and Gunnery Range in July 1945. They came to test a new super weapon that they aptly called "the gadget." If the War Department had not made clear that a new land-use ethic had come to south-central New Mexico, the explosion of the first atomic weapon at the Trinity Site assured that many ranchers would never return to their homesteads. As rumors of a permanent military installation swirled through local communities, radiation monitors tried to measure fallout across the region. The embryonic science of nuclear weaponry had come to the militarized desert of south-central New Mexico.

2

ATOMIC ATTRACTIONS

In July 1953 the Atomic Energy Commission (AEC) hired the Albuquerque construction firm Campbell & Kay to fill in the large crater created by the first test of an atomic device at Trinity, New Mexico. The AEC had deemed the site chosen by Manhattan Project personnel for the July 1945 blast a potential health hazard. Because of its radioactivity, scientists had classified the green glassy-like substance called Trinitite found in the crater (sand fused by the extreme heat of the blast) as dangerous. Since the test, Trinity had become a desert laboratory where scientists funded by the AEC (created in 1946) could study the intersections between nature and radiation. It also had value to the military, which sought to know the role of radiation in employing nuclear weapons in warfare. Once the commission had filled in the crater and removed the Trinitite, the Soil Conservation Service planned to plant grass on the site. If no one protested, Trinity would return to New Mexico's rural desert environment despite its profound significance to the atomic age.[1]

But not all were happy with the seemingly logical plan for the still radioactive environment. Local tourist boosters from nearby Alamogordo and White Sands National Monument and state politicians had encouraged the AEC to reconsider the proposal. By bringing visitors to the site of the first nuclear explosion they believed Trinity could act as an economic bulwark for the state as well as a monument to scientific ingenuity at the dawn of the nuclear age. On August 11, 1945, two days after the bombing of Nagasaki and less than a month since Trinity, the Alamogordo Chamber of Commerce wrote a letter to Hillory A. Tolson, the acting director of the National Park Service (NPS). The letter emphasized the importance of the test and explained "people will want to see the spot where this great event occurred bringing in a new era the same as they have wanted to see the spot where the first Pilgrim set foot on this continent." Trinity held the potential to attract tourists to the area.[2]

Throughout its early history Trinity was contested terrain neither fully secured from public memory nor open to public audiences. Two seemingly divergent narratives shaped the Trinity Site at the dawn of the Cold War. The first was defined by the ecology of radiation and its value to the military. A second revolved around an appreciation for Trinity as public domain. Boosters tried to sell Trinity as a tourist site. This was the first crusade to delimit America's nuclear landscape as tourist haven. Between those two narratives stood an unpredictable desert environment that challenged radiation monitors to make sense of fallout. Along with the increased military activities in the region, wind, rain, and desert sand thwarted attempts to build meaningful and informative museums and monuments at Trinity.

Even as the AEC sought to understand Trinity's nuclear landscape and despite the proving ground's expanded missile testing, the proposed designs for a public site of commemoration remained alive and well. For the Park Service, Trinity could act as another draw to White Sands National Monument (established in 1933) on the missile range's eastern edge. For local towns the site was one more reason for travelers to stop and visit southern New Mexico. In the wake of the plan to fill in the crater, New Mexico governor Edwin Mechem would directly appeal to the chairman of the AEC to reassess the move, and New Mexico representative Antonio Fernandez would introduce a bill in the U.S. Congress calling for designation of Trinity as a national monument. Both ultimately failed. After 1945 missile and ordnance testing was a weekly occurrence on the growing White Sands Proving Ground (in 1953 alone the missile range carried out 425 tests). At a meeting in 1952 the NPS reluctantly agreed with the Department of Defense (DOD) and AEC in their assessment that national security and concerns of radiation overshadowed public access to a planned tourist site. But this would not end the conflict over Trinity.[3]

As the historian Ferenc Szasz explains in his seminal study on the site, Trinity does not hold the same significance as does Gettysburg, Pearl Harbor, or Harper's Ferry. But it remains as important, if not more so, than all of those places. Trinity is a peculiar war monument. Still situated on White Sands Missile Range, Trinity is open to the public only on the first Saturdays of April and October, the most inviting times of the year in an otherwise challenging desert environment. The site is a barren and isolated place marked by a simple obelisk. At ground zero there are remnants of the tower that held the bomb. With the exception of a small area protected by a shelter, there exist few reminders of the Trinitite or crater. The Jumbo encasing (which if used would have preserved the precious plutonium core had the test failed) sits outside the fenced-in obelisk. A tour bus shuttles visitors to and from the nearby McDonald ranch house (owned by George McDonald, brother of Dave McDonald) where the device was assembled in preparation for the test. Missile Range authorities have recently resurrected one of the dilapidated observation bunkers. After that, though, there is little left to experience but the surrounding natural landscape.[4]

To truly understand Trinity's monumental present we must examine its contested environmental past. Trinity was more than simply a site where Manhattan Engineer District (MED) scientists exploded the first atomic weapon. The military and Atomic Energy Commission wove a narrative where national security met environmental uncertainty. Between 1945 and 1952 radiation monitors examined soil, water, plants, and animals with little initial sense of the degree to which radiation from the test had contaminated the environment. Wind storms, arid soil, and rain played a vital role in undermining how radiation monitors understood the intersection between nature and fallout. As a safety measure the AEC not only bulldozed the crater and observation bunkers but also removed monitoring equipment, scooped up most of the Trinitite, and removed contaminated cattle. Although stories of the irradiated livestock rippled through New Mexico, the public never truly understood the problem of environment and fallout. Neither did the AEC or DOD, for that matter.

Knowledge of the effects of fallout from the new weapon (and thus a value in keeping it secret) aided those scientists keenly interested in understanding the dynamic interplay between a new destructive human technology and the nonhuman natural world. As the historian Sharon Kingsland notes, "ecosystem ecology was nurtured in the bosom of the atomic age, funded largely by government agencies that evolved from the Manhattan Project." The University of California, Los Angeles became a primary recipient of AEC research dollars at Trinity. In 1954 famed ecologists Howard and Eugene Odum did research for the Atomic Energy Commission on the Eniwetok Atoll in the Marshall Islands (a site of nuclear weapons research). Most of these funds did not directly support ecosystem science. However, they did encourage research into interactions between the biotic and abiotic worlds that would establish and reaffirm the fundamentals of ecosystem ecology.[5]

More broadly, as the historian Donald Worster notes, it was the bomb that produced "a new moral consciousness called environmentalism." Through their research, scientists joined concerned citizens in driving a movement that by 1970 would take on not only the bomb but also toxic waste in rivers and lakes and the ill effects of pesticides on birds and the human body. Trinity would come to hold significance for environmentalists, pacifists, and antinuclear activists. Well before that Trinity had evolved into a place with competing uses and meanings. The relationship between the science of radioactivity, militarization, and the dynamics of the nonhuman natural world stood in stark contrast to its material value as tourist haven and monument to scientific ingenuity. Between 1945 and 1970 the NPS and local monument boosters lobbied to keep the site as intact as possible and even sought to build a museum there. They saw the site as an economic bulwark for a region that once relied on the limited productive capacity of the desert for cattle grazing.[6]

The Cold War transformed regional demography from one mostly made up of ranchers to one dominated by scientists, military personnel, and their families. But for those not tied to the bases and proving grounds in south-central New Mexico, tourism was another important source of income. Trinity was cast as a sacred space tied to the end of World War II, the American Cold War struggle against global communism, and the ultimate fate of human societies in the nuclear age. Boosters recognized that those narratives of Trinity would not only attract tourists to New Mexico but could also challenge the idea of Trinity as only a military-scientific site. For better or for worse, boosters believed Trinity belonged to the public.

That the first contest over America's nuclear landscape happened in the American West is hardly surprising. As mentioned in the introduction, those lands west of the Mississippi were the heart of the American nuclear industry. Beginning in 1942 several federal agencies, including the U.S. Army (1942–46), the Atomic Energy Commission (1947–74), the Energy Research and Development Administration (1974–77), and the Department of Energy (after 1977), time and again chose the open spaces of the West for nuclear weapons research, development, and waste disposal. New Mexico in particular has nurtured the nuclear weapons industry from mining uranium to the storage of radioactive waste. As the anthropologist Jake Kosek suggests, "from cradle to the grave (many would say beyond the grave), New Mexico is 'Nukes 'R' Us.'"[7]

At the same time, the historians Bruce Hevly and John Findlay argue that while the Atomic West materialized from federal schemes, "westerners themselves—old-timers and new arrivals both—toiled to make nuclear power a reality and to shape the forms it would take." The nuclear weapons industry did not simply take over the region. Westerners worked for the military in both a civilian and an armed forces capacity. They both promoted its presence and challenged its place in transforming their communities. They made sense of militarization as a part of everyday life. While the predominant story suggests a profound unease with the emergence of the nuclear industry in the region, westerners also used the new nuclear state to fulfill their own desires. Nuclear tourism would become a part of that history.[8]

Tourism is, of course, nothing new to the American West, since the late nineteenth-century westerners (and easterners) had shaped a tourist economy that touted the diverse cultures, landscapes, and prominent myths of the region. Tourism was big business in a region home to the most famous national parks: Yellowstone, Yosemite, and the Grand Canyon. In the early twentieth century Anglos trekked west (or east) to experience and exploit Indian cultures, go skiing, and find wilderness. For Aspen, Colorado, Santa Fe, New Mexico, and Moab, Utah, tourism has both revitalized town centers and transformed them into places tied to the business of other places. This was perhaps clearest in the hotel chains and outdoor-leisure financiers who employed westerners, but whose capital base was elsewhere.[9]

It should thus come as no surprise that in 1952 tourists gathered in Las Vegas, Nevada, to watch the AEC test weapons at the Nevada Test Site. In fact Casino owner Wilbur Clark and the Las Vegas Chamber of Commerce used the specter of the nuclear blast to bring Americans to the city. The usually secret weapons tests often made their way through the local grapevine so that local casinos, including the Desert Inn, which promised a bird's-eye view of blasts from its Sky Room, could promote atomic tourism alongside gambling.[10]

Alamogordo is not Las Vegas, and Trinity was not the Nevada Test Site. However, as America's first nuclear shrine, Trinity was at the vanguard of atomic tourism *as a part of the state*. The battle for Trinity was the first attempt to make a federally mandated tourist site from a federally controlled nuclear landscape. The environmental history of the first nuclear weapons explosion underlies Trinity's dirty past. That story begins on July 16, 1945, when a cadre of scientists and military personnel gathered before dawn to see what they had created as members of the Manhattan Project.

THE TROUBLE WITH FALLOUT

The Trinity test was the culmination of the American secret mission to beat the Germans to a nuclear weapon during Word War II. Major General Leslie R. Groves, a crude but efficient army official, directed the program, established in 1942 and dubbed the Manhattan Engineer District. Plutonium production occurred at Hanford, Washington, and uranium enrichment at Oak Ridge, Tennessee. Los Alamos, New Mexico, served as the site of research and development. Led by J. Robert Oppenheimer of the University of California, Berkeley, the group of international scientists on "The Hill" at Los Alamos included the A-list of mid-twentieth-century theoretical physicists and mathematicians (many had fled fascism in Europe during the 1930s). In addition to Oppenheimer the list included Italian physicist Enrico Fermi (winner of the 1938 Nobel Prize), physicist Edward Teller (father of the hydrogen bomb alongside physicist Stanislaw Ulam), and mathematician John von Neumann (a whiz in artificial intelligence and architect of the first game theory models), among many others. The first bomb design employed the radioisotope U-235. Because of its simple design (described as a "gun assembly" technique, a nuclear reaction occurred by simply shooting one subcritical mass of U-235 at another), scientists expressed confidence that it would work. Therefore, no test was planned. The second weapon used plutonium and turned on implosion. Employing conventional explosive "lenses" as a trigger, scientists hoped to concentrate plutonium so it reached supercritical mass. Uncertainty about its design led to calls for a test shot, later named Trinity.[11]

The ideal landscape for the test needed to be flat and isolated and enjoy clear skies. While Manhattan Project personnel had explored seven other potential locations across the West (including several areas in New Mexico and one in California), they chose south-central New Mexico on the Jornada del Muerto. By the approval date in September 1944 the proposed site (swapped with the state of New Mexico for lands in the eastern section of the state) was already under the auspices of the military as Alamogordo Bombing and Gunnery Range. Site selection was influenced by not only the presence of the bombing range but also its proximity to Los Alamos, sparse human settlement, and advantageous geographical and climatic conditions (namely, low rainfall and flat terrain hemmed in by the San Andres and Oscura mountain ranges).[12]

Even before Trinity, questions about weather and the potential spread of fallout swirled among scientists and military personnel. Fallout was initially seen as one of the lesser theoretical concerns within the secret

2. Trinity explosion, 1945. Courtesy of the National Nuclear Security Administration–Nevada Field Office.

program, but during the weeks leading up to the test physicians and radiologists attached to the Manhattan Project raised concern about fallout (namely the radiologists Louis Hempelmann and Stafford Warren). This science of how radiation affected people, plants, and animals went by the thinly veiled title of "health physics." The MED hired meteorologist Jack Hubbard to deal with the impossible task of predicting rain and wind patterns for the day of the test. How much fallout would harm humans remained an ambiguous matter as scientific guesses ranged from 60 roentgens to 100 roentgens (R) over two weeks. In the name of secrecy there was no strategy for pretest evacuation. Thus, the wind direction had to be taken into account. That it blew from the south-southwest toward uninhabited areas of New Mexico would play a vital role in minimizing human exposure to radiation immediately following the test. Project personnel only planned to remove local residents in

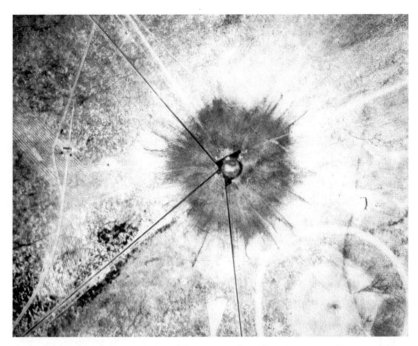

3. Trinity crater, 1945. Courtesy of the National Nuclear Security Administration–Nevada Field Office.

the event of an emergency after the explosion. Herein lay a problem. Even with Hubbard keeping track of wind and precipitation patterns, the weather could change.[13]

When the device exploded at 5:29:45 a.m. Mountain War Time, July 16, 1945, one observer recalled that "when it let go, it lit up 180 degrees of the horizon, not like one but a dozen brilliant suns. It stayed lit up and made chills run up my back because I knew what might happen if it was not controlled." The blast scorched flora and exterminated every moving creature from snakes to ground lizards. In historian Ferenc Szasz's words, "the stench of death lingered about the area for three weeks."[14]

Manhattan Project officials employed a cadre of radiation monitors, each of whom had several instruments including gamma ray survey meters, counters for detection of alpha particle radiation in the presence of beta and gamma radiation, and a meter for the detection of gamma and gamma plus beta radiations. As result of changing weather the fallout cloud did not move with uniformity, and monitors gathered an uneven series of readings. The cloud first split into three parts, but the bulk of it moved northwest and then shifted northeast. It moved at a speed of fifteen miles per hour and rose in altitude at fourteen thousand feet per hour, eventually reaching nearly fifty thousand feet, producing initial readings beyond the crater at levels far lower than expected. Significant readings on the ground did not appear until more than two hours after the test and over an area far wider than projected.[15]

Reflecting the uncertainty about fallout after Trinity, safe levels of radiation exposure have changed as the scientific community has come to learn more about the health effects of human contact with radioactive materials. Since 1945 acceptable exposure levels continued to drop. For the one-hundred-ton TNT test shot that preceded the Trinity explosion, exposure levels were set at 0.1 R per day. For the members of the Manhattan Project at Trinity, a "voluntary limit" for external exposure rose to 5 R. A pretest conference near ground zero set acceptable levels of the "integrated gamma ray dose for the entire body" at 75 R over a 336-hour (or two-week) period. In 1960 acceptable public doses leveled at 150 millirem (1 rem is equivalent to one roentgen) for continuous exposure and 500 millirem for infrequent exposure levels. In 1993 the National Council on Radiation Protection and Measurements set the annual whole body levels for continuous and infrequent exposure levels at 100 millirem and 500 millirem, respectively.[16]

At Trinity, measurements varied by distance from ground zero, time of reading, and position of radiation monitors. When radiation readings finally appeared at ground zero, levels jumped off the scale. A tank driver wearing a catastrophe film badge (used to show gamma readings) amassed as much as 15 R over three trips to the site. Readings were high elsewhere. At 8:30 a.m., just beyond the town of Bingham (about eighteen miles due north of the Trinity Site) at Army Search Light Station L-8, physical chemists Joseph Hirschfelder and John Magee captured readings of 2.0 Roentgens per hour (R/hr), at which point army personnel "buried steaks which were cooking on an open fire because they

4. Members of the Manhattan Engineer District in protective clothing. Courtesy of the National Nuclear Security Administration–Nevada Field Office.

thought they were too much contaminated . . . and pulled out." East of L-8 monitors stumbled upon a car "heavily contaminated" under the fenders and chassis with a reading of 4.0 R/hr. Dirt and dust seemed to have clung to the car's underbelly. After noon, readings near the junction between U.S. 161 and U.S. 146 reached 6.0 R/hr. At the small gorge on the Chupadera Mesa two miles from the junction and nine miles east of Bingham, readings read 20.0 R/hr three hours after the explosion and 7.0 R/hr six and a half hours after that. Scientists quickly dubbed the area "Hot Canyon."[17]

Scientists measuring fallout knew several important factors would complicate monitoring even before the test began. Radioactive sand particulates would fall from the cloud in different places due to varying wind directions at different altitudes. They also understood that a period of time would elapse before monitors could accurately measure the intensity of the radioactivity and that decay depended upon where and at what rate the particulates settled. Moreover, rain could potentially wash particulates further into the ground. In all cases natural conditions meant that the geometrical division of fallout would vary considerably.[18]

Warren realized that "energy developed in the test was several times greater than that expected by the scientific group." In effect, monitors had tracked radiation from the explosion as far as Las Vegas, New Mexico, more than 150 miles north of ground zero. As wind and rain affected how radioactive ash and debris moved across the desert, monitors found that results varied by both time and place. Uncertainty best characterized initial analysis of the test's environmental impact.[19]

In August 1945 Joseph G. Hoffman, leader of the Health Group section of the Manhattan Project, had measured high levels of exposure at Bingham and White Store and in Hot Canyon. Hoffman suggested levels on the ground in Hot Canyon reached as high as 139 R total over two weeks. Stafford Warren, head of the UCLA group (which did the brunt of the research on radiation at the site), later suggested that the canyon might have received as much as 230 R in the days after Trinity. Hoffman found that numbers were decidedly lower for Bingham, where ground levels measured at 14.7 R. At the town of White Store the ground dose peaked at 26.2 R on the ground. By Hoffman's own admission, those were conservative numbers. It remains clear that scientists did not totally understand how the environment altered the dispersal of radioactive materials. Their attempts to measure fallout were simply trial and error.[20]

During the same month Louis Hempelmann, head of the Health Group sector of the project in Los Alamos, had made a preliminary trip to several of the areas most affected by fallout. In Hot Canyon they interviewed the Raitliff family, whose home had not appeared on the maps used to find people in case of evacuation. Having neither heard nor seen anything at the time of the test, the older couple had learned of the event from a grandson who lived with them. For the two weeks following the test, they went on with their lives tending to ranch business. Importantly, rain had fallen in the canyon the night after the test, making it probable

5. Rada cows, 1945. Courtesy of the National Nuclear Security Administration–Nevada Field Office.

that "some of the activity was carried into their drinking water and may have been drunk on the following day and thereafter." They showed no symptoms of exposure, but Hempelmann estimated the dose of gamma radiation received by the Raitliffs during the first two weeks after the explosion at 47 R, which exceeded the tolerance does by 33 R. Yet the family seemed in good health.[21]

There remains little doubt that with such high radiation levels the livestock, wildlife, and desert plant life of south-central New Mexico felt the effects of fallout. Many ranchers complained that their cattle had burns in the weeks following Trinity as "atomic calves" and "rada cows" became the talk of New Mexico. Louis Nalda of the Red Canyon Sheep Company noted that cattle grazing in the area most affected by the fallout showed a loss of hair accompanied by blistering on their backs. The hair grew back but with a substantial amount of gray follicles where it had once been red. Of over 300 company cattle, 136 showed effects. Nalda explained to Hempelmann that he received word of similar symptoms from both the Bursum Cattle Company and Harvey Cattle Company.[22]

In November 1945 rancher Ted Coker explained to Hempelmann his cattle also showed a graying of hair on their backs. At the same time, his fences and windmill looked as if they had been "painted white" when seen during the night. At the Raitliff ranch two dogs had started to limp and eventually their footpads became raw and bloody. For a time one could no longer walk, and the other had formed white hairs on its back. The Raitliffs recalled that the ground and fences seemed "frosted" by what looked like snow at a time that would have been immediately after the explosion. The two dogs eventually recovered.[23]

A follow-up report led by Hempelmann suggested that between five and six hundred cattle displayed symptoms of beta radiation exposure as had cats, dogs, and some lambs. Holm Bursum's cattle had shown the greatest effects. Ten to fifteen animals exhibited epilation and scab formation on their backs. Graying of hairs seemed more noticeable than on cattle studied at the Nalda Ranch. In December Hempelmann and his team also studied suspect cattle from both the Bursum and Coker ranches. Most had symptoms similar to those at the Nalda Ranch: significant graying of the hair, epilation and scabbing of the skin, and bleeding lesions. One showed bloody mucoid discharge from the nostrils. Of seventy cattle showing symptoms that the AEC examined in 1949, only a few had long-term effects from exposure to radiation. But it was also noted by the AEC that some of those animals with burns on their backs did develop cancer.[24]

A sense of disorder surrounded the earliest examinations of animals as lack of uniformity characterized readings around ground zero. As winds blew, rain fell, and animals moved about the desert, it became a tall order to accurately measure the dynamics between radioactive fallout and the desert ecosystem. While prior to 1947 it was the MED that completed fallout studies at Trinity, after 1947 the newly created AEC took over the area. A group of University of California, Los Angeles scientists (led by the head of the UCLA Medical School, Stafford

Warren) joined the AEC Division of Biology and Medicine to conduct of environmental studies of the region.[25]

There remains little record of the immediate impact of the test on wildlife in the region. But when the AEC took control of the site in 1947, UCLA-led radiation investigations expanded to include feral birds and rodents. The findings were not conclusive. An adolescent jay with a severely damaged foot "showed considerable radioactivity [when] exposed to 'counter' tests." Five horned larks possessed deformations to their claws and feet. Biologists also found that mice trapped just outside the fenced-in crater area had significant cataracts most likely caused by exposure to the test. Of white-footed mice captured, 26 percent showed symptoms. Among kangaroo rats 62 percent had cataracts, which far exceeded the average for normal mice populations.[26]

But further examinations of feral birds, reptiles, and other mammals found within the vicinity of the radiation path showed only trace amounts of radioactivity. Of 402 animals collected between 1947 and 1948 only 38 showed "significant values" for beta and gamma activities. Of those, 33.3 percent of birds, 7.3 percent of mammals, and 4.7 percent of reptiles displayed effects. For those showing significant activity, it usually occurred in the digestive tract. Fecal samples suggested that because of no absorption into the bodily tissue, radiation often entered the body as small particulates and then passed through the digestive process. Nevertheless, uncertainty of the effects of long-term exposure led the health physics group to classify the Jornada del Muerto and surrounding areas as potentially unsafe for humans.[27]

Prior to the UCLA studies, Los Alamos completed some studies of plant life. In August 1945 the first analysis of plant life occurred at the behest of Kenneth T. Bainbridge, a physicist for the Manhattan Project. Those studies could explain both how radiation moved and how animals consumed it. A group of observers drove stakes into the ground at up to five hundred yards from ground zero. Each spot denoted a measurement. The radiation survey offered a myriad of results that ranged from as high as 0.53 R/hr near the crater to as little as 0.013 R/hr at the furthest measured point. Those findings informed the first of a series of studies that sought to explore how radiation settled in the ground, how plants reacted to it, and how wind and erosion spread radiation. Levels of radioactivity detected between 1949 and 1950 by UCLA teams remained constant with patterns measured during earlier studies. The highest levels of activity beyond ground zero again were found on the Chupadera Mesa twenty-seven miles northeast of the fenced-in area. There, plutonium was found in the feces of cattle as well as in the tissues of wood rats. Probably the result of the age of the animals, their feeding habits, and even the physical and chemical characteristics of radioactive materials at ground zero, kangaroo rats and squirrels showed little exposure within the immediate cratered area.[28]

In 1947 the soils section of the UCLA group completed several follow-up studies on plant life. They found that not only had the explosion destroyed vegetation within five thousand feet of ground zero, but also in certain areas along the fallout path cattle had produced radioactive fecal matter as a result of the consumption of contaminated grasses. In particular, waste samples taken from cattle in the Hot Canyon area of the Chupadera Mesa "were found to be definitely radioactive." If a one-thousand-pound cow consumed an average of thirty pounds of dry material per day, it would have ingested about 7.2 millicuries of radioactive material per year. While relatively low, those numbers did not take into account soil attached to digested plant life. Thus monitors felt that dung from cattle present in the Hot Canyon area in the month immediately following the test did not accurately measure the radioactivity of the landscape. Too many factors could not be measured, creating doubt about the level of radiation in the region.[29]

The UCLA group again showed a great deal of concern for the ability of dust and rain to transport radiation that settled in the hours after the test. Wind was a serious problem for radiation monitors. Researchers explained: "dust storms have been observed in the valley where the crater is located. These storms transported large amounts of fine soil great distances from one place to another." The number of storms, their impact on different types of vegetation, the condition of the soil, and the velocity and duration of the storm mitigated how radiation spread across the region (particularly alpha emitters from plutonium). Importantly, the team admitted, "in the unique and rapidly changing conditions in and around the crater region there can be no control. One has only to experience the five heavy dust storms (so far)." Natural forces often mitigated where radiation ended up and the degree to which it concentrated in any particular area.[30]

Environmental studies completed in 1951 reiterated that climatic conditions had complicated readings across south-central New Mexico. Erosion of topsoil due to wind was again believed to have played an important role in transporting radioactive materials from the crater area. The period between 1945 and 1950 had brought dry and windy conditions to the region, allowing large quantities of radioactive material to spread from the northeastern edges of the crater area, making it weaker and thus less measurable by instruments. Water runoff had a less noticeable effect on the spread of radioactive materials. Yet, the uneven character of radioactivity at ground zero after an August 1950 flood (considered rare) suggested at least a cursory role for water in the transfer of fallout. Just as importantly, they found that "even finely powdered Trinitite is only sparingly soluble in water and dilute alkali solution, and only slightly more soluble in dilute acids." The study's authors suggested: "The problem outside the Fenced Area is entirely different for there are many potential long term insidious hazards from the present low level contamination which is the focal point of these studies." Potential risks existed not only within the crater, but also for surrounding environments. An entire region was contaminated. As fallout swirled across the desert environment the true degree of contamination remained unknown. The ambiguity that came out of early studies on fallout affected the trajectory of a monument for the Trinity Site.[31]

SELLING TRINITY

As scientists completed studies of radioactivity, monument promoters sought to build a place of commemoration at ground zero. As early as August 1945 the Alamogordo Chamber of Commerce garnered support for the plan from New Mexico's governor and congressional delegation.

Charles S. McCollum, a former local official with the Farm Security Administration (created during the New Deal) applauded the monument idea as a potential international "peace monument" with the crater left untouched "as evidence of the terrible force that can be utilized against any nation that might have thoughts of making war on any other country." Hinting at the economic utility of the site, he argued that it would become a "mecca for many, many tourists and visitors to our state, not only to see what the bomb had accomplished but to be able to say they had been to this shrine."[32]

While some New Mexicans reveled in the idea that the bomb was built and exploded in their home state, many citizens and public officials also translated Trinity to a boon for the changing economy of New Mexico, which after World War II was increasingly defined by not just military-scientific dollars. Trinity as a monument would bring visitors to Alamogordo and White Sands National Monument. In 1945 New Mexico ushered in the age of nuclear tourism.

It is important to note that the public knew of radioactivity at Trinity. In fact, the NPS had made it a point to gather clippings on the effects of fallout. From September to December newspapers printed stories on contaminated cattle and soil. The New Mexico Stockman reported on the changing color of cattle hides and the whitened corral fences at Coker's ranch. Regional papers including the Santa Fe New Mexican and Alamogordo Daily News also reported on the changing color of cattle hairs. A Visalia, California-based newspaper reported that there existed no plant life for eight hundred yards from the center of the crater. It reported on the "crude glass" fused at the point of explosion. The Albuquerque Journal reported vegetation "denuded" as "white footed men of science" conducted tours of the site. It also reported that X-rays "emanate from billions of atoms in sand, dirt, stones, and from the glass which the heat created on the surface."[33]

At the same time, advocates for the commemoration of Trinity recognized that the War Department would not readily cede the land, which remained under the control of the Alamogordo Army Air Field (renamed Holloman Air Force Base in 1948). Acting Secretary of the Interior Abe

Fortas sought permission for a full site investigation. However, citing security reasons, the Army Corps of Engineers had refused to allow anyone near it. Nevertheless, in September Fortas forwarded his request to the secretary of war, hoping for an opportunity to assess ground zero for its inclusion in the national monument system.[34]

In October 1945 the Department of War granted permission for a survey of the site at the end of the year. Yet because of ongoing radiological tests, military personnel gave no indication whether the department would hand over the land to the Department of Interior (DOI). Nevertheless, monument plans went forward. By the summer of 1946 DOI officials lobbied to have several issues implemented. They needed to bring together an accurate timeline that explained the history of the test, compile scientific facts to explain the engineering of the bomb, and collect historical objects vital to telling the story of the device. The following year DOI officials also sought to create an interagency panel with the DOD to deal with questions about the monument program and its relationship to increased weapons testing in the region.[35]

The DOI wanted to include the planes used in the bombings of Hiroshima and Nagasaki at a Trinity monument. In January of 1946 Secretary of Interior Harold Ickes had asked Secretary of War Robert Patterson to consider the transfer of the *Enola Gay*. He suggested, "The B-29 plane that carried the bomb to the target links this site with Hiroshima and vividly demonstrates the ease with which atomic power could again be devoted to the destructiveness of war." In March a bill introduced in the U.S. Senate by New Mexico senator Carl Hatch called on the secretary of war to "reserve and maintain" the *Enola Gay* and *Bockscar* (the plane that delivered the bomb to Nagasaki) for the purposes of display in a nationally and internationally focused museum within the proposed monument.[36]

While neither plane came to Trinity, in August 1946 an interagency meeting in Los Alamos encouraged the completion of several aims to further an interpretive blueprint for the site. They asked that all unclassified information on the test be made available to the DOI. The army would also recommend the transfer of the tanks that had carried scientists to the crater after the test. Finally, the army would not do any "house-cleaning" until DOI officials could complete studies of the area.[37]

In 1946 a draft proclamation had reached President Harry Truman. In a letter to the president, then secretary of the interior Julius Krug asked that the proclamation set aside 4,190 acres of land as allowed by the 1906 Antiquities Act. Truman did not sign the proclamation. By 1950 the area remained under the control of Holloman Air Force Base (although the Atomic Energy Commission maintained authority over the area around Trinity). Continued uncertainty about the degree of radioactivity stifled the push for a national place of commemoration. The Department of Interior in part recognized that fact. An NPS official believed "it will be some time, probably several years, before the National Park Service can take over."[38]

In April 1947 NPS personnel given the opportunity to inspect Trinity spent only two hours at the still contaminated site. Following a second visit in September, the Park Service's chief historian, Ronald Lee, argued that preserving at least a portion of the substance Trinitite (which he called "Atomsite") was vital to maintaining the crater's integrity. They also hoped to protect bunkers and the McDonald ranch house. By covering dead plant life with buckets, the Park Service also hoped to protect charred vegetation for future use in an onsite museum.[39]

The same year E. T. Scoyen, acting regional director for the Park Service, asked for the preservation of the actual clock used during the test, several observation bunkers, the wiring that connected the bunkers to ground zero, and the McDonald ranch house, where initial staging for the test occurred. Once completed, the Trinity experience would take visitors not only to the crater but also through the original base camp and to the ranch house.[40]

Trinitite had a strange story of its own. In 1946 Scoyen sent to Arthur Demaray, associate director for the NPS, a sampling of the substance. He suggested that the Department of Interior display Trinitite on a sand bed brought from the Trinity Site to the agency's museum. In October 1952 the Smithsonian Institute asked for fifty pounds of Trinitite, which would act as an artifact in an exhibition on the bomb. The request was granted. In removing it from the crater, the NPS offered no story about ecological degradation or an uncertainty about public health. Instead, it became merely a remnant of the bomb itself.[41]

Fragments of the bizarre substance also held material value among local residents. People living near the test site found ways to get their hands on the unusual green glass. In 1947 Don's Chevron service station in Socorro sold the material for fifty cents apiece. A chunk of the Trinitite purchased by a Sandia National Laboratories (established in 1948) employee measured 0.4 milliroentgens per hour. The Atomic Energy Commission reported that a woman who had trucked gas to the Trinity Site wondered if her uterine tumor and spleen condition had resulted from the shoebox full of Trinitite she had taken from the site. In both cases questions of liability and public safety became issues for the Atomic Energy Commission and Holloman Air Force Base. That the public could potentially scour the site for similar shards of Trinitite concerned military and scientific personnel.[42]

Along with the national and global significance of Trinity, monument boosters also argued that individual contemplation and reflection would also act as part of the visit. In unexpected ways the beauty of the desert environment necessarily acted as an important but ironic factor in discussions about making a monument at Trinity. Lee explained: "It is difficult to describe the strong appeal of this barren spot. Some persons might find the area disappointing; to me, the visit was unforgettable." He described the Trinity base camp as "a wind-blown desert outpost" with a "near grandeur" natural setting. The mountains in the distance acted as "a sort of wild and appropriate stage, on a huge scale, for the atomic explosion." Yet the desert also remained "unfriendly near at hand" (one of the few intimations that the site's contamination could influence a visitor's experience).[43]

By 1951 Park Service hopes of creating a commemorative site with significant interpretation began to fade as scientists continued to monitor the extent of fallout and as military activity increased in the region. A year later Charles Porter III, acting chief historian for the Park Service, relayed to the regional director that Paul Pearson, of the AEC

Division of Biology and Medicine, had suggested that little remained of the original crater. At the same time, most of the equipment used during the test was no longer housed in the region. Hinting at the removal of materials from the site and the reality that the area would remain off limits to the general public, Pearson wondered "if it would not be sufficient if the National Park Service simply erected a marker at the site."[44]

Memorial advocates within the DOI and NPS recognized that the fused sand at ground zero remained radioactive. Yet they still strove to retain a portion of the substance for use in a larger museum setting at the site. At a March 11, 1952, meeting at New Mexico governor Edwin Mechem's office, Tillotson relayed the AEC Division of Biology and Medicine's belief that while in its present form Trinitite posed little threat to human visitors, "as it weathers and becomes powdered it presents an inhalation problem and a certain hazard from a public health standpoint, because it has a tendency to cause lung cancer or other diseases of the respiratory organs." The radioactive threat remained, in Mechem's words, "indefinite and in the future." All involved recognized the infeasibility of the project until DOD relinquished the site.[45]

The day before the meeting in the governor's office and in the wake of the revelation that the AEC planned to bulldoze the site, monument boosters staked their claim to Trinity. New Mexico congressman Antonio Fernandez introduced a House resolution for the establishment of the Trinity Atomic National Monument. Fernandez's bill had also stipulated that the monument would not materialize "until the Atomic Energy Commission determines that the public health and safety will not be endangered by its use . . . as a national monument." In a letter to the House Committee on Interior and Insular Affairs, the Secretary of the Interior Oscar Chapman compared Trinity to the first human airplane flight, suggesting that "the establishment of the site of the first successful use of atomic power as a national monument will commemorate one of the most significant steps forward which man has taken in his mastery of the world about him." In Trinity Chapman found a place of transcendent significance to the human race.[46]

Like other boosters, Mechem objected to the covering up of the original crater, reiterating its importance as part of the monument. The Park Service attempted to protect what Trinitite remained at ground zero despite uncertainty about the potential health impact on visitors. In April 1952 various New Mexico politicians and national representatives meeting with NPS and DOD officials agreed to protect the residual Trinitite for inclusion in a museum exhibit, even though there remained little likelihood of the site opening to the public in the near future.[47]

On May 20, 1952, several air force, Park Service, and AEC representatives visited the site. Their report reiterated many previous NPS demands. All parties agreed to continued protection of remnant Trinitite under an erected wooden shelter. They understood that the AEC planned to bulldoze the area, but asked that the crater remain otherwise undisturbed. Similarly, the report requested that the remains of the tower that held the device along with several observation bunkers remain intact. Importantly both sides recognized that Park Service officials could take no action until the DOD no longer needed the land. By August 1953 the crater was gone, radiation remained a concern, and missile testing increased on White Sands. Nonetheless, the site existed as a site of conflict between the military, NPS, and state and local politicians and business communities. The AEC and the DOD never fully owned Trinity.[48]

CONTESTED OBELISK

Early monument proposals met little public protest. In 1946 a lone dissenting voice challenged the NPS on its plan for Trinity:

> According to a news notice in Desert Magazine you are planning to make a national monument out of the spot where the first atomic bomb was exploded in New Mexico and also to have on display the B-29 which dropped the second atomic bomb on Nagasaki. I wonder whether you have given thorough consideration to the controversial nature of this action. There are many Americans, including some of the top men in the Navy and Army, who consider the dropping of

the bombs on the Japanese cities a national disgrace. In view of this fact, isn't the placing of the plane that dropped one of the bombs on public display a rather questionable act?[49]

Either way there seemed little likelihood of any large-scale museum opening at the site. In late 1952 the expanding White Sands Proving Ground gained control over the Trinity Site. In March 1953 Colonel Homer D. Thomas within the Ordnance Corps on the proving ground had written to P. P. Patraw, acting regional director for the NPS, explaining that "our firing program is becoming heavier and indications are that the range may soon be in full use every day of the week. If this program materializes, any construction work in the area will of course be out of the question." In September 1953 radiation levels had "subsided" enough to allow the public to visit the Trinity Site. More than seven hundred visitors came to look around. Yet during the next twenty-two years the missile range opened Trinity only at irregular intervals.[50]

Enthusiasm for Trinity never totally subsided. In the mid-1960s there came a second major wave of interest in making the site a national monument open to the public on a regular basis. Despite military activity and studies that showed continued radioactivity at ground zero, the Park Service again emerged as the key player in pushing for a commemorative site. As William Brown, NPS regional historian, explained in 1967, "in due course, if we don't blow up in the meantime, the Trinity Site will be an international monument commemorating the birth of the atomic age."[51]

In 1970 Clinton Anderson, U.S. senator for New Mexico, introduced a bill to establish Trinity National Historic Site (in 1965 Congress designated Trinity a National Historic Landmark district). An accompanying Park Service report provided data to support the bill, reemphasizing the site's global implications: "Consider the transcendent significance of this scientific and technological triumph; its implications for world military and political history, both in World War II and thereafter; and the resultant impact of accelerated nuclear science in peaceful fields ranging from metallurgy to medicine. All of these mark the atomic bomb project as a great turning point in universal history. . . . Thus there is no question of the national, indeed the international, historical significance of the Trinity Site."[52]

The bill ultimately failed. But with former White Sands National Monument supervisor Donald Dayton named as NPS liaison to the project, the NPS drew up the 1970 Master Plan for the Trinity National Historic Site despite continued uncertainty about fallout there. In 1967 the park naturalist for White Sands National Monument had reported to Dayton that "by word of mouth we heard that: Trinity Site is hot enough to give a person a dose of 3 milliroentgens per hour in the enclosed area" and what remained of the instruments from the test both at ground zero and at the dilapidated observation bunkers were also deemed "hot."[53]

In 1967 Frederic L. Fey Jr. of Los Alamos National Laboratories completed a health-physics survey of Trinity and noted gamma readings near ground zero at 3mr/h, but those numbers rapidly diminished as monitors moved away from the center. While he argued, "it does not appear that anyone could receive any radiation injury through a visit to Trinity Site," Fey also acknowledged those who spent more time there, namely guides, "should wear an accepted radiation dosimeter." A study by Los Alamos National Laboratories published in 1973 showed that plutonium concentrations at ground zero were ten thousand times higher than those registered for other soils in New Mexico (as much as 262,720 microcuries per gram). While those numbers were relatively low in the grand scheme of things, there remained uncertainty about fallout at Trinity. Despite the filling in of the crater to reduce exposure, plutonium intensity in flora and fauna remained suspect. Radioactivity had traveled as far as thirty centimeters into the ground, and Trinitite understandably remained "an order of magnitude" higher than other ground zero soils. In fact, small pieces of the substance remained spread around the site where visitors might take it as a souvenir.[54]

In the master plan, Dayton stressed the broader implications of the test by stating: "It touches some face or another in each of us and has been described, analyzed, moralized, and possibly romanticized. Suffice it to be said, the world in that instant, became a much smaller place."

He also called for the incorporation of ground zero, the two remaining structures at Camp Trinity, the McDonald ranch house, the Jumbo encasing, and several bunkers, as well as any remaining concrete footings to the tower and wires used during the test. A "system of trails" would connect several sites. Interestingly, the Park Service wanted to maintain "the loneliness, the desolation, and the mystique of the region." The museum idea was no longer a consideration. In fact, extensive interpretation might "compromise this scene, therefore any such elements to be added must be planned accordingly." This was the middle ground the Park Service hoped to reach with the military. Dayton believed that as many as 150,000 people would visit annually.[55]

Eight years before the Park Service's master plan, the missile range had erected a simple obelisk at ground zero. Raised in 1965, the same year Trinity was designated a National Historic Landmark district, it reads simply:

TRINITY SITE

WHERE

THE WORLD'S FIRST

NUCLEAR DEVICE

WAS EXPLODED ON

JULY 16, 1945

Erected 1965

White Sands Missile Range

J. Frederick Thorlin

Major General U.S. Army

Commanding[56]

Yet conflict over the preservation of Trinity remained. In 1973 the Park Service claimed that the army had bulldozed bunkers and allowed personnel to shoot up the McDonald ranch house. Citing the National Historical Preservation Act of 1966, NPS argued that any federal agency "prior to the approval of the expenditure of any federal funds on the undertaking or prior to the issuance of any license, as the case may be, take into account the effect of the undertaking on any district, site,

6. Trinity monument. Courtesy of White Sands Missile Range Museum and Archives.

building, structure, or object that is included in or eligible for inclusion in the National Register." That same year Trinity was entered into the National Register of Historic Places, which included the McDonald ranch house and what was left of the instrument bunkers. White Sands would have to maintain the site although it remained off limits on a regular basis. Trinity no longer existed as just a radioactive site. It had become a vital place in America's nuclear heritage landscape.[57]

It is impossible to understand how every person experienced and understood Trinity. However, the fiftieth anniversary of the first nuclear test offers some hints into how visitors from diverse backgrounds came to write their own pasts onto the obelisk. On July 16, 1995, over 5,300 people descended on the Trinity National Historic Landmark to remember the fiftieth anniversary of the first atomic explosion. Entering through White Sands Missile Range's northern Stallion Gate near San Antonio, New Mexico, many came before dawn to observe the exact moment, 5:29:45 a.m., when the device exploded. Diverse in character, the crowd included World War II veterans, former Manhattan Project personnel, a Japanese television crew, and a number of protestors. Near the obelisk that marks the center of the site, a woman held up a string of a thousand origami cranes crafted by children from the Japanese cities of Tokyo, Hiroshima, and Nagasaki, as well as nearby Albuquerque, New Mexico. She explained that the cranes would become part of a "Children's Peace Statue" in Albuquerque.[58]

It is important note that protests at Trinity on the occasion of its fiftieth anniversary reflected the site's national and international implications in the post-1960s world. There is little doubt a visit to Trinity some forty years earlier would have aroused different emotions. Equally important, the event revealed how a simple obelisk could hold so many meanings for so many different people. The gathering was less concerned with Trinity as a place and more concerned about the past fifty years of nuclear weapons. The simple monument that emerged from the long contest over the Trinity Site framed that discourse. As thousands lined up to enter the landmark, it was entirely predictable that the throngs would include protestors. One of them placed a copy of the *Bhagavad Gita* at the foot of the monument. Immediately following the first atomic explosion, Manhattan Project lead scientist J. Robert Oppenheimer had famously quoted from its pages, "I am become Death, the destroyer of worlds." Several protestors sang, played drums, and chanted in an effort to mend the first "atomic wound." Many brought signs. One read:

"We are the new abolitionists." Another lamented, "We're sorry about Hiroshima and Nagasaki." A protestor flung "symbolic blood" onto the obelisk (in 1995 a similar incident happened at the *Enola Gay* exhibition in the Smithsonian Institution's Air and Space Museum).[59]

Protestors enjoyed a high profile, but a vast array of visitors came to the site. Melvin Burks, a veteran of World War II, came "to see the place that saved my life." A crew from the Japanese television network Nippon TV came to report on the event. Journalist Saburo Kawakami explained that while he did not blame the United States for the bombings of Hiroshima and Nagasaki, he felt no nation held the absolute right to utilize "such cruel weapons." Few if any of these visitors voiced consternation with the contaminated landscape on which they stood.[60]

None of the many news reports from the fiftieth anniversary at ground zero mentioned the environmental history of Trinity or its role in making the monument. A sign posted at the site discourages visitors from eating, drinking, chewing gum, or putting on cosmetics. The brochure handed out by missile range personnel to visitors offered some information on local radiation levels. It underlined the knowledge of uncertainty about the potential impact of fallout on human visitors. It cautioned: "Although radiation levels are low, some feel any extra exposure should be avoided. The decision is yours." Small children and pregnant women were particularly at risk. The brochure claimed that an hour at Trinity equals substantially less radiation exposure than a year's worth of contact with cosmic rays or radioactive minerals, or from the general consumption of food and water. The brochure discouraged visitors from picking up Trinitite.[61]

The brochure said nothing about the historical problems with the radioactive desert environment that drove concerns about visitor exposure. Moreover, little interpretation marked Trinity. The War Department had removed ranchers, tested a weapon with uncertain consequences, and sent radiation monitors into the desert to make sense of fallout. The lack of interpretation and contextualization was rooted in the site's long and complex links to the burgeoning science of radiation, the dynamics of a desert environment, and security at the missile range. As Szasz explains in his seminal study on the site, Trinity does not hold the same cache as does Gettysburg, Pearl Harbor, or Harper's Ferry. But it remains as important, if not more so, than all of these places. Monument boosters sought to exploit Trinity to bring tourists to the region, and the military and AEC sought to contain it. But even without significant interpretive framing, every visitor would find meaning in Trinity.

As White Sands repeatedly wrestled with demands for access to Trinity, its mission as a proving ground expanded exponentially during the early Cold War. In 1955 alone White Sands tested 1,250 rockets and missiles. For the year 1960, the number reached more than 2,000. Even as the first AEC scientists explored the ecology of fallout and monument boosters lobbied for public access to Trinity, a group of American and German scientists had already come to White Sands to build the American rocket program. Like radiation at Trinity, the weapons and space program at White Sands often defied the expectations of scientists working there. As radioactive fallout puzzled the MED and AEC, missile testing changed a burgeoning proving ground into a wide-reaching borderlands institution.[62]

3

Boundaries

On the evening of May 29, 1947, a V-2 rocket launched from White Sands Proving Ground fell to Earth just outside the border town of Juárez, Mexico. It startled residents of Juárez and "jarred" windows from the central fire station across the Rio Grande River in El Paso, Texas. The rocket hit with such force that residents on both sides of the U.S.-Mexico border believed that it must have carried some sort of explosive material. In reality the V-2 carried only measuring instruments. However, at a speed of more than one thousand miles per hour it had the kinetic energy to create both a loud explosion and a massive crater.[1]

Revealing the local interest in the event, hundreds of Mexicans gathered at the site. Narcisco Vargas, caretaker of the Tepeyac Cemetery near where the rocket crashed, explained: "Suddenly there was a terrible noise and a ball of fire, which seemed to engulf me. . . . I must have bounded into the air because the next thing I knew I was lying face down. There was a black cloud of smoke and dust all around me. I could hardly breathe." Recognizing the commotion the V-2 created, the United States sent a letter of regret to the Mexican government following the incident.[2]

The errant rocket that hit just across the border was not the first to stray off course, nor would it be the last missile launched from White Sands to cross into Mexico. Missile prototypes often failed. Between

1947 and 1970 at least three different rockets hit Mexico. Numerous others fell in parts of New Mexico, Utah, Colorado, and Texas.

Since 1945 the federal government had set legal boundaries for the missile range. But its mission of testing uncertain technologies made it an institution that contradicted its own perceived geographical fixity. Errant missiles reflect the tensions between militarization, imperialism, and national sovereignty that permeated the U.S.-Mexico borderlands since the end of the Mexican-American War. Both Americans and Mexicans lived under the forming and dissipating contrails of White Sands. What went on at White Sands was often disorderly and unpredictable. At an outpost of the national security state, encounters between the American military and civilians mutated with new rocket technologies.

Yet as much as missile testing collapsed boundaries between military site and local and regional communities, states, and nation-states, it also reaffirmed the power of the Department of Defense in the borderlands region. Containment was no longer merely about secrecy within the missile range. For missile range personnel it was also about containing the fiascoes that brought White Sands beyond its secure borders and into public light.

At the same time, scientists challenged the mission of White Sands from within. Was White Sands merely a missile and ordnance testing facility? Were missiles only to be understood as weapons? Who owned White Sands? Like the National Park Service and local tourism boosters who attempted to wrest the Trinity Site from nuclear scientists and the military, how rocket scientists understood their creations challenged the boundaries between militarization and science and between science and the public. White Sands was never totally a "black space," as Tom Vanderbilt has dubbed Cold War military sites. As much as errant missiles reaffirmed power structures in the region, they also established a militarized landscape that remained visible and vulnerable. White Sands was no fortress.[3]

When historians think about the Cold War West, one word comes to mind: *nuclear*. Nuclear weapons development, testing, and waste disposal had an ineffable impact on western environments and communities.

So too did mining for plutonium, the maintenance of bombs, and the storage of radioactive waste. In 1950 the Nevada Test Site became the primary site for nuclear weapons testing. In all, the Atomic Energy Commission tested more than nine hundred nuclear devices in North America. While most testing occurred at the Nevada Test Site, as part of the peaceful Project Plowshare several tests also took place in New Mexico and Colorado. At Hanford Site in Washington, Los Alamos and Sandia National Laboratories in New Mexico, Rocky Flats in Colorado, and Pantex in the Texas Panhandle, nuclear weapons design and construction emitted radiation that seeped into regional water supplies, polluted soils, and affected human and nonhuman bodies. At sites in the Four Corners region, uranium mining created a series of occupational and public health hazards that infected miners and civilians with cancer and other diseases. Uranium tailings piled in slag heaps remain a part of the landscape today. While now mostly abandoned, the missile silos of the northern Great Plains were ready to launch nuclear warheads at a moment's notice. The messy history of toxic waste and social dislocation produced by weapons testing sites has led to important discussions on the Cold War military-scientific apparatus in the West. It is in part a story of environmental decay and community exploitation.[4]

Between the sites of atomic America lay the history of the rest of the militarized West. Military bases, aircraft testing facilities, naval stations, and proving grounds could be found in every western state. From Naval Base San Diego to Edwards Air Force Base on the California high desert and Cannon Air Force Base near Clovis, New Mexico, to Francis E. Warren Air Force Base in Cheyenne, Wyoming, military sites dotted the western landscape. Rather than see them as outside the nuclear weapons apparatus, those sites were a part of a web of militarization engaged in a constant program of readiness during the Cold War. Planes stationed at Cannon could carry weapons tested at the Nevada Test Site, and ships stationed at San Diego could carry the missiles maintained at Sandia National Laboratories in Albuquerque. Nuclear weapons left the most obvious mark on the environments of the West, but the other militarized places, which have their own environmental history, were a part of the same massive military-scientific garrison of North America.

Between 1945 and 1977 the missile range carried out 54,808 missile tests. Another 5,230 happened between fiscal years 1978 and 1980. For the fiscal years 1994 and 1995, the number had dropped to only 521. Despite a Freedom of Information Act request for records from 1981 to 1993, the missile range claims "no record exists." As the premier missile testing facility in North America, White Sands played a vital role in several Cold War–era missile programs. In addition to V-2 shots, the missile range tested the Aerobee, Viking, Hermes, Nike-Ajax, Nike-Zeus, Honest John, Little John, Athena, Pershing, and several MX prototypes, among many others. Often under contract with private firms ranging from General Electric to Honeywell, the U.S. Army, Navy, and Air Force have all tested at White Sands. Holloman Air Force Base also uses the site for test firings and as a bombing range.[5]

This chapter tracks missiles across the U.S.-Mexico borderlands into outer space and back to Earth over the first twenty-five years of the missile range's existence. But it does not attempt to retell the entire history of missile testing at White Sands. Instead, I use two incidents to explore that history. First, for all of their destructiveness, missiles did not merely explode. As biologists and health physicists at Trinity tracked radioactivity across the desert, scientists and engineers led by Wernher von Braun tested forty-six V-2 rockets and other missile designs. Many carried cameras.

The early rocket programs at White Sands were at the vanguard of the science of seeing the Earth from the upper atmosphere and outer space. Scientists working for the Applied Physics Laboratory (APL) at Johns Hopkins University and the Naval Research Laboratory (NRL) captured the first images of the planet's curvature from rockets launched from the missile range. While they did not have the same cultural cache as *Earthrise*, shot in 1968 by the Apollo 8 crew as they took pictures of the lunar surface for research purposes, or *Blue Marble*, captured in 1972 by the crew of Apollo 17 and reoriented before NASA distributed it to a public audience, the first gritty shots of the curvature of the Earth made their way into national media outlets. In 1950 *National Geographic* published a story that presented two large-scale panoramas that showed the curvature of Earth to public audiences.[6]

Those images had complex stories. Knowing nature from space found its roots not simply in a benign expansion of scientific knowledge about space travel, but instead in the intertwined relationships between early Cold War militarization and the scientific exploration of the upper atmosphere. Tensions arose between the value of Earth photography to the Cold War military-industrial state and the technological utopianism promised and promoted by postwar "big science." Scientists told stories that complicated the narrative of a military site bound only to military readiness. White Sands became not merely a weapon testing facility but also a place that cultivated the dreams of big science.

The second event was the series of errant missiles that happened between 1945 and 1970. Missiles not yet perfected defied the boundaries of White Sands Missile Range. In 1967 and 1970 two highly publicized misses sent military teams over the U.S.-Mexico border in search of downed rockets. One contained contaminated materials. Local, regional, and transnational people became part of the military-scientific apparatus in south-central New Mexico in unexpected ways. The incidents became legendary episodes as people on both sides of the border relayed to the media and the military their experience in hearing, seeing, and finding wayward missiles.

In both obvious and unexpected ways the primary mission of the missile range reveals its historical ties to people and landscapes not only beyond the fences that marked the borders between secure military reserve and public or private lands, but also between nations. As they honed rocket technology in the first twenty-five years after World War II, scientists and engineers both played a role in the metamorphosis of White Sands and its value to everyday peoples.

"AN ALL-SEEING FLYING EYE"

In October 1950 the popular magazine *National Geographic* published an amazing image of the American West.[7] Rather than accompaniment to

7. "V-2 Rocket-Eye View from 60 Miles Up," 1948. Courtesy of the Johns Hopkins University Applied Physics Laboratory.

an article on the intricacies of American Indian art or the awe-inspiring landscape of a national park, the black and white image instead offered an approximately eight-hundred-thousand-square-mile vista of a vast part of the region.[8] The photograph captured an area from Mexico and the Gulf of California far to the southwest and Wyoming deep into the north. Looking through scattered wispy high clouds and building thunderstorms viewers could cast a gaze upon Arizona, Utah, and parts of Nevada and California. Distance to the horizon was 720 miles.[9]

Although most of the West was visible, the image centered on New Mexico (the result of the camera shooting at an oblique angle), where viewers could see the San Mateo Mountains, Mount Taylor, the Rio Grande River, and the town of Lordsburg. The picture does not immediately reveal the intricacies of the desert landscape. The image's author therefore added a series of numbered markers to orient the view for readers.[10]

Captured in July 1948 by Clyde T. Holliday of the APL and titled "V-2 Rocket-Eye View from 60 Miles Up," the image exists as one of a handful of pre-NASA photos that offered a large-scale geographic view of the Earth.[11] Like *Earthrise* and the *Blue Marble*, Holliday framed "V-2 Rocket-Eye View from 60 Miles Up," but with a very different intent. He was no novice photographer, having utilized photography to track missiles and document artillery fuze bursts aimed at airplanes during World War II.[12]

Holliday's work began when German scientists and engineers came to the United States after World War II. In May 1945, as the Third Reich collapsed, a team of Americans led by Major General Holger N. "Ludy" Toftoy had the specific task of finding and confiscating V-2 rockets and interrogating the scientists that worked for the German program. Wernher Von Braun was the lead technical chief. While recommendations for bringing as many as 600 scientists to the United States swirled among personnel in what became known as Project Paperclip, Toftoy decided to lobby the Pentagon for 300. In his initial cable to military brass he emphasized that the German rocket program was in theory twenty-five years ahead of the American program. In late June, after Toftoy had pled for the program in person, the military agreed initially to allow 100 Germans to enter the United States. As Toftoy and Von Braun handpicked the selected group, potential numbers swelled to 120. While the Soviet Union would also capture German engineers and scientists, 118 scientists would eventually go to Fort Bliss and White Sands.[13]

Originally signed to one-year contracts, the team began building the American V-2 rocket program (also known as the A-4) with a host of American scientists. Yet they were not the first to tinker with rocketry in the Southwest. Physicist and inventor Robert H. Goddard initiated the earliest rocket research in New Mexico after leaving the less than inviting community and climate of New England. New Mexico's mild winters and open spaces made for a more suitable site for testing. A Guggenheim grant, secured with help from Charles Lindbergh and Harry Guggenheim, in part allowed for the experiments in the Southwest. Goddard's rocket research began in the region at the end of 1930 and lasted until his unanticipated death in 1945. Missilery continued to evolve over the next several years. In 1944 Major General Gladeon Marcus Barnes gave the okay for tests of the relatively simple Private A Rocket at Camp Irwin, near Barstow, California, and later the similar Private F on the Hueco Range at Fort Bliss. They were a part of the rapidly expanding ORDCIT program discussed in chapter 1. The Private A and F tests were followed in the fall of 1946 by experiments with the WAC-Corporal rocket (a reference to its military rank above prior rockets), which laid the groundwork for the V-2 program at White Sands.[14]

Before 1952 the V-2 became the most extensive and well-known rocket and missile program at the proving ground. The V-2 is a large machine. Early designs measured forty-six feet in length with fins that extended almost twelve feet. The projectile reached 52,000 pounds of thrust behind a turbopump feed rocket engine run on an oxygen-alcohol propellant. The rocket weighed an average of 9,218 pounds with no fuel. The payload or warhead alone could weigh more than 2,000 pounds. By 1951 V-2 rockets had undergone modifications allowing for an almost 50 percent increase in total payload. Of all the rockets tested under the White Sands experimental program, scientists considered about 68 percent of flights successful.[15]

While initial experiments had happened a month earlier, on May 10, 1946, scientists completed the first "full scale" test of a V-2 in the United States. The V-2 was incorporated into the Hermes Project, which since 1944 had tested American rocket designs including the A-1, A-2, and Hermes B. Many V-2 shots began at Launch Complex 33, designed specifically for the early trials of the rocket. The flight path took the rocket 68.7 miles across the stratosphere and ionosphere and drew more than one hundred journalists and photojournalists representing newspapers, newsreel outlets, and other media sources. Unlike the Manhattan Project, scientists had successfully lobbied Toftoy (then in the Army Ordnance Department) to keep upper atmospheric research open. Stories of V-2 tests recorded in local and national newspapers told of speed and height records without significant censorship. White Sands Proving Ground announced the first tests to the public by suggesting that rockets could soar one hundred miles into the sky at velocities reaching 3,500 miles per hour. In October 1946 a rocket reached a height of 102 miles at a speed of 3,600 miles per hour. In December a rocket achieved a new velocity record of 5,000 feet per second. By 1948 knowledge gathered from V-2 tests had led to the emergence of new rocket technologies, including the Aerobee, a rocket that could climb 70 miles at 3,000 miles per hour, the Viking system (including Viking I and Viking II), a program also involved in high-altitude research, and early tests on the Nike rocket series.[16]

The V-2 shots at White Sands Proving Ground became the first significant American intrusion into space. The early tests included no animals, humans, or plant life, but at least one test included "man-made meteorites" used as part of spectrographic analysis. What today might constitute space junk was at the time described as "small metal slugs, weighing only a few grams." During a December 1946 test, scientists hoped they could shoot the projectiles from V-2 rockets at a speed sufficient to shoot across Earth's atmosphere. On the night of the shot Lieutenant Colonel Harold R. Turner, the first commander of White Sands, encouraged several regional observatories to watch for the glow of the projectiles. Shooting them from the side of a rocket at an altitude of 113 miles, rather than from Earth's surface, would ensure that the small, fast-moving meteorites would not immediately burn up because of intensive heat in the upper atmosphere. Even as scientists hoped to study the act of disintegration at the atmospheric level (and while the firing mechanism for the slugs did not function correctly), they considered slugs hurtling into space "a symbolic milestone in man's exploration of space."[17]

Three short years after the first V-2 tests, the scientists reached a milestone. On February 24, 1949, a WAC-Corporal carried by a modified V-2 reached empty space. As part of Project Bumper, itself a part of the Hermes tests, the V-2 left Earth at 3:14 p.m. Mountain Standard Time, rising into the air at nearly a mile per second. When the WAC-Corporal initiated, the combined force moved the rocket to an even faster 1.39 miles-per-second. The rocket had ascended to 250 miles above sea level and beyond Earth's atmosphere.[18]

Scientists had immediate interests other than those of the military. In early 1946 a group of individuals met at Princeton University to form the V-2 Upper Atmosphere Panel (later the Upper Atmosphere Rocket Panel). The ultimate goal of the panel while first working with V-2 rockets was not only space travel but also an expanded knowledge of the upper atmosphere, weather patterns, and climate. The panel included a virtual who's who of American scientists, including James Van Allen of the APL at Johns Hopkins University and Fred Lawrence Whipple of Harvard University. Others came from the NRL in Washington DC, the University of Michigan, and Princeton University. It also included representatives from the General Electric Company, who would carry out the test firings at the White Sands Proving Ground as part of the Hermes Project.[19]

As much as high-altitude rocket research was about the exploration of space, it was also about exploring Earth. As early as the late nineteenth century scientists had toyed with using balloons, kites, pigeons, and crude rockets to take pictures of the planet. In 1897 Alfred Nobel successfully photographed a part of Germany from about a hundred feet in the air. In 1906 photographer George Lawrence used a camera fixed to seventeen kites to capture the rubble of San Francisco following that city's worst earthquake. In 1935 a National Geographic Society–Army Air Corps balloon named *Explorer II* reached the stratosphere with "aeronauts" aboard. Their hazy view of the planet led them to remark that Earth seemed "a foreign and lifeless world."[20]

Yet it was the first rocket tests at White Sands that ushered in the age of seeing Earth from space. Led by Thor A. Bergstralh of the NRL and Holliday of the APL, White Sands personnel used rocket testing to explore the nature of the planet when photographed from the upper atmosphere. On October 24, 1946, an APL team working at White Sands sent a rocket carrying a Holliday-designed camera protected by a layer of duraluminum beyond the stratosphere. The motion picture captured images from one hundred feet to sixty-five miles. The grainy photographs included more than forty thousand square miles of space. The film ran for four and a half minutes as the V-2 reached its apex and then made an initial descent. Of the many pictures taken, one showed the horizon of Earth from sixty-five miles above the launching point. A press release from Johns Hopkins explained, "If there had been an observer in the rocket, able to look all directions, he could have seen approximately 1,600,000 square miles of the earth's surface and have had a clear view of San Diego, Salt Lake City, Kansas City and San Antonio." An image from the test published in the *Albuquerque Journal* gave a "rocket view of earth" with clouds stretching west to the curved horizon.[21]

Between 1946 and 1954 cameras that accompanied rocket tests captured similar shots of the planet. On March 7, 1947, a Bergstralh-designed camera affixed to a V-2 Rocket captured the first images of Earth from one hundred miles up. A reporter for the *New York Times* called it a "triumph of technical skill and of photography." The infrared sensitive film used by Bergstralh had allowed for clearer pictures through the hazy troposphere. On March 31, 1947, the grand picture of two hundred thousand square miles of Mexico and the American West taken at one hundred miles up was named *Life* magazine's "picture of the week."[22]

Early Earth images had several important research purposes. They helped in measuring how cosmic rays hit the rocket. They also allowed for scientists to understand the orientation of rockets in flight, how their jets worked, and how other inflight systems behaved at high altitudes. Similar tests proved valuable as a way to explore how cameras could help to scout enemy movements in battle. For meteorologists the pictures corroborated theories on the formation of cumulus clouds and the relationships between cloud formation and topographical variations. Yet the images of Earth held something more than scientific data. They took on new social meanings for scientists at the dawn of the Cold War.[23]

In July 1948 Holliday captured the clearest and most expansive photos of the curvature of Earth. Originally published in an APL brochure titled "So Columbus was Right!," one magnificent image, titled "V-2 Rocket-Eye View from 60 Miles Up," acted as the centerpiece of the seventeen-page story in *National Geographic* penned by Holliday. It did not include the original title, the date it was taken, or its ties to the V-2 Panel. But through the story itself, which included several images of scientists improving rockets, measuring craters, and other shots of Earth at lower altitudes, readers were offered insight into the value of Earth photography for scientists, the military, and the public.

The camera used for "V-2 Rocket-Eye View" was experimental. Exposure times ran at a shutter speed of 1/500 of a second with an aperture of f:5.6. The camera operated continuously until the film was exhausted. Eastman Aerographic black-and-white infrared film shot through an 89a filter proved the most successful filter-film pairing for capturing clear shots. Color film was tried, but above thirty thousand feet it proved unsuccessful in shooting images through the haze of the upper atmosphere. The cameras often returned to earth broken, but a heavy steel cassette protected the film. Importantly, because the early V-2's were not fully guided and their trajectory not totally controlled, the images captured by the cameras were at the mercy of the rocket's uncertain path.[24]

Holliday clearly understood the social value of photography as a medium. His *National Geographic* article offered two overlapping yet differing understandings on Earth photography to its viewers (in 1950 the magazine had a circulation of over 1.8 million). He explained that "V-2 Rocket-Eye View" revealed both the possibility for improved human relationships with atmospheric environments (namely through rocket-based meteorology) and, through his use of a wide optical perspective, the possibility of using such an image to make a military map. Though some Earth images might bring on new imaginations of environment and society, as the geographer Denis E. Cosgrove suggests, they may also "induce desires of ordering and controlling the object of vision." In the same spirit the photograph's structure and content reflect the role of early rocket photography in contributing to the militarization of the skies.[25]

Yet Holliday's *National Geographic* image speaks to notions of scientific progress and utopianism at the dawn of the Cold War. The atom was central to that promise. In the 1950s scientists promoted the potential for nuclear-powered cars and airplanes, cancer-curing drugs, agricultural antidotes, and weather patterns made predictable by the atom. Enumerated in President Dwight Eisenhower's 1953 "Atoms for Peace" speech before the United Nations, nuclear energy's peaceful applications offered a counternarrative to the anxieties of nuclear obliteration. But more generally the emergence of "big science" based in large research parks and university labs pledged a transformation of life for the better through chemistry, biology, and physics. Artists, architects, and even scientists sought to visualize this potential society through drawings, blueprints, and photography.[26]

Holliday framed "v-2 Rocket-Eye View" in part to fit that narrative. Holliday constructed the photograph with only eight panels selected from nearly two hundred images. With an obvious nod to American westward expansion, the mosaic faces west toward the Pacific Ocean. The composite image taken above New Mexico offers a subtle statement on the post-1940 transformation of the coastal and western United States into a "gun belt." Holliday made sure to direct the viewers' gaze upon Earth at the western horizon instead of out to space and was careful to mark directions south, west, and north.[27]

Demonstrated by the distorted scale that resulted from the camera's oblique angle (the background of the photo is on a much smaller scale than the foreground), the structure of the panorama reveals the limitations of the rocket-bound camera that could not, on its own, capture a total view in a single image. Holliday had to step in and create a complete image by piecing it together; it was an image constructed to reflect his own notions of Earth and to convey to the reader the everyday value of rocket-based earth photography. His panorama, in part, harks back to the production of cyclorama paintings and panoramic photographs (often of cities or warscapes) that gained popularity in the mid-nineteenth century. The approach is also reminiscent of landscape artist Albert Bierstadt, who employed artistic license in his paintings both to conjure awe in the viewer and also as a measure to promote the values of western environments as divine and ultimately national places. Not unlike viewing Bierstadt's work, readers of Holliday's photograph could take note not only of the triumphant human mastery of the West but also its ties to the cosmos.[28]

The image, in short, conveyed the "technological sublime" (to use the historian David Nye's phrase), promoting the idea of scientific and technical progress to readers. A more natural bird's-eye view was no longer necessary in the age of rocketry. While scientists could not yet control the high clouds and clusters of storms in the panorama, such phenomena might be made more predictable. Flipping between written word and the photograph itself, Holliday's readers learned that the U.S. Weather Bureau (the precursor to the National Weather Service) could benefit from further data collection: "if guided missiles carrying cameras could be sent out crisscross over the entire continent of North America every day, photographing in a few hours all the cloud banks, storm fronts, and overcasts, weather forecasts could be made more accurately than now." In "V-2 Rocket-Eye View" viewers journeyed above the clouds and watched storms form and dissipate with a new sense of mastery over nature. Photography would make life easier for meteorologists and by proxy everyday Americans who needed the most accurate weather forecast.[29]

Much like the American space program a decade later, which NASA at times cast as outside the Cold War, Holliday's panacea to the vagaries of weather and climate contradict V-2 rockets as weapons. His description of the panorama revealed the nebulous mission and meaning of White Sands in the early Cold War. A second glance at the image reveals a parallel perspective: of military control over the environment, a capability revealed in Holliday's article. Black-and-white infrared film significantly alters the representation of subject matter. This process follows what the cultural theorist Paul Virilio called the "splitting of viewpoint" or "the sharing of perception of the environment between the animate (the living subject) and the inanimate (the object, the seeing machine)." In the image the ground and foliage have become a bright white (almost melding with clouds), while rivers and mountaintops glow a deep black. The grand mosaic conveys an alien scene that readers may not have noticed at first glance. The military had used the film type first developed by Kodak to differentiate flora from camouflage during World War II. Holliday had constructed an image to show the viewer things down there as they are, but ironically he ends up also offering the viewer something that could not be seen without the aid of technology (in this case an infrared planet with the potential to reveal enemies trying to hide).[30]

With that in mind, there remained the series of small numbered dots that speckled the image to guide the reader to notable markers in the photographs and make the alien familiar. A corresponding legend helped readers to find the mountains, rivers, states, and towns in the picture. But the markers were indicative of another purpose: the use of such photography to identify possible targets of Cold War adversaries. "V-2 Rocket-Eye View" can be seen as a military map wherein the American West was a proving ground for rocket-based surveillance. Holliday directed audiences to see its military values: "Cameras mounted on guided missiles might be shot out over enemy territory and brought back with a photographic record of troop concentrations, fortifications, and airfields." Published about one year after the Soviet Union tested its first nuclear weapon, "V-2 Rocket-Eye View" was not merely a benign statement about innovation, but it was also a statement about the military competition to establish scientific and technological control of space and the Earth. In turn, the image raised the possibility that the American West, too, could be a region of targets in the Cold War struggle.[31]

"V-2 Rocket-Eye View" was in part an experiment in reconnoitering people and places from the upper atmosphere. In 1949 Secretary of Defense James Forrestal paid lip service to an earth satellite vehicle as a future military tool.[32] It remained only a theoretical possibility at the time. Thus Holliday's intense focus was on the planet rather than the things "out there" better captured by ground-based telescopes.[33] The image is carefully laid out with the author and his team mapping the major sites in the foreground. The plotted sites again orient the image, but they now can be read as directional orientation aids that would make images from future unmanned military satellite vehicles useful for reconnaissance.

In Holliday's words the mosaic puts the viewer in the place of an "all-seeing flying eye."[34] Reminiscent of the English legal scholar and philosopher Jeremy Bentham's plans for eighteenth-century English prisons, "V-2 Rocket-Eye View" suggests a space-based Panopticon.[35] As the historian-philosopher Michel Foucault notes, "The Panopticon functions as a kind of laboratory of power. Thanks to its mechanisms of observation, it gains in efficiency and in the ability to penetrate into men's behavior."[36] Although not identical to the state of confinement found in Bentham's prison, Holliday's interpretation of his effort as an "all-seeing flying eye" reproduces the concept of the Panopticon's efficiency and power. The clouds obscure some locations, and thus suggest the impediments in using rocket-based images for military purposes. Yet the ability of the viewer, guided by the author's cues, to connect the dots on New Mexico's landscape lessens that limitation. Here "V-2 Rocket-Eye View" conveys the aspirations of U.S. state and military power.

In other words, for Holliday the technology of early Earth photography offered potential solutions for national security planners who hoped to establish their own version of control over Earth's environments. Holliday explicitly saw the capability for even more precise reconnaissance in his image. Television "could send back a running report of what the camera 'saw' as it flew." Once the process of using color film was perfected, "camouflage would hide little from such an all-seeing flying eye if the pictures were taken in color, for the varying wave lengths of light recorded by color film penetrate almost any kind of artificial concealment." Such an "eye," too, could map weather patterns, facilitating the military's capability to operate over the entire Earth—a statement of mastery over terrestrial and sublunary environments.[37]

"V-2 Rocket-Eye View" did not create the same splash as its famous kin, but it holds its own importance in exploring the relationships among science, technology, and the environment. Holliday consciously produced a panorama that employed the era's belief in "big science" as a hopeful development for humanity. At the same time, it had profound utility for the military at the dawn of the Cold War. The mosaic took viewers on a rocket-driven ride that promised better times on terra firma, but via a technology that in Holliday's words was "built to spread death." Rockets had meaning, and that meaning was complex.[38]

While the military on the missile range had a particular vision for rockets, scientists continued to see a technological utopianism in Earth photography. On October 5, 1954, the NRL, using an Aerobee rocket with two moving-picture cameras, captured 116 images of Earth. The final mosaic was published in the American Meteorological Society journal *Monthly Weather Review* and included 1.25 million square miles of Earth from Nebraska in the east to the Pacific Ocean in the west and Texas and the Gulf of Mexico in the south. The tinge of color made it different from the images shot before. The mosaic was made up of ninety frames, and the AMS found usefulness in the image because for the first time scientists had a good picture of a tropical storm from above (this one brewing near Del Rio, Texas). Such images held a potential to help meteorologists map and follow weather patterns. L. F. Hubert of the U.S. Weather Bureau and Otto Berg of the NRL explained that the image had "tremendous" implications for studying weather, and that the ability of rockets to provide "truly simultaneous data" would supplement technologies, including aircraft reconnaissance, already in use.[39]

Despite the composite value of rocket technology, the actual projectile always plummeted to the ground; the success or failure gauged the development of American rocketry. In a moment when scientists sought to improve a form of technology so fundamental to military power after World War II, there emerged a most unexpected moment when Americans could look upon Earth from sixty miles up. Earth photographs might make everyday life easier for the average American, but from sixty miles up they also revealed the vast geographic range of White Sands as a weapons testing facility.

CONTRAILS OUT OF TOWN

In the attempts to improve rocket designs, engineers and scientists tinkered with an unproven technology. Beginning with the V-2 crash near Juárez, Mexico, errant missiles were a visible reminder of the scale of White Sands and brought the site into the consciousness of local, regional, and national communities. The American states that bordered New Mexico became a de facto part of the testing area. Beginning in 1958 overland tests started at the Fort Wingate Launch Complex east of Gallup, New Mexico, and in 1964 from the Green River Launch Complex about forty-five miles northwest of Moab, Utah. Missiles followed flight corridors that crossed southeast over most of New Mexico and parts of Utah and Colorado. As much as failed rockets revealed the ephemerality of borders, they also affirmed the powerful role of the military state in the region.

White Sands National Monument felt the immediate burden of the increased military presence in the region during World War II and the early Cold War. The missile range encroached on the monument's mission of preserving and promoting the ancient gypsum dunes. Military personnel visited the monument for leisure, driving over dunes to preferred sites for family picnics and barbeques.[40]

In other ways the monument was simply a part of the missile range. In 1957 monument superintendent Johnwill Faris showed alarm with the growing disregard that both the missile range and Holloman Air Force Base had for White Sands National Monument. The military planned to use it for impact areas, military personnel laid down paths through the monument to instrument stations, and both military installations sought the right to use monument lands for launch complexes. While not all measures would go into effect, the co-use agreement signed in 1948 (see chapter 1) made parts of the pristine dunes accessible to the missile range (in 1963 a second co-use agreement was signed). An environmental impact statement released in 1975 showed that over the prior thirty years the missile range had maintained tracking equipment and communication lines across the sand dunes. Moreover, evacuations and the frequent closure of U.S. 70 shaped how the monument did business. Under the co-use agreement a special use permit allowed for impacts and the retrieval of missile fragments. Between 1963 and 1974 the missile range had completed 260 planned impacts in the co-use area of White Sands National Monument. Potential pollution and alterations to natural resources from ground- and air-based emissions also proved a concern for the Park Service. Missile and aircraft created considerable noise disturbances as they flew overhead. Those tests affected both wildlife and how tourists experienced White Sands. By the mid-1970s the monument tallied an average of 160 roadblocks on U.S. Highway 70 per quarter (there was most likely more than one at a time) hindering the passage of as many as a hundred drivers per incident.[41]

In March 1957 V-2 test number 21 crashed at White Sands National Monument. Homer E. Newell, then a scientist with the NRL, reflected upon searching out the downed rocket as "a glorious hunt riding up and down over the snow-white dunes of gypsum sand that stretched as far as the eye could see!" In March 1953 another missile hit the sand dunes. Faris tracked down a "fragment of tin" and other parts of the rocket. The information was relayed to the proving ground, which explained that the test was secret. As Faris later explained in a memorandum to the Southwest Office of the National Park Service, "I certainly don't like to gripe but I want to repeat—the Army pays about as much attention to us on the whole as we were afflicted with scarlet fever, or some other dreadful disease."[42]

Ranchers whose land bordered the range also experienced the unexpected impact of missiles. In January 1959 a Nike-Hercules guided missile hit within seventy-five yards of the ranch house occupied by the Charles Lee family. Members of the family were knocked down and temporarily deafened. The missile was fired from the McGregor Range, and its guidance system and self-destroying device had failed.[43]

By the mid-1950s improvements to long-range missile technology and the subsequent increase in test flights led to a slow creep of White Sands Missile Range into places outside south-central New Mexico. In February 1957 a Matador guided missile, a tactical weapon that travels at speeds of 650 miles per hour, launched from Holloman Air Development Center failed to operate properly, crashing "somewhere in western Colorado." The military dismissed unsubstantiated claims from the public that the rocket passed either near Jensen, Utah, or Casper, Wyoming.[44]

In 1964 a Pershing missile launched from Fort Wingate, New Mexico, crashed near a school in Ramah, New Mexico, less than fifty miles from the launch site. During the same year a missile launched from the Hueco Range south of White Sands Missile Range strayed four hundred miles north of its impact zone on White Sands Missile Range and crashed in a mountainous area near Creede, Colorado. Henry Larson, sheriff of Creede, recalled "a real loud shock in the office building" in the wake of the impact. Athena prototypes seemed to have the most trouble. In February 1964 the first Athena test failed to hit the missile range, instead crashing close to Durango, Colorado. In August 1965 an Athena missile launched from Green River, Utah, hit eighteen miles southeast of Fabens, Texas. No damage was noted, as military personnel explained it hit "way out in the boondocks."[45]

Some failed tests were downright strange. In August 1969 an "emergency parachute" slowly dropped an unmanned aircraft into Los Alamos Scientific Laboratory. Citizens of the town saw the projectile fall to Earth. The U.S. Air Force, which fielded questions from the media, refused to answer queries about the program. Yet journalists knew something was up when they pressed as to whether or not the drop was part of a covert program called "Firefly." White Sands had accidentally leaked the covert program to the press the year before. While it had to do with missiles, details were sketchy. The military conceded that it was indeed Firefly but offered no more information.[46]

The problems of managing the flight corridors from Fort Wingate and Green River revealed the problems that White Sands might face with longer launches. White Sands public information officer John B. Nieland explained the situation in a disposition form completed at the missile range. Between 1964 and 1973, twenty-four motors from Athena missiles hit in the Datil impact area near the Cibola National Forest in west-central New Mexico. Yet not all effectively dumped in the 1,318-square-foot military area named for a nearby town. In August 1979 a second stage Athena motor was found in the Cibola National Forest, and the hermitically sealed C-4 explosive destruct package had been forcefully removed.[47]

Nieland expressed concern about an accidental detonation of the explosives. Yet responses to the issue were complicated from a public affairs position. The army could simply take no action. Yet Nieland noted that if "WSMR says nothing or does nothing about this matter, perhaps no one will ever be injured as result of finding one of the motors. Then again this might well occur 'tomorrow.'" Furthermore, releasing information at so late a date would leave the army "damned" for neither having warned the public nor cleaning up the scattered parts. In other words, the legal implications of doing nothing were "enormous." On the other hand the missile range could publicize the issue. Yet then White Sands would "be damned for having kept that problem a 'secret' for so long." Moreover, local peoples might seek out the motors knowing that they were there. Finally, the army could send army personnel out to the impact area to clear the area of missile parts (the solution eventually employed).[48]

From Utah to Texas, the tentacles of the missile range reached out across the American Southwest. As communities went about their everyday business, missiles whizzed overhead. White Sands occupied a range far beyond its boundaries. With the missile range's southern border just thirty miles from the city of Juárez, it should come as no surprise that as weapons testing increased in frequency and distance, missiles crossed into Mexico.

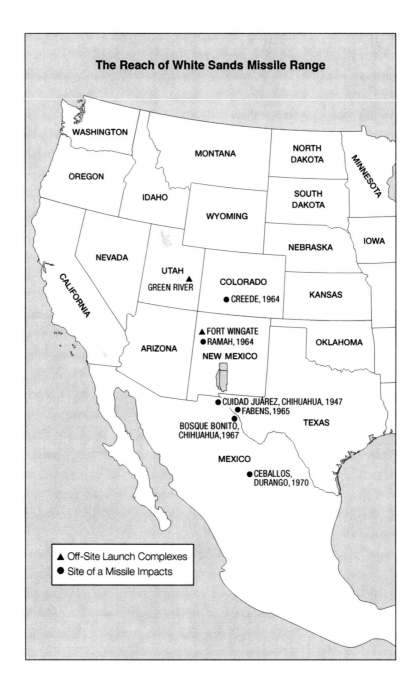

MAP 3. The Reach of White Sands Missile Range. Author's collection.

The U.S.-Mexico borderlands have always been a complicated landscape defined by conflicts over race, citizenship, and nationalism. In the post–World War II years it took on marked national security significance. The U.S. Border Patrol led the charge. During World War II the United States had relaxed the stringent immigration policies of the Great Depression. Via labor contracts under the Bracero Program, more than 4.5 million immigrants crossed the border to fill wartime labor shortages, namely in the agricultural sector. Labor-starved communities in the West also welcomed immigrants who would have been deemed illegal by the U.S. government. After the war the U.S. Border Patrol, often with the help of the Mexican Border Patrol, cracked down on illegal immigration under the banner of national security and crime control. The notorious 1954 Operation Wetback acted as one of the major postwar attempts to expel illegal immigrants from border states.[49]

At the same time, questions about race and citizenship permeated the Hispano communities of the American Southwest. During the 1950s and early 1960s organizations such as the Los Angeles–based Community Service Organization and the Mexican–American Political Association sought to organize candidates and voters to promote civil rights through the political process. By the late 1960s, as participatory democracy took hold among antiwar and civil rights organizations, Chicana/Chicano communities brought border politics to the fore of political protest. Organizations such as the Movimiento Estudiantil Chicano de Aztlán and the First National Chicano Liberation Youth Conference adopted the idea of an Aztlán homeland to emphasize the problem of dispossession and the movement toward cultural self-determination in the borderlands.[50]

By 1965 the borderlands were a site of political discourse and social conflict. But the roots of American militarization and social conflict in the borderlands ran deeper. As discussed in chapter 1, the American military presence in the Southwest stretched back to the Mexican-American War as outposts aimed at protecting settlers from Indian raids dotted the landscape. While conflicts with Indians would dissipate by the turn of the century, the Mexican Revolution renewed the heavy military presence in the region. As the revolution raged, the U.S. military garrisoned troops along the border. It also carried out counterraids from New Mexico and Arizona. Notoriously, General John J. Pershing led the Mexican Expedition to capture Mexican revolutionary Pancho Villa. Pershing had commanded Fort Bliss during the early part of World War I and at the height of the Mexican Revolution. Pershing's 8th Brigade had the task of guarding the border, and when Villa and his compatriots attacked Columbus, New Mexico, in the spring of 1916, Pershing sought Villa deep into Mexico but was unable to capture him.[51]

The missiles tested at White Sands would eventually be aimed at the Soviet Union. But prototypes spoke to the historical place of the military in the region. Like Fort Bliss and its antecedents, White Sands was a reminder of the symbolic power and complex national imagery that lay in the border. Two events captured the imagination of people on both sides of the U.S.-Mexico border. As instruments for understanding boundaries, wayward missiles also raise questions about the place of northern Mexico in the American national security state.

On September 12, 1967, a Pershing missile broke into pieces in the wooded Bosque Bonito, about 140 miles southeast of Juárez not far from the Texas-Mexico border. Ironically, the rocket was named for General John J. Pershing. First tested in 1958, a Pershing missile measures thirty-five feet long, weighs ten thousand pounds, can travel 100–400 nautical miles, and flies at supersonic speeds with a two-stage propellant. It can carry a nuclear warhead. In the mid-1960s scientists carried out initial experimental shots from off-site launch pads. Most began at the Green River Launch Complex in Utah, followed the 400-mile flight corridor over Utah, Colorado, and New Mexico, and eventually impacted at White Sands Missile Range. The Pershing that landed in Mexico caused no injury to people or property, and in the hours after the test, range officials had yet to find a cause for the failure. Mexican officials from the state of Chihuahua allowed an immediate aerial survey of the region. Yet missile range officials did not find any trace of the rocket.[52]

8. Mexican rancher Felipe Chavez-Garcia holding a piece of a downed Pershing missile, 1967. Courtesy of the U.S. Army, White Sands Missile Range Public Affairs.

A week later the missile made headlines in northern Mexico. Felipe Chavez-Garcia, a laborer on the Puerto Alto ranch near the Bosque Bonito, told the Juárez-based newspaper *El Fronterizo* that he had found a metal fragment from the rocket. In a front-page story, he recalled that in the early morning hours of September 12 a loud explosion followed by two other loud noises had startled him from his bed. For almost a week Chavez-Garcia thought little more of the event until nearby residents explained to him that they had heard radio reports of a downed missile in the Juárez Valley. The rancher had stumbled upon the piece of the missile as he herded cattle. U.S. helicopters made the first passes over where Chavez-Garcia had found the metal fragment but with little success of locating the Pershing.[53]

The missile crash initially caused little outcry, despite the potential damage the missile could have caused had it hit a populated town or city. The information office at White Sands explained in a press release that the missile had fractured into several pieces, which were most likely scattered across the desert. Under a September 20 special order the Mexican government gave permission to missile range officials to cross the border and search for the remnants of the Pershing. In coordination with Lieutenant Colonel Jorge Mario Rojas Madrigal of the maintenance section of the Director General of Materials of War within the Mexican Army, a recovery team formally planned to recover the missile. The group included Lieutenant Colonel Fred Dean, Carlos Bustamante, a test facility design engineer at White Sands, civilian electronic expert Oved Gonzales, Madrigal, and several other U.S. and Mexican personnel. They first met at the missile range to discuss operational plans. Range Commander General H. G. Davisson briefed the team on the Pershing missile. Missile range personnel promised Madrigal that they would take appropriate steps to make sure that errant missiles were not a common occurrence in the future.[54]

On September 22 the ground teams convened at White Sands Missile Range in preparation for a border crossing at Van Horn, Texas. By plane they flew over the Sierra de Los Pilares to survey the impact area. After landing, the search crew inspected the crater, which measured 13 feet in diameter and nearly 5 feet deep. The party found pieces of sheet metal and cast steel at distances between 164 and 328 feet from the initial site of impact. At one-third of a mile another piece was found. The following day the search continued with some men on horseback. The guidance and control sections of the Pershing included some hints as to the missile's failure. Gonzales suggested a short circuit mostly likely caused an electronic failure in the rocket. In all, the team recovered part of the thrust reversal mechanism for the second stage, the fin, fragments of the tip of the rocket, portions of the guidance mechanism, and housing for radio instrumentation (the piece found by Chavez-Garcia). The team made no mention of radioactivity or toxicity.[55]

In all, the incident ended with little fanfare. The lack of significant evidence of impact on the Mexican landscape or harm to local communities may have hindered protest from government officials or the local populace. But the stray rocket shows that there was a potential for harm to Mexican communities from missiles launched by White Sands. Davisson commended Madrigal for his support in recovering the failed Pershing and extended gratitude to the Mexican government for their support. Madrigal attended a "hail and farewell" party at the Officer's Club on the missile range, where he received "many respects and references to Mexico."[56]

Three years later a more controversial incident occurred. On July 11, 1970, an Athena missile launched from Green River, Utah, and set to impact at White Sands Missile Range hit more than 400 miles south of the U.S.-Mexico border near the town of Ceballos in the state of Durango. This time the missile carried Cobalt-57, a radioisotope with a half-life of 270 days. In 1964 the missile range had initiated the first Athena tests. Following its successful completion of the Trailblazer II reentry physics test program, the Atlantic Research Corporation began work on the Athena project. The sixteen-thousand-pound surface-to-surface rocket with a technical range of 450 miles was usually launched from the Green River Launch Complex and would hit the missile range.[57]

In a press release after the failure of the test, the missile range's Public Affairs Office advised its personnel to respond to questions of potential radioactivity by saying "yes a small amount of radioactive material was in the instrumentation and is not dangerous to human or animal life, if it survived reentry, unless it is ingested or handled."[58]

But conflict and confusion surrounded reports. Mexican nuclear expert Colonel Manuel Vasquez Boreto described the Cobalt-57 as potentially dangerous, despite reports to the contrary from the U.S. Air Force (the branch that carried out the test). An air force spokesman explained to a reporter for the *El Paso Herald Post* that "if carried in a pocket for two weeks, [it] might cause a skin burn." Those measurements assumed that the radioisotope had not escaped its tungsten-based protective sleeve. White Sands Missile Range also reported the rocket carried only "minute quantities" of Cobalt-57. As in the case of the errant Pershing, local residents found remnants of the missile and called authorities from the state of Durango. The Mexican Nuclear Agency encouraged any person who found the projectile to leave it alone. Boreto explained that "although the capsule is radioactive, it is inside a special container and there is no great danger, but we have warned people in the area that if they find it they should stay away and notify authorities."[59]

Concerned with human contact and potential soil and water contamination, the Mexican government again allowed missile range personnel to enter Mexico and retrieve parts of the missile. Locating the downed Athena happened in two stages. First, the U.S. Atomic Energy Commission authorized a plane carrying the Aerial Radiological Measuring System (ARMS) to survey the site of the impact with the hopes of finding the wreckage. For fourteen years ARMS had helped to measure radiation from a series of nuclear weapons tests and for experimentation with peaceful uses of nuclear weaponry under the Plowshare program. NASA had also used ARMS to measure radionuclide fuel levels during the Apollo space program. Atomic America had invaded Mexico.[60]

The seemingly shapeless desert terrain and no accurate maps made ARMS important in the recovery of the Athena. If employed correctly the system held the capability of honing in on the small amount of Cobalt-57 using its gamma radiation detection system. On August 5 the crew made several flights over the area, successfully located a site of increased radioactivity, and dropped bags of flour to mark the location of the Athena. Importantly ARMS showed that rather than contained within its protective casing, "the sources [of Cobalt-57] were not intact but distributed." As a result ground teams completed measurements of contamination at the site. Of sixteen soil samples, four sand samples, two air samples, and two foliar samples, twenty-two returned positive for Cobalt-57. The missile range continued to say that the radiation posed little threat to the public.[61]

Led by again by Carlos Bustamante, a ground team sought out the rocket following the ARMS survey. The ground search was a significant undertaking. The crew included fifteen individuals, including interpreters, health physicists, Lockheed Martin representatives (a key contractor in the Athena program), and a member of the Judge Advocate General's office. Like the Trinity Site, health physicists were there to deal with the effect of radiation on bodies. Trains trucked in a large number of vehicles and supplies. The crew carried shovels, pickaxes, combat rations, cameras, radios, rakes, and a number of other materials and provisions.[62]

Once the team was given clearance to enter Mexico, Bustamante's field notes show that local residents emerged as important sources of information as to the rocket's trajectory, speed, and failure. A rancher named Felipe Silva relayed to Bustamante that he had observed a projectile move on, in Bustamante's words, "a southern track heading [three] miles west of Escalón [Chihuahua]." To Silva it moved slower than a falling star. A hired hand at the La Victoria ranch "saw a fireball come to earth slower than a meteorite." Inocente Vasquez compared the falling rocket to what looked like a soccer ball.[63]

In the weeks after the discovery and cleanup of the Athena missile fragments, a new issue arose: how to dispose of the contaminated soil. The White Sands Missile Range Public Affairs Office answered questions about radioactivity at the crash site by revealing that soils read between 0.5 and 1.5 milliroentgens per hour. They again argued that the radiation posed no real threat to the public. Yet the fact that tests showed contamination of soil and plant life raised questions about what to do with the contaminated materials. The Mexican government called for the removal of radioactive soils, and the United States acceded to the request. On September 25 a forty-man team traveling by rail arrived at Ceballos to assist army personnel and nuclear engineers who had been at the scene since late August.[64]

The Army dubbed the mission led by Colonel Thomas Kearns Operation Great Sand. An information document for the public affairs branch of the mission explained what had happened: "When the payload (nosecone) landed, it dug out a sizeable crater. The soil in the crater and from ejecta became sufficiently contaminated to require the United States to take proper steps to decontaminate the area." Altogether the recovery team took sixty drums of contaminated materials by train back to the United States. From Orogrande, New Mexico, near the southern end of the missile range, personnel trucked the contaminated soil to its disposal site.[65]

Mexican officials called for the removal of Cobalt-57 contaminated soils in an era of increased fears about the impact of even small amounts of nuclear fallout on environments and bodies. Moreover, the United States had breached Mexican sovereignty, an event in a long line of military incursions across the border. In July the United States had apologized to Mexico for the failure of the Athena missile. Yet during the recovery period secrecy and vague information undermined coverage by U.S. and Mexican media. While the Athena's failure made headlines on both sides of the border, the extent of radiation exposure remained a murky issue. In fact, the army's Office of Information (OCINFO) within the Office of the Assistant Secretary of Defense for Public Affairs (OASDPA) placed tight restrictions on information allowed to the press. Public affairs officials could draw upon several prepared guided questions, but "queries which can not be answered within this guidance will be referred with suggested response to the OASDPA through OCINFO."[66]

Coverage in Mexican newspapers concerning the cleanup of soil appeared in the few days leading up to the transportation of contaminated dirt back to the United States. Reporters from a Torreón, Coahuila, radio and television station and from the Mexico City newspaper *Excelsior* visited the American crew at the train station. A reporter from Chihuahua's *Heraldo* also visited the site. White Sands personnel hoped to quell any protest of the cleanup efforts as it could bring unwanted questions about the mission of the missile range. A fear within the White Sands Missile Range Public Affairs Office arose that "some elements of the

Mexican press are not too friendly toward the U.S. and could use this incident to accuse the U.S. of imperialism by indiscriminately permitting radio-active elements to impact on Mexican soil without regard for the sovereignty of the Mexican government."[67]

The Mexican press reported on the cleanup, but the fears raised by public affairs officers at the missile range did not materialize. The newspaper *El Siglo de Torreón* reported on the arrival of U.S. personnel to the site and the timeline for removal of the soil. *La Opinion*, another Torreón, Coahuila, newspaper, also reported on the cleanup efforts. Confusion arose as to whether the Athena caused the contamination or if radiation on the ground had brought down the missile. A story in the newspaper *Correo* thought that the team of scientists had come to find the "unknown" cause of the radiation and how it may have caused the crash rather than to uncover the extent of soil corruption as a result of the Athena impact. The relative isolation of the area and the speedy recovery of the Athena in the months after it crashed may have helped to quell any hostility from the Mexican public. At the same time, the ambiguous information that came out of the missile range created confusion as to the extent of exposure for the communities near Ceballos.[68]

The failure of both the Athena and Pershing missiles suggests that White Sands Missile Range was a place with a geographical scope beyond south-central New Mexico. Regardless of the environmental impact of the tests, landscapes neither within the geographical boundaries of White Sands nor even a part of the United States felt the impact of weapons testing. The presence of American military personnel in Mexico challenged concepts of state sovereignty as wayward missiles transformed the pastoral landscapes of Chihuahua and Durango into proving grounds. It also increased the visibility of White Sands as a military site in the region.

At the end of the day, most missiles successfully hit White Sands, leaving behind craters, debris, and pollution. The speed of a rocket or missile, the angle of impact, the design of the projectile, and the target environment would play a role in the shape, size, and level of "displaced masses" at the site of a rocket impact. A 1976 comparative study of missile craters and lunar environments showed that when projectiles with the highest velocities hit the earth, "destruction of the missile is so complete that it is difficult, if not impossible to find pieces of it anywhere." The ejection of soil, rock, and floral debris caused by a cratering event varied by the type of weapon tested and the condition of the terrain. Missiles scattered with natural ejecta across the area surrounding the target. Below the surface, missile parts mixed with destroyed soil materials in the center of the crater. Moving towards the rim, fractured zones included open breaks in the subsurface soil.[69]

Ordnance testing had similar effects. The three largest nonnuclear high explosive tests carried out by the United States happened at White Sands. In the 1980s the missile range conducted a series of blasts that ranged in force from about 550 tons to more than 4,000 tons of TNT. The largest of the tests, the 1985 Minor Scale event, measured at the equivalent of more than 4,300 total tons of TNT; 4,440 tons of ammonium nitrate fuel oil triggered the explosion. The crater left behind was 345 feet in diameter and 80 feet deep; the test threw ejecta into the air and created an immense air blast and an intense ground shock.[70]

Craters offer some obvious hints about environmental damage, but the secrecy surrounding testing makes it difficult to measure the environmental impact of the thousands of ordnance and missile tests at White Sands. The payload a missile carried, whether or not it was to impact at the surface, and the simple size of a rocket determined the effect on nature. Unexploded munitions offers another area of concern, but few open documents offer verification on the problem. In 1998 the missile range's commanding general, Harry D. Gatanas, organized the Unexploded Ordnance Hazards and Munitions Management Team to deal with issues related to military munitions and waste military munitions at White Sands. The missile range also trained employees, tenants, contractors, and visitors working inside and outside the missile range cantonment area how to recognize unexploded ordnance and when to report them.[71]

One still secret environmental impact comes from depleted uranium. Depleted uranium occurs in the process of enriching U-235, a desired form of uranium for use in weapons. It has about one-half the activity of naturally occurring uranium, which emits 0.68 microcuries per gram, while depleted uranium emits only 0.39. Because of its abundance, pyrophoricity, and value as an armor penetrator, depleted uranium became a primary element for use in missiles and smaller weapons projectiles during the Cold War. After 1989 the tie between Gulf War syndrome and weapons that employed depleted uranium led to inquiries from both veterans of the war and environmentalists.[72]

The missile range was not the only place in New Mexico where depleted uranium was tested. Environmental and peace organizations, including Citizens for Alternatives to Radioactive Dumping, the Albuquerque Peace and Justice Center, and Peace Aware, brought issue with depleted uranium tested at the New Mexico Institute of Mining and Technology (NMIMT) in Socorro, New Mexico (just a twenty-three-minute drive from the northwestern corner of White Sands). At a six-thousand-acre site on Socorro Peak the Terminal Effects Research and Analysis Group (TERA) at NMIMT carried out explosives tests that included experimentation with both U-238 and depleted uranium. By the 1980s New Mexico was one of two states that stored and tested the greatest amount of depleted uranium in North America (an honor shared with California). While there remains no clear evidence to connect the health of Socorro's populace to testing of depleted uranium, opponents claimed that the city had experienced increased levels of cancer. TERA's meticulous guidebook to handling the radioactive materials suggests that protestors had a substantive claim. The manual encouraged all employees to wear appropriate safety gear because of the chemical toxicity, pyrophoricity, and potential health implications for human bones and kidneys.[73]

In the 1998 and 2009 range-wide environmental impact statements, White Sands revealed it had tested missiles with depleted uranium but did not give total numbers. In 1994 a report completed by Los Alamos National Laboratory explored four sites where depleted uranium–tipped Pershing missiles had crashed on the missile range. At three of the sites, Chess, Salt Target, and Mine Impact, the team took soil samples.

Between 1991 and 1992, the team put in a monitoring well at a location called Site 65. In 1976 a Pershing missile carrying approximately eighty pounds of depleted uranium had hit the site located near the southern end of the missile range.[74]

While during the two-year study at Site 65 the Los Alamos monitoring team found uranium only in the realm of natural occurrences, in the Salt Target and Mine Impact areas they discovered negligible levels of depleted uranium. However, such findings remain suspect as water from rain and runoff could have carried the depleted uranium from the site either at the surface level or underground. Water analysis at the Chess Site revealed the potential for the dispersion of depleted uranium. Tests showed missile fragments present and that "the total uranium in the water was high, ranging from a low of 13 to 489 [micrograms per liter]." Reflecting the potential for the natural transfer of radioactive materials, at Chess Site "the uranium was leached from the missile fragments and is moving with the water in the gypsum." Until White Sands opens its records we may learn little more on depleted uranium testing.[75]

It might be tempting to bookend the environmental history of White Sands with the Trinity Test at one end and depleted uranium at the other. Since 1945 the military had displaced ranchers, tested a nuclear weapon, and transformed a vast area of the U.S.-Mexico borderlands into a missile testing facility. It had in the process disintegrated the fixed property lines that demarcated missile range from public and private lands and affirmed that the greater U.S.-Mexico borderlands were auxiliary landscapes to White Sands. Errant rockets affirm that boundaries are hardly tried and true. Paradoxically they also reveal the power of certain states and agencies to dictate the significance of borders and border crossings to everyday people.

At the same time, a sole focus on the specter of missilery has the power to shroud a more nuanced environmental history of the missile range that emerged under the contrails of rockets. As the struggle for the Trinity Site suggests, what White Sands and its environments meant were a matter of perception. Similarly, as rockets lifted into space, they created new opportunities for comprehending the earth. In the process

Clyde T. Holliday found in White Sands not only a landscape of war but also a landscape of scientific utopianism. It is impossible to know the many conversations everyday Americans had about early Earth photography. But the ambiguity that permeated Holliday's explanation of "An All Seeing Flying Eye" suggests that the scientific imagination from inside the military-scientific machine was not beholden to a particular vision of wartime readiness.

Between 1945 and 1970 White Sands was never totally a military "black space." Secured from public access, it could yet be observed and reimagined. At the same time that White Sands occupied the Southwest, the nonmilitary public crafted new visions of a militarized landscape to meet their own needs and desires. It was not only those boosters and national monument officials interested in the Trinity Site nor the scientists who saw in the missile range the promise of technological utopianism.[76]

In 1969 the New Mexico Department of Game and Fish introduced an exotic African antelope to the missile range as viable big game for leisure hunters. White Sands was not only a weapons testing facility—it also became a consumer's landscape. By the end of the century White Sands would face an environmental calamity that had nothing to do with missile testing.

4

A Consumer's Landscape

In the autumn of 1969 excitement filled the halls of the New Mexico Department of Game and Fish. Just a few short weeks after the Athena debacle, the gemsbok (*Oryx gazella gazella*), commonly referred to as the oryx, had come to New Mexico. On the second day of October department officials released seven of the antelope onto White Sands Missile Range. The long-legged animals had never before inhabited the area. As the department's fiscal report testified, the "highlight of the year was the first release of animals into the wild under the current exotic introductions program." The department believed that the long-horned native of the Kalahari region in southern Africa would not only make an excellent trophy for hunters but, through hunting licenses, could create considerable revenue for the state's game and fish division.[1]

South-central New Mexico had not only become a site of weapons research but was now remade a consumer's landscape. Supported by scientific studies on the region's desert environment and the potential for the oryx to survive there, state game officials exploited, for their own purposes and profit, the transformation of private ranches and federal grazing lands into a massive missile testing facility. By the 1960s the missile range was not a landscape contained by the Cold War national security state. Instead it became a site of competing visions for a newly emptied desert environment. With the first public hunts in 1974, New Mexico wildlife officials and their clientele recast White Sands as a safari of the Southwest.

By 2000 a resilient oryx population had reached near five thousand, creating unique environmental consequences for a landscape that was not simply pockmarked by missile craters. Even as hunters tracked and killed their trophies, in just twenty-five years oryx numbers skyrocketed, challenging native wildlife for food and habitat and carrying diseases dangerous to other ungulates. The missile range, ranchers in communities surrounding the testing facility, and White Sands National Monument found themselves managing a wild animal that had come to dominate the militarized environment of south-central New Mexico.[2]

While missile testing had a troubling environmental impact on the region, the oryx hunt at White Sands argues for a reconsideration of how we understand the post-1940 "Ugly West." Through limited public access, militarized landscapes have acted as sites of unintentional wildlife productivity. From Rocky Mountain Arsenal, now a national wildlife refuge, to the Naval Air Weapons Station at China Lake, which has played an integral role in the conservation of the threatened desert tortoise, places once deemed environmental wastelands have ironically emerged as sites of native wildlife protection and regeneration. Removing cattle from the missile range has led to a resurgence of antelopes in the White Sands region. In turn, all branches of the military, as well as the Department of Energy, have found themselves managing a myriad of animal species, many protected under the 1973 endangered species act.[3]

The oryx hunt at White Sands is different. It offers a history of Cold War militarization, science, and the rise of a post–World War II consumer economy unique to the open spaces and sometimes-struggling rural economies of the West. From the oryx program's inception, wildlife and environmental scientists supported the release and its continued success. They did not see the missile range as a destroyed military wasteland; instead through comparative studies they recast it as an environment similar to that of the oryx's native Kalahari habitat in South Africa. The New Mexico Department of Game and Fish saw the oryx as an authentic animal of the African safari and thus a boon for hunters. Restricted public access to White Sands would protect the

9. An oryx on White Sands Missile Range. Courtesy of White Sands Missile Range Museum and Archives.

nascent population from poachers and prying eyes. With little interference the oryx population irrupted.

Behind expansive prosperity and increased leisure time, the postwar period became the golden age of leisure hunting in the American West. As part of its mission, the New Mexico Department of Game and Fish both managed and promoted tourism in New Mexico's wild spaces. Increased opportunities for leisure and vacation after World War II allowed for new forms of rural consumption that brought revenue not only to state government but also to hotels, bait and tackle shops, and convenience stores. The idea of exotic game offered another reason for tourists to come to the state. The introduction of the exotic oryx to the missile range acted as the cornerstone project in a wider exotic game introduction program. In south-central New Mexico, seventy-plus years of livestock production had pushed large game out of the lower lying areas of the region. The rationale of the Game and Fish Department was that the oryx would fill one environmental niche without native big game.[4]

Importantly, the oryx program shows that not all ecological and wildlife-based studies, many produced from local sources, supported the preservationist agenda of post-1960 environmental movements. Early scientific studies of the oryx in New Mexico sought not to warn against the potential environmental degradation exotic ungulates could create in the region, but instead to encourage their release. After 1945 the ties between New Mexico's peculiar tourist economy and the local value of environments and animals within the Game and Fish Department mitigated the relationships between national environmental thought and knowing nature through science. Citing the apt physiology of the oryx, the ecological similarities between south-central New Mexico and the Kalahari, and the perceived lack of significant impact on native ungulates and domestic livestock, wildlife biologists offered rationale for introducing a resilient exotic antelope into a perfectly suited ecosystem. But there was little effort to understand the negative impact the animal could have on native animal populations and the environments proposed for introduction. The exotic game program reflected the long history of seeking to both restore and improve the productivity of western landscapes with little consideration for the long-term consequences of those changes.[5]

Because White Sands remained an active weapons-testing facility, hunting would remain limited and would require specially trained guides. Studies of oryx adaptability were also limited. By 1990 the dramatic expansion of the oryx population compelled wildlife biologists to address the adverse effects of the exotic ungulate on regional flora and fauna. As the herd grew exponentially and increasingly defied the boundaries of the missile range, studies revealed that the oryx challenged native species for forage and carried diseases detrimental to endangered animals. By the mid-1990s evidence suggested that the oryx played at least some role in the collapse of mule deer populations across south-central New Mexico.[6]

The oryx program was not an anomaly. Wildlife irruptions have happened across North America both naturally and as a result of game management practices. With European colonization, ecosystem disruption allowed non-indigenous horses, pigs, and sheep to flourish in the Americas. More recently, humans have induced population explosions among certain species. During the 1930s the deadly mixture of drought and exhaustive farming allowed for grasshopper, Mormon cricket, and rabbit irruptions in the southern Great Plains. The destruction of predators to promote deer on the Kaibab Plateau of Arizona led to an explosion of deer herds that consumed much of the forage in the area and a collapse in their population. This led Aldo Leopold to famously call on Americans to "think like a mountain" (that is, to respect the interplay between deer and predators in ecosystem health).[7]

From the late nineteenth-century introduction of alien fish into California's aquatic ecosystems to the transplant of bison herds to Alaska during the 1920s, experimentation with exotic and transplanted species in the West had a long history. Those programs were not necessarily well conceived and did not always play out as expected. For example, in 1944 the U.S. Coast Guard introduced 29 reindeer to the Alaskan island of St. Matthew. The herd exploded to 6,000 head. By 1966 their numbers had dropped to 42 as a result of the relationship between available fodder and climatic factors.[8]

It is also important to note that exotic game introductions were not just state programs. Private interests both imported exotic animals and bankrolled exotic game initiatives. Between 1963 and 1988, Texas experienced an estimated surge from about 14,000 to more than 161,000 exotic hoofed animals. Private ranches primarily purchased those exotics, but the animals nonetheless expanded onto publicly controlled lands. Imported from India, free-ranging nilgai antelope numbered as many as 36,400. Free-range sika deer, from Asia, roamed in numbers as high as 5,600 in parts of the state. Although the oryx program was managed by the New Mexico Department of Game and Fish, hunting organizations helped bankroll it.[9]

By the time state and federal agencies initiated new ecological and biological studies of the potential impact of the oryx on the region, the popularity of hunting the animal led to calls for the management of a smaller herd (rather than outright removal) as the best situation for the people, plants, and animals of south-central New Mexico. Despite recent protests from ranchers and White Sands National Monument officials, the oryx's fate remained tied to military control of the basin and the exotic animal's place in the New Mexico Department of Game and Fish hunting agenda.

THE SAFARI OF THE SOUTHWEST

The release of oryx at White Sands Missile Range acted as the culmination of a broader New Mexico Department of Game and Fish planned exotic game program. Beginning in 1950 State Game Warden Elliott S. Barker selected the Canadian River Canyon as the ideal location for the introduction of fifty-two Barbary sheep. Private individuals had imported a number of species including carp, ringneck pheasants, and brown trout. Beginning in 1961 the newly appointed chairman of the State Game Commission, Dr. Frank Hibben, anthropology and archaeology professor at the University of New Mexico and avid African big game hunter, expanded exotic experimentations with fauna. He argued that the introduction of exotic animals would enhance local environments by bringing new birds and mammals to an already vibrant landscape. After 1961 the department assayed plant species including wheatgrass and mammal and bird species including kudu, Afghan white-winged pheasant, sandgrouse, gray francolin, and coturnix quail as viable for New Mexico environments.[10]

Exotic introductions did not go uncontested. Under pressure from conservationists, federal authorities passed legislation to control future programs. The Lacey Act of 1900 served as the first significant push to undermine the introduction and adverse impact of exotic animals. The act addressed problems associated with migratory game and insectivorous birds and required that the Department of Interior "regulate the introduction of American or foreign birds or animals in localities where they have not heretofore existed." But it was the flood of environmental legislation during the 1960s and 1970s that offered the most powerful legal counter to programs that sought to introduce non-indigenous species. In particular the 1969 National Environmental Policy Act in part required environmental impact statements for all federal and state actions on federal lands that would have an effect on the natural conditions of those particular places. It required similar statements for private activities on federal lands. Wildlife protection under the Endangered Species Act ostensibly created new powers to undermine the introduction and continued development of exotic species programs in the United States. Similarly, Executive Order 11987, signed by President Jimmy Carter in 1977, encouraged federal agencies to use all legal means to undermine the introduction of exotic species into ecosystems. Finally, the 1990 Non-indigenous Aquatic Nuisance Prevention and Control Act sought to prevent the expansion of exotic fish species in the United States.[11]

The oryx release reveals the unique role of a U.S. state in rethinking the shift from private landscapes of production to ones controlled by the federal military scientific apparatus. Closed to the public and lacking huntable big game, White Sands offered a place perfect for experimentation with nonnative ungulates. In New Mexico hunting became part of the postwar culture of leisure and consumption. More generally, economic studies encouraged greater emphasis on the use of New Mexico's vast recreational resources. In 1954 nearly 1.3 million people had visited the state's national forests for recreational purposes. Ten years later, the number had jumped to nearly 4.6 million. Despite a clear success in bringing visitors to New Mexico, management consultants who had completed tourism studies for the state raised concerns about other underutilized recreational resources. The greatest alarm came with the uneven sales of hunting and fishing licenses. Between 1951 and 1959, resident big game hunting licenses had grown by a staggering 90 percent from 46,566 to 88,525. Yet for the year 1959 the state had sold only 2,772 nonresident big game licenses. Between 1959 and 1964, total resident and nonresident hunting and fishing licenses increased by only 7 percent. Those numbers were less than the total increase of New Mexico's population for the same period. The exotic game program would act as another way to bring hunters to New Mexico.[12]

Initiated prior to the January 1970 enactment of the 1969 National Environmental Policy Act, the programs for the African oryx and the Persian ibex became the success stories of New Mexico's exotic game program. From its inception the program hoped to produce "new hunting opportunities in New Mexico." The transfer of exotic ungulates from their native lands to their adopted home started with fact-finding missions led by Hibben and a team, who traveled to South Africa to search out viable species. While New Mexico financially supported the program, private donors subsidized the purchase of exotic species seen as capable of surviving in New Mexico ecosystems. Once purchased, the animals were transplanted to the Albuquerque Zoological Park, where they would live out their lives in captivity. Under U.S. Department of Agriculture regulations at the time the Game and Fish Department could release only the progeny of exotic animals into wild North American environments.[13]

Between 1964 and 1965 state game officials began pasture studies at the zoo with the presentation of mesquite grass, tornillo, catclaw, and chamisa to ibex, oryx, and kudu in an effort to measure the adaptability of exotics to regional forage (the kudu was eventually rejected for introduction because it was believed that it would adapt to New Mexico environments only with "great difficulty"). During 1965 and 1966 oryx, ibex, and kudu were moved to the department's newly built 350-acre enclosed pasture at Red Rock in the southwestern area of the state. There the different exotic animals underwent further assessment to determine their viability for regional ecosystems and potential impact on native plant and animal species. In December 1970 game officials released fifteen ibex into the Florida Mountains, and with adequate natural reproduction, hunting commenced five years later.[14]

But Hibben gave the oryx introduction program first priority. In 1962 the department purchased two males and six females, and the fiscal year report for 1963 and 1964 reported that the small herd produced its first progeny. First at the zoo and later at Red Rock, oryx numbers increased steadily. By the summer of 1965 the Game and Fish Department had three offspring, and two years later department officials at Red Rock began to "determine their food preferences and behavior and additional facts about their life histories." By June 1968 oryx numbers had reach twenty-three at the Red Rock pasture.[15]

From the beginning the exotic game program was controversial. But early opposition was not from local environmentalists, ranchers, or military leadership. While some ranchers showed concerns about oryx competing with cattle for forage, in September 1969 Tom Ela, staff park ranger for the National Park Service, raised an early voice of concern. Speaking to the future of White Sands National Monument, he suggested to Frank Koski, the National Park Service's regional director, oryx "are being planted in the White Sands area on military ground but eventually they may be on us." Ela's fear would become reality only ten years later.[16]

The National Park Service was not alone in protesting the program. Arizona's State Game and Fish Department raised similar concerns with reference to the oryx releases and the need to protect native flora and fauna. Director Robert Jantzen explained: "Our principle interest is to protect and preserve native wildlife." The destruction of any animals trespassing in Arizona remained the department's official policy on New Mexico's exotic introduction program. Yet in 1969 the small number of successful introductions and the lack of public understanding of how the oryx might affect environments in New Mexico muted any challenge to the release. Wildlife officials justified the program by arguing that invasive species programs had long since undermined any so-called balance of nature. William Huey, former secretary of natural resources for the state of New Mexico, acknowledged that the few who were opposed to the program had valid arguments about the nuisance of certain exotic species. But, he explained, "the contribution which they might make toward breaking down the balance of nature is certainly among the least important."[17]

Most opposition from state residents and public officials concerned financing behind the oryx program. Former Game and Fish commissioner Hibben and Dr. Bruce Stringer, director of the Albuquerque Zoological Park, charged the department prematurely sold off kudu not yet released into the wild. In response, New Mexico governor Bruce King organized the Advisory Exotic Mammal Task Force to probe financial dealings of the exotic game program generally and the sell-off of kudu specifically. By 1981 the reality that kudu did not adapt to New Mexico's winter climate made the issue moot. At the same time, the passage of the National Environmental Policy Act and the requirement that similar programs carry out federally mandated environmental impact studies curtailed further release of exotic game.[18]

Due to the small number of oryx scheduled for release and little evidence of interference with the mission of the weapons testing facility, on May 26, 1969, missile range commander General H. G. Davisson agreed to allow the department to release a few oryx on the missile range. In October seven were set free. By 1974 the oryx had adapted to the missile range, and that year the state issued five licenses to hunt the exotic antelope.[19]

There was another reason the program went forward on the missile range. Hunting was not new to White Sands. Even before the New Mexico Department of Game and Fish released the oryx on the missile range, the military had permitted controlled deer hunts there. White Sands allowed campsites at the edge of the military reserve, and hunters, many of them military personnel and their families, sought out game. While Hibben later tried to justify the exotic game program by suggesting that the department helped protect many of the species from their endangerment in Africa, there remains little doubt that trophy hunting was the sole purpose of the release of ibex and oryx into New Mexico.[20]

Although for different purposes, like the recent "Big Open" and

"Buffalo Commons" proposals for parts of the post-agricultural Great Plains, the department hoped to stock the missile range with big game that could attract tourists. White Sands had become a consumer's landscape. After 1972, under the new state game commissioner, Ladd Gordon, officials emphasized that "hunting opportunity in areas of the state where there were no existing big game populations" remained the primary goal of the program. The oryx would replace other big game that had dwindled in the years prior to World War II. To encourage the hunter-tourist to come to New Mexico, the Game and Fish Department remade a militarized desert landscape to fulfill the needs of regional big game enthusiasts and create revenue for the state.[21]

The value of the oryx as a commodity for hunters far outweighed any environmental concerns raised by White Sands National Monument or the state of Arizona. As leisure hunting opportunities expanded in the postwar years, hunting clubs appeared as well. Between 1962 and 1971, individual donors and several organizations not based in New Mexico, including the Shikar Safari Club (founded in 1952 by an alliance of international hunters) and the Southern California Safari Club (founded in 1966), contributed more than $65,000 to the exotic game program. Hunting the oryx in New Mexico would offer a similar experience to hunting on the Kalahari, but closer to home. Reflecting the desires among sportsmen to hunt the animal, Albuquerque lawyer Thomas Cornish wrote a letter to Governor Bruce King that explained while hunting had "deteriorated" during his lifetime, the exotic game program offered future trophy game for his sons, who took pleasure in the same outdoor pastimes that their father had long enjoyed.[22]

By 1971 the New Mexico Department of Game and Fish could safely suggest, "of all the exotic animals recently imported, the [oryx] has made the greatest strides." Hunters jumped at the opportunity to hunt the animal. By 1983 the department had received a total of 1,188 applications for oryx hunting licenses. Usually guided by missile range personnel and Game and Fish officials, hunters found themselves led to the known haunts of oryx herds. While utilizing all environments on the missile range, oryx amassed in greater numbers at the Small Missile Range

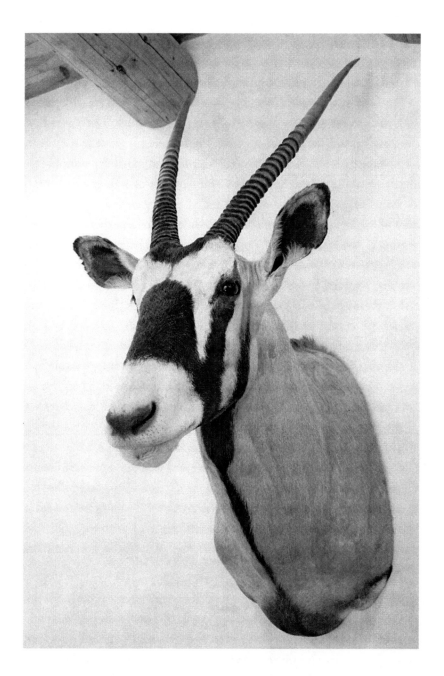

10. Oryx trophy, Tesuque, New Mexico. Author's collection.

area near the center of White Sands and the Stallion hunt area at the northern end of the missile range. Both areas were grassy playas that offered significant fodder for the resilient antelope.[23]

The number of licenses issued by year varies but has increased steadily with the growth of oryx numbers. Historically licenses were based on a lottery system, and oryx hunts at the missile range were a once in a lifetime experience. More recently hunts happened for a mobility-impaired youth, Iraq/Afghanistan War veteran, or holder of a WSMR security-badged license (for those with security clearance). The oryx hunt at White Sands is not so different than the safari experience in the southeast African nations of Tanzania and Kenya. Experienced trackers, usually members of safari outfitter companies own and run by white hunters, lead the hunts in Africa from regional towns and cities. Yet, rather than a privately run venture, on White Sands those duties were carried out first by the Department of Game and Fish and later through interagency collaboration with the missile range's environmental office.[24]

Hunters faced unique restrictions because White Sands remained an active missile testing facility. On what is usually a two-day trek, hunters show up at the missile range before dawn on the first day. Because of the size of the range, hunters often do not run into one another during their trip. It is legal to take both male and female animals, but hunters prefer males because of the size and thickness of their horns. From a distance, the two sexes look markedly similar, as do adolescent and adult oryx. Animals are tracked by truck until a suitable animal is located. Hunters dismount to shoot. After the kill, the animal is loaded onto a truck and hauled away.[25] One hunter relayed the experience of shooting the animal:

> We were staying at a little motel in Alamogordo and at dawnish the next morning off we went to the range. We drove around a couple of hours not seeing anything at all and then off to our left appeared a small group at about one hundred yards. Perhaps they were lying down and just stood up. There looked to be 10-12 cows and several bulls. After a few minutes of binocular examination, we found a really

nice bull in the middle of the group. As we looked, they ambled off further to our left out to about 150 yards. The decision was made to pursue the bull. I got out of the truck while the guide kept track of him within the group. I kneeled down in front of the truck and found him in the scope. I had to wait until several animals cleared away to allow a shot. I found his shoulder in the scope, lowered the crosshairs to the racing stripe and squeezed the trigger. At the shot, he dropped to his knees as the group took off.[26]

The popularity of the oryx hunt in its early years bolstered the nascent exotic game program. By all accounts the natural increase in oryx numbers and the large number of applications for the hunt shows that in very little time Hibben's dream of establishing a premier African trophy species in New Mexico had come to pass. As much as it was a greater emphasis on outdoors leisure as an antidote to the lack of big game in the region, the oryx program evolved from meticulous scientific study and experimentation on a militarized landscape. In those studies there was little effort to predict the environmental damage that might result from the release.[27]

MAKING THE CASE

The oryx adapted to White Sands Missile Range better than expected. In 1977 Richard Saiz, a wildlife scientist and graduate student who completed the first study of the oryx at the missile range, calculated that in the year 2000 the population would reach 402 animals and support a harvest of 90 annually. During the 1991–92 fiscal year oryx already numbered somewhere between 1,800 and 2,100, far more than the number Saiz projected. For the same years hunters harvested only 96 oryx. A myriad of environmental and biological factors and limited initial hunting allowed the oryx populations to swell to 5,000 by the end of the century. The exotic species survived and thrived in a place designed for missile testing because it remained isolated. It would eventually vie for food with native animals, trample plant species on White Sands National Monument, and act as a host to diseases detrimental to deer and cattle. In the 1990s wildlife officials began to take greater notice of those issues only with the irruption of the oryx population and the decline in native ungulates at White Sands.[28]

Resiliency in acute desert environments appropriately describes the disposition of oryx populations both in their native southern African habitat and in their adopted home in south-central New Mexico. On arid African steppe, brush lands, and savannas the oryx run in herds of fifteen to fifty but may also operate in significantly larger aggregations. On White Sands Missile Range they can congregate in herds as large as thirty to forty animals. Despite their large stature and sometimes hostile nature, oryx almost always use flight as a defense mechanism when pursued by predatory animals. Breeding among oryx occurs aseasonally, and females begin reproducing as early as two years of age. Needing a mere three liters of water for every hundred kilograms of body weight per day, oryx can survive without significant water for extended periods of time. In native habitats the animals uses a variety of strategies to keep hydrated when water sources remain scant and desert temperatures rise. The oryx allow body temperatures to elevate to 45 degrees Celsius, from a regular 36 degrees, before allowing the onset of dehydration through sweating and panting. The animal may also retain water from urine concentration and absorption of fecal moisture. By feeding on certain roots, tubers, bulbs, melons, and cucumbers, oryx can also utilize plant moisture for hydration.[29]

During 1968 and 1969 the New Mexico State University Agricultural Experiment Station retained John Wood of the Division of Wildlife Sciences at the University of Nevada, Jackson Durham with the U.S. Bureau of Land Management, and independent researcher Ronald White to carry out the foundational research for exotic introductions to the state. The study recognized aseasonal and early patterns of gestation among oryx herds. More importantly, in suggesting that oryx made use of a variety of water sources, the team understood the hardy nature of the species and its adaptability to arid landscapes. While the animal remained in captivity at Red Rock, Wood and his team recorded an average of forty-eight hours between waterings. In 1968 researchers recorded a thirty-day span when one animal did not return to observable water sources.[30]

Just as importantly, the team sought to bridge the gap between the oryx and adopted environment. Wood and his team noticed that the small herd had started to take to southern New Mexico's varied flora. The antelope fed on several grass and grass-like plants, including Johnson grass, Bermuda grass, and fluff grass. In all, the team of researchers observed the oryx feeding on twenty-seven types of flora common in the region.[31]

Wood and his colleagues also suggested, "It appears that the range of the [oryx] is very similar to the Lower Sonoran" (the southwestern vegetational zone where the Red Rock pasture existed). Climographs that compared Lordsburg, New Mexico (near Red Rock), and Pretoria, South Africa (near the oryx's homelands), showed a considerable degree of variety in annual rainfall and seasonal temperature. While the team discerned such factors "might prove limiting," they argued that the oryx (and ibex) showed "promise of being adaptable and establishable big game species for New Mexico."[32]

The work of Wood and his colleagues coincided with the October 1969 release of an experimental herd of oryx to the missile range, an environment not studied by the researchers. Wood recognized that releasing the animal into wild spaces would most likely create problems for monitors tracking the success of the oryx but said little about the likelihood for environmental problems following the release. The studies of food and water done at Red Rock offered some evidence of the potential success of introduction at the missile range, but little was said about release sites. White Sands Missile Range became the primary introduction site because it possessed no big game for hunting, its environment was not unlike Red Rock or the Kalahari, and the area included few lands used for grazing domestic livestock. Moreover, White Sands also remained closed to the public and thus ideal for experimentation with the oryx. Game officials and wildlife scientists did not list any fear of the potential negative impact of the program, including possible irruptions, disease, or competition with other foragers and grazers. Exotic game boosters, hunters, and scientists transformed an apparatus of the American Cold

War defense industry into a place for testing something as foreign to south-central New Mexico as the missiles that appeared there some twenty-five years earlier.[33]

Like fish and wildlife personnel, Wood and his colleagues reiterated that the oryx would fill "vacant niches of the creosote and mesquite brush land." Similar environmental conditions between home and adopted habitat acted as rationale for the selected site. Beginning in 1972 Richard Saiz, at the request of the New Mexico Department of Game and Fish, carried out the first study to determine how well the oryx had adapted to the missile range environment. Range commander Major General Arthur H. Sweeney had allowed for studies of the oryx to be conducted on the missile range. Personnel within the Facilities Resources and Requirements Division of White Sands and "range riders" (security patrol officers) aided Saiz as he completed his work.[34]

Following climographs similar to those used by Wood and his team at Red Rock, Saiz recognized crucial parallels between the home and adopted habitats of the oryx. While reversed cyclically, the two regions had similar seasonal precipitation with rainfall peaking at between 1.5 and 2.0 inches in the late spring and reaching a nadir of less than 0.5 inches during the winter. The temperatures at White Sands reached a maximum average of 93.5 Fahrenheit during the summer while the Kalahari peaked at a maximum average of 93 Fahrenheit. Similarly an average eight-degree differential separated the two environments during their coldest months (a number marked as promising despite the disparity).[35]

The range also consisted of at least fifteen plant families similar to those found in the oryx's native habitat. Saiz saw the oryx eat at least five of those. The animal consumed plants from the dropseed family, Russian thistle, and various grasses. Oryx also fed on mesquite and creosote bush, two species similar to plants found in the Kalahari region. While Chihuahuan desert scrub and desert grasslands (where primary food sources exist) acted as the primary territory for the herds, oryx exploited many vegetational zones in the region, from pinyon and juniper ranges in the Oscura and San Andres foothills to (less frequently) the gypsum dunes on White Sands National Monument.[36]

One of the most important aspects of Saiz's work argued that south-central New Mexico lacked significant predators to impinge on oryx population growth. While coyotes, bobcats, and mountain lions seemed like potential threats to the small herd on White Sands, actual predation remained limited to coyotes stalking newborn calves. Reflecting the realities of continued natural reproduction on the missile range and successful adaptation to the environment, Saiz could safely suggest that the small oryx population "show[ed] potential of becoming successfully established in New Mexico."[37]

As engineers experimented with new military weaponry, wildlife scientists experimented with an exotic animal species in a desert landscape closed to the public but still in need of big game. They cultivated an ecological disaster that had nothing to do with weapons testing. The separate studies done by Wood and Saiz had not adequately considered the potential negative implications of the oryx release for native ungulates and the nonhuman natural environment. The rapid and extensive irruption of the oryx population created concerns that would challenge the value of the animal in the region.

In 1969 Wood and his team of investigators had suggested that oryx "could possibly compete with domestic livestock for available grass." Yet, they concluded: "On ranges where competition could be controlled by manipulation of livestock and [oryx] numbers, competition for food need not develop into a problem for either the animals or the range." Saiz argued only a few years later that the oryx "were not found to compete significantly with native big game of White Sands Missile Range due to differences in habitat preferences." While early studies maintained that there existed little environmental overlap between the exotic species and imported livestock or indigenous ungulates, by 1977 the natural increase in oryx numbers led to the first call for new management strategies.[38]

Oryx challenged native foragers and grazers for food. Moreover, biological and environmental factors not adequately discussed before the release also played a role in the irruption of the species. The oryx carried a series of diseases harmful to mule deer, pronghorn, and the endangered bighorn sheep. Drought held the potential to create greater competition for less food. Recognizing that the oryx had emerged as the primary ungulate in the region, wildlife biologists moved from supporting the release of a nascent oryx population to calling for a cautious reconsideration of the exotic animal's place in a complex New Mexico habitat.

Yet throughout the 1970s the early notion that no competition occurred between oryx and native ungulate populations remained a key rationale for the release. In 1971 William Huey, then associate director of operations for the New Mexico Department of Game and Fish, reiterated the work of Wood and Saiz by suggesting in *National Sportsman's Digest* that "no competition is anticipated among the [oryx] and native wildlife populations since the feeding habits of the native deer and pronghorn are significantly different from those of the [oryx]." He went further, arguing that the program would succeed without any "adverse effects."[39]

The limited access to herds on the missile range only encouraged oryx population growth. In two follow-up studies completed by Saiz between 1975 and 1977, the New Mexico Department of Game and Fish acknowledged that the non-indigenous antelope had thrived far beyond expectations. At the same time, between 1974 and 1975 the number of hunting applications rose from 241 to 507. Between the 1981-1982 and 1982-1983 fiscal years, they rose again from 1,301 to 1,451. However, the second study advised that because of aseasonal breeding habits, hunters should not shoot a cow with its calf. Such a practice would undermine oryx population growth. Management proposals promoted the expansion of the species but did not consider the potential need to control the animal's numbers. As oryx numbers exploded, so too did interest in the program. Yet limited yearly hunting on a militarized landscape with only controlled access could not alone cull the herds.[40]

IRRUPTION

Between 1969 and 1975 the oryx population had grown to 200. Researchers argued for continued analysis of herd numbers and the animal's relationship with natural environments on the missile range. Most research explained that south-central New Mexico could most likely support larger populations. Since "oryx still were not found to compete significantly with the native big game of White Sands Missile Range," Saiz believed that the missile range could support as many as 11,224 total oryx without negative impact. That approximation derived from a USDA estimate that the region could hold 67,348 total animal units. At the same time, wildlife biologists knew very little about the herd's growth, most likely because these scientists had limited access to White Sands.[41]

The 1977 call for management strategies urged that while the missile range could carry "several thousand" head of oryx, "a management plan for the [oryx] should be proposed to hold the population below a maximum of 500 animals." Such an idea seemed to preclude any suggestion that too many oryx would create adverse effects for the regional environment. Nor did it consider managing an animal species on a closed military landscape. The continued popularity of the oryx hunt and the considerable state revenue generated from licenses gave credence to management rather than significant reduction or total removal of the species. Even as hunters consumed more oryx, the exotic antelope's population expanded across White Sands, creating a widening gap between annual harvests and hunters afield.[42]

It took little time for the unexpected consequences of the exotic game program to appear in south-central New Mexico. By 1983 oryx numbers had reach more than 500 total for the region. Oryx often strayed onto the gypsum dunes at White Sands National Monument, where they fed on a myriad of plant species. During a study carried out during the year, wildlife biologists witnessed 115 oryx eat forage on the national monument, including large amounts of buffalo gourd. Wildlife scientists suggested that the oryx "presence poses questions for Park management," but that the animal could also become an economic benefit. They said this despite the fact that the oryx ate the very plants that added to the aesthetics of the dunes. They also seemed to hint that so long as the oryx's impact on the monument was minimal, the exotic animal could become an attraction for tourists visiting the national monument.[43]

By the 1990s the cost of management outstripped any economic benefits the animal had held for National Park officials. Between 1993 and 2001 the National Park Service estimated that the removal of oryx from White Sands National Monument by nonlethal measures would cost upwards of four hundred thousand dollars. In 1996 the NPS constructed a six-foot high, sixty-seven-mile-long fence at a cost of over a million dollars. Although nonlethal reduction using helicopters and tranquilizing darts had actually reduced oryx numbers on the monument, the removal of 228 animals proved both tedious and costly. Monument officials thus encouraged a shift to lethal reduction on the grounds that it would reduce removal costs. They believed the process would "improve natural ecosystem functions by removing the cause of existing impacts on soil/vegetation such as game trails, trampling, digging roots, grazing, and browsing." Animal rights activists eventually undermined the lethal removal program, forcing the National Monument to maintain herding and nonlethal strategies for expelling the oryx from White Sands.[44]

While park officials struggled to deter oryx from trespassing on the monument, the exotic antelope increasingly challenged indigenous species for forage. Recent biological studies suggest that because of variations in habitat usage by season coupled with forage availability, oryx dietary overlap with mule deer and pronghorn remained relatively low. However, both pronghorn and oryx favored similar forage, leading researchers to encourage further studies of oryx population dynamics. Depending on the vegetational zone, the overlap in mule deer and oryx dietary preferences varies. For example, in Chihuahuan semi-desert grasslands, one researcher found that annually oryx diets consisted of about 61 percent grasses, 22 percent shrubs, and 15.5 percent forbs compared to about 16.5 percent grasses, 58 percent shrubs, and 24.5 percent forbs for mule deer. While seen as relatively negligible, those findings remained an issue for wildlife biologists studying the expanding oryx population.[45]

In the mid-1990s, the mule deer population crashed. Drought between 1993 and 1995 acted as a primary cause. However, like the recent concerns over a transmission of brucellosis between transplanted bison, indigenous elk, and livestock in the Yellowstone area, disease was also seen as a contributing factor. Wildlife biologists argued: "anecdotal evidence suggests that dramatic population declines coincided with large increases in [oryx] population densities and expansion of the oryx range." Researchers explain that the exotic species had emerged as "superior competitors" in the region. Yet competition for food remained only one of many concerns. Research into diseases carried by the oryx offered more evidence that it undermined not only mule deer populations, but also the endangered desert bighorn sheep. A study done in 1988 offered the first evidence of disease in oryx at White Sands Missile Range. A newly found vesiculovirus named Malpais Spring virus occurred in 65.8 percent of oryx populations. Indigenous pronghorn and mule deer also carried the disease, suggesting a possible connection between the expansion of oryx numbers and the potential for future declines in the native ungulate population.[46]

Whereas earlier studies had offered no consideration of negative elements of the oryx release, a 2003 study completed by wildlife biologists examined oryx exposure to several diseases adverse to wildlife. The study found high seroprevalence for three diseases. The overwhelming majority of oryx (98 percent, 49 of 50 animals) tested positive for malignant catarrhal fever, a disease that could be fatal to deer at a time when the mule deer had just experienced a significant decline in numbers. Oryx also carried bluetongue fever (96 percent, 48 of 50 animals), a condition known to affect elk, bison, mule deer, and desert bighorn sheep. They also carried bovine respiratory syncytial virus (66 percent, 33 of 50 animals), which created a concern that the disease could undermine the recuperation of endangered desert bighorn sheep populations on the missile range and at the nearby San Andres National Wildlife Refuge (the primary site for the sheep's potential recovery).[47]

In February 1999 President Bill Clinton signed Executive Order 13112 as a measure to "prevent the introduction of invasive species and provide for their control and to minimize the economic, ecological, and human health impacts that invasive species cause." The order called for "science-based" management plans evaluated by the newly created

Invasive Species Council as a measure to prevent further invasions and control exotic species already affecting North American ecosystems.[48]

The 1999 order resulted in two decisive reports that measured oryx physiology and the animal's environmental impact. Conducted in 2000 under mutual agreement between wildlife biologists at White Sands Missile Range and the New Mexico Department of Game and Fish, the *Comprehensive Oryx Management Plan* examined oryx biology, monitoring strategies, population growth, and potential measures toward controlling the population within the missile range and eliminating its presence outside of the range. It also reaffirmed that the missile range was forced to undertake environmental management programs well beyond those required under the National Environmental Policy Act and monitored by the Environmental Protection Agency. Unlike earlier studies, the plan revealed that "oryx diets overlap extensively with domestic cattle" and that a "potential for displacement of native ungulates" existed. A second report completed in 2006 explored the dynamics of the oryx in south-central New Mexico with the hope of understanding oryx fecundity, movement patterns, and its part as a carrier of contagious diseases. With members of its environmental stewardship office playing a role in both reports, White Sands Missile Range had emerged not only as a military-scientific reserve but also as a hunting ground co-managed by the military.[49]

The acknowledgment of the adverse effects of oryx on native ungulates and domestic livestock acted as an about-face from earlier studies of the exotic animal in New Mexico. The explosion of herds allowed for a greater understanding of the oryx and raised concerns among biologists within the New Mexico Department of Game and Fish, at the missile range, and from neighboring New Mexico State University. Yet several factors challenged an outright end to the oryx program in south-central New Mexico. Some wildlife biologists and state game officials remained wedded to the program. Despite recognizing that without control of herd numbers the oryx would spread across the Southwest, White Sands Missile Range wildlife biologist Patrick Morrow suggested that the goal of interagency management plans "is to reduce the population to a manageable level [while] maintaining optimum hunter opportunity. We are not trying to reduce oryx numbers to zero."[50]

Morrow tempered his assessment of the program, explaining: "I am, however, always concerned with the potential [effects] this exotic species has on native species and habitats, so reduction of the population to a much lower, maintained number is in the best interest of WSMR, the State, and native species." The *Comprehensive Oryx Management Plan* suggested the latent impact of the oryx on indigenous flora and fauna, but most parties remained committed to the oryx hunt. The report argued, "hunters directly benefit from oryx hunting as recreation, supply of meat, and prized trophy harvest." In 1997 Morrow estimated the number of requests for oryx hunting licenses at between five thousand and eight thousand applications per year. Yet as the *Comprehensive Oryx Management Plan* explained, "A harvest of 613 oryx in 1997 reflects the gross underestimation of the oryx population growth potential."[51]

White Sands National Monument followed its plans for an elimination of the species from the national monument. In management reports nearby federal and state-administered areas, including the neighboring San Andres National Wildlife Refuge, the Bosque del Apache National Wildlife Refuge, and the Sevilleta National Wildlife Refuge, fell under New Mexico Department of Game and Fish plans for a total reduction of oryx numbers to zero outside the missile range. Recently, private individuals have also raised greater concern about the program. In particular, ranchers have tied the oryx to the decline of the local livestock economy. Local rancher Jim Grider argued: "A few years ago, the oryx were so thick we had to pull the cattle off the ranch." He was particularly disturbed by competition for water and the decrease in grasses on land he leased from the Bureau of Land Management. Grider explained that "when I had to pull my cattle and continued to pay those leases, to graze and water oryx, I didn't think that was fair." While thousands of prospective hunters waited for permits from the New Mexico Department of Game and Fish, some local residents argued that the oryx undermined the regional ranching economy by competing with domestic livestock.[52]

Yet the issue of oryx in south-central New Mexico remains complicated. Not all ranchers have sought the elimination of the exotic species. In fact, ranchers used what they perceived as an assault on the livestock economy to call for hunting oryx on private lands. In recent years, if ranchers can prove destruction to property by the exotic antelope, they now qualify for depredation permits. At a price of $1,000 to $3,000 per permit, many landowners have rethought their position on the oryx in south-central New Mexico. At Ted Turner's Armendaris Ranch on the western edge of White Sands Missile Range, land manager Tom Waddell sees a value in the oryx. As productive eaters they efficiently turn food into protein, a benefit for humans that consume them. More importantly, like other ranches, Turner's property benefits from oryx hunts, selling permits for as much as $1,500 apiece. Such value offsets questions of production on many ranches that abut or are near the missile range.[53]

While oryx compete with native ungulates for forage, hunters continue to hunt and kill the animal on the missile range and on private ranches. Despite environmental concerns, the monetary value of the oryx remains high for hunters who want the safari experience, ranchers who can capitalize on the expansion of oryx populations off the missile range, and the New Mexico Department of Game and Fish, which benefits from license sales. Recently White Sands has established special hunting fees collected directly by the missile range as a measure to offset the cost of the hunt. Moreover, by 2006 efforts to keep the oryx in check reduced the total population by at least 1,500 animals. Yet, as Morrow had suggested, "maintaining optimum hunter opportunity" remains a key goal of the program.[54]

By 2006 hunts had successfully reduced herds to between 3,000 and 3,500 animals.[55] Yet for the mule deer and the desert bighorn sheep, the oryx, at the very least, still exists as competition in an arid environment dominated by the exotic antelope. In 2001 Frank Hibben reflected on the program he had started forty years earlier: "We have more oryx in New Mexico than all of the Kalahari, I'm thrilled that they're doing so well." Hunters continue to flock to White Sands Missile Range to track and kill the exotic species, despite its historically negative environmental impact. Much of the success of the program hinges upon the resiliency of the oryx in a desert habitat not only similar to its home region, but also with viable forage, no predators, and negligible competition from other ungulates.[56]

As the oryx took to the desert environment, White Sands had transcended its mission as a military-scientific facility. The transformation of public grazing lands and private ranches into a massive federally controlled landscape allowed diverse communities to reconsider the value of the region. Emptying south-central New Mexico of its one-time abundant cattle herds and creating an immense open landscape offered the New Mexico Department of Game and Fish a place perfect for experimentation with exotic big game hunting. A desert environment presumably destroyed by weapons testing had ironically become the safari of the Southwest. Yet even as the first herds of oryx skulked the landscape, ranchers remained determined to contest the taking of their homes. In the meantime the missile range had become a site of consumption for both hunters and oryx.

5

RANGE WARS

Early on the morning of October 13, 1982, eighty-one-year-old Dave McDonald and his niece Mary crept quietly onto White Sands Missile Range. Carrying two rifles and a pistol, they intended to reclaim the family's former homestead, which the McDonalds had ceded to the federal government forty years earlier. Not far from the haunts of oryx herds, the two constructed a crude barbed wire fence and erected signs reading "No Trespassing" and "Road Closed to the U.S. Army." In 1942 officials from within the Army Corps of Engineers had compelled McDonald and nearly three hundred other landowners and mine claimants to lease or sell their lands to the federal government as a wartime necessity.

The McDonalds (with two journalists in tow) had come to the missile range to dispute the forty-year-old occupation of more than six hundred acres of private land and the loss of state and federal grazing leases. They alleged that the federal government had underpaid them for their property by not accurately calculating the long-term value of claims on grazing permits and the capital lost to an idle ranch. More importantly, the Department of Defense had reneged on the promise to eventually return property taken during and immediately after World War II. The McDonald family understood their former homestead as an occupied landscape once part of a vibrant ranching economy. This was a war over the missile range.[1]

11. Dave McDonald with a member of the White Sands Missile Range Public Affairs Office, n.d. Courtesy of the U.S. Army, White Sands Missile Range Public Affairs Office.

In 1982 Denny Gentry, who had joined the New Mexico Cattle Growers Association as communications director three years earlier, came across the McDonalds at a hearing on grazing fees in Carrizozo, New Mexico. Alongside Bob Jones, then president of the Cattle Growers Association, Gentry sat down with Dave and his niece Mary. The McDonalds notified the two men on the situation at White Sands and their idea of returning to the family ranch. Later on Gentry received a call from

Mary, who explained that she and her uncle planned to carry out their occupation. They asked Gentry if he would "run interference" for them, which he agreed to do. Sometimes using a pay phone at a hamburger joint in San Antonio, New Mexico, Gentry made sure the story got to the *Albuquerque Journal* and *El Defensor Chieftain* in Socorro. Once it reached the Associated Press, the McDonalds' story went national. As Gentry later explained, the McDonalds seemed to be "pulling a John Prather" just as the conflict over lease and suspension agreements heated up.[2]

Missile range officials saw things differently. They characterized the McDonalds' unlawful occupation as "potentially a trespassing situation." Yet rather than remove them by force, security personnel let the two remain at the dilapidated structure. Eventually escorted off the range by New Mexico senator Harrison Schmitt and Representative Joseph Skeen, the McDonalds celebrated their three-and-a-half-day occupation as a symbolic victory. "We had to get their attention," explained Mary McDonald. "We tried everything else and we finally decided to treat it like a mule: first, you've got to hit him between the eyes with an axe handle to get his attention." Despite their protest and subsequent media coverage, they would never return to the family's ranch. By the 1960s White Sands Missile Range was for all intents and purposes a permanent weapons testing facility.[3]

While compensated $216,000 over the twenty-year term of the lease, and later $220,000 to buy the land outright, the McDonalds believed those payments fell far short of the total value of the property. During condemnation litigation in the 1970s, Dave McDonald had asked for $960,000 to cover private property, suspended state and federal grazing permits, and loss of capital due to ranch inactivity. Yet no judicial avenues remained for McDonald and the other ranchers seeking either to go back to their homes or receive proper payment for their lands. In November 1988 the U.S. Court of Claims denied a final appeal by the landowners to seek further payments for property taken to create the military reserve in south-central New Mexico.[4]

On top of remuneration for private property, between 1971 and 1988 ranchers at White Sands argued that true total payment should include the yearly take from livestock sales and their interests in public grazing lands regulated by both federal and state agencies. Yet most ranchers had already received payments over the term of lease agreements. To both military officials and federal politicians it seemed that ranchers in south-central New Mexico had made as good of a living ranching the government as they had once made running livestock on their lands. Ranchers countered that the military had no right to hold them hostage under the lease and suspension agreements. While the McDonalds' protest symbolically called for a return of private land, the quarrels over the minute details of animal units, property improvements, and the value of idle ranches suggested that the broader legal battle brought by ranchers acted as a form of protest against the way the federal government had handled the lease and suspension agreements.

The demands made by ranchers did not only stem from a desire for appropriate compensation for lost property and income. Their struggle was also about community and ties to the land. Many, like the McDonalds, had ranched in the region for generations. Like any other rural community, they knew one another and did business together. They traded advice and borrowed each other's equipment. The got together for social functions and met at the local coffee shop or bar. South-central New Mexico held deep meaning for ranchers.[5]

The life and death of a community often shaped how rural westerners understood their ties to the federal government. By 1970 consensus did not characterize the relationship between rural westerners and the state. The conservative political base that helped elevate Barry Goldwater to the Republican candidate for president in 1964 and Ronald Reagan's successful 1966 gubernatorial race in California reveal that the suburban Sunbelt and Far West emerged as bastions of a new grassroots conservatism. Steeped in libertarian economic policies and conservative social ideology, communities from suburban Atlanta, Georgia, to Orange County, California, developed a new conservative political movement in America.[6]

The relationship between rural western communities and federal land management agencies, namely the Bureau of Land Management and the

Forest Service, shaped a uniquely rural version of this new conservative ideology. Two movements came to the fore. First, in the late 1970s and early 1980s the Sagebrush Rebellion emerged as a voice of concern over federal control of public lands in the West. Backed by President Ronald Reagan, congressional representatives from western states (including Orrin Hatch of Utah and Ted Stevens of Alaska), industry groups such as the National Cattlemen's Association, and private enterprises including Boise Cascade, the organization fundamentally believed in the New Right's emphasis on individual property rights. But its national message often hinged on more traditional notions of state's rights.[7]

Second, in the late 1980s and early 1990s the conservative Wise Use movement employed greater grassroots organizational tactics to oppose public land policies and environmental legislation. Similar to the Sagebrush Rebellion, their rhetoric emphasized the danger public lands management posed to individual property rights. Wise Use advocates were explicit about that stance. The organization circulated a "video syllabus" titled *The Western Family: An Endangered Species*, which flipped the idea of "endangered species" on its head in promoting individual property rights and rural economic growth. Fundamentally, Wise Use proponents perceived urban environmentalists and public land agencies as key adversaries in their battle to salvage a rural producer economy that they believed had historically stood at the heart of western life. As the organization saw it, through the regulation of public lands and creation of environmental agencies, the federal government acted as the environmental movement's comrade in arms in undermining the independent family ranch.[8]

Ranchers in south-central New Mexico were an antecedent to the politics of Wise Use. But their struggle was distinguished by the place of the military in the region and later the role of environmentalists in defining militarized landscapes (see chapter 6). White Sands was a bastion of American military readiness during the Cold War. Property owners displaced at White Sands thus faced a catch-22: their land-use ideas often matched well with other rural westerners, but they confronted the DOD, an agency that many western politicians (both liberal and conservative) refused to touch politically or economically. Rather than passive casualties of the military build-up in the rural American West, ranchers challenged the geographical boundaries and legal reach of a dynamic national security landscape in New Mexico. They faced an insurmountable struggle.

The legal campaign pursued by ranchers depended in part on an imagined economic past. They argued for measuring the value of an idle ranching landscape as fully productive over the course of lease and suspension agreements. The ranchers also cast themselves not only as the victims of federal deception over a twenty-year period, but also as the collective owners of the lands inhabited by White Sands. The DOD was simply a tenant. Like the McDonalds, some ranchers hoped to go back to their homesteads and return to grazing livestock to make a living. However, most understood that the eviction of the military was impossible. At best, ranchers would receive compensation for their lands. Seeing themselves as rightful owners of the now militarized landscape, a pecuniary plundering of federal coffers was a powerful move that would bring justice and equity to their fight against the seizure of property. Ranchers were methodical in their legal battle with the Department of Defense. They used the media and hired lawyers. They created an organization, White Sands Missile Range Ranchers. Direct action was never out of the question.

From the Homestead Act to the National Park System, displacement of western peoples in the name of economic progress, nationalism, and manifest destiny critically marked (and marred) the history of the American West. This is particularly true in the case of American Indians, who lost lands for the creation of national parks, homesteads, and wilderness areas. Cold War–era militarization exists on a longer continuum of displacement. The historian William Robbins argues that "the historical tension between private claims and the common good" has long driven questions about land use in the region. Across the twentieth-century rural West, deep fissures between the federal public land bureaucracy and private ranchers instructed the meaning of private property in a time when grazing permits increasingly blurred the distinction between public and private landholdings. Because it created a sense of private right in grazing leases, the 1934 Taylor Grazing Act was perhaps the most significant piece of legislation in transforming the political economy of ranching in rural western communities. At White Sands the act reverberated through the struggle to define the perimeters of private property as argued in condemnation litigation and congressional hearings. As important, the struggle for lands on White Sands shaped what the common good meant in the age of large-scale militarization.[9]

The push by the federal government to acquire title to private ranches and state-owned grazing lands occurred first through condemnation on property already leased to the DOD under the auspices of the U.S. Army. By the mid-1970s a series of court cases initiated by both ranchers and the state of New Mexico sought to justly compensate the state and former landholders who had not settled with the federal government. Ranchers found little solace in the outcome of those proceedings. With the ranchers having lost in the judicial system, New Mexico's bipartisan congressional cadre, including Republicans Pete Domenici and Joe Skeen and Democrats Jeff Bingaman and Bill Richardson, initiated a series of legislative bills that requested compensation for the ranchers displaced during the war. The significance of federal grazing leases in defining the market price of landholdings condemned by the DOD shaped the legal and legislative campaigns to compensate the well-organized White Sands Missile Range Ranchers. In the end the value ranchers held for their former homesteads yielded to a restricted interpretation of property offered by the federal government. By the early 1990s the death of most of the ranchers effectively ended the controversy. Nevertheless their struggle against White Sands reflects the missile range as contested place.

DEPENDENCY

As explored in chapter 1, in 1942 President Franklin Delano Roosevelt signed Executive Order 9029 withdrawing public lands for the construction of a bombing range in south-central New Mexico. That order allowed the War Department to remove large sections of grazing lands from use. A public land order passed during the same year permitted the taking of similar lands for the creation of an air base later named Alamogordo Army Air Field. In 1952 Public Land Order 833 extended the Department of the Army's use of 2,394,384 acres in south-central New Mexico for an indeterminate amount of time (the tally in 1958 was 2,215,450.07 acres total). Importantly, the order stated "when the lands described herein are no longer needed for the purpose for which they are reserved they shall be returned to the administration of the Department of Interior, the Department of Agriculture, and any other federal agency according to their respective interests of record." At that time most ranchers would agree to twenty-year leases on their private property with the assumption that they too might see the return of their property.[10]

The condemnation of federal grazing lands and the taking of private property in south-central New Mexico was a reflection of the vast changes that the Second World War created for the use of both public and private lands in the North American West. In 1942 the War Department condemned the Los Alamos Boys School for use in the Manhattan Project. In 1943, to the surprise of landholders in the Richland irrigation district, Leslie Groves and Colonel Franklin "Fritz" Matthias selected the Columbia Basin as the site of plutonium production for the atomic bomb project. To secure the necessary land the War Department condemned the region surrounding what would become Hanford. Upset local residents were heard making "angry and excited assertions" in the wake of the decision. Groves also selected Oak Ridge, Tennessee, for uranium production at least in part because of the low cost of purchasing private lands (property was sold for as little as thirty dollars an acre).[11]

While the exigencies of war made for a common experience of displacement in the rural West and elsewhere, the situation in south-central New Mexico was unique. Instead of simply condemning the land, lease and suspension agreements became a most curious way to acquire lands. Property was not purchased outright by the War Department or later the Department of Defense. The 1934 Taylor Grazing Act, enacted during the New Deal, sought to curtail farm and ranch overproduction and concomitant ecological degradation through a permit system. By the 1940s most ranchers in south-central New Mexico relied on the Grazing Service in daily cattle operations. In fact, they owned only 4 percent of the area by the end of World War II.

At the same time, the creation of the Alamogordo Bombing Range, White Sands Proving Ground, and eventually White Sands Missile Range stemmed directly from the Department of Agriculture's increased control over lands in south-central New Mexico as a result of the environmental collapse of the desert grasslands. The isolation of the region and its climatological benefits proved crucial to the establishment of the missile range. But the large swaths of grazing lands regulated by the Grazing Service and later the Bureau of Land Management allowed for an interagency exchange of most of south-central New Mexico. This would not halt fights over the meaning of public lands. No matter their legal state, those lands remained highly politicized. Ranchers could asserted a privilege in defining property rights at White Sands even though the region remained federal domain.[12]

During the war, most ranchers had reluctantly ceded their private landholdings to the army. Many expected to reoccupy their homesteads at the end of the war. The continued need for those lands as a result of the onset of the Cold War led to the negotiated lease and suspension agreements or formal condemnation hearings on private landholdings. Most arrangements lasted for a period of twenty years. Fast forward to June 30, 1970, when leases on private property and state and federal grazing lands would expire. A month earlier ranchers with land under lease to White Sands Missile Range met to discuss their fate. Prior to that most received yearly compensation for the entirety of their ranch units, including interests in state and federal grazing leases. Replacing the initial agreements arranged between 1942 and 1952, leases drawn up in 1970 maintained no stipulation for payment on suspended grazing permits on federal public lands. Prior to that decision permit holders had received compensation as required under section 315q of the Taylor Grazing Act.[13] A measure added during the war to relieve property owners whose land the federal government seized for military purposes, section 315q states that those with grazing permits cancelled for national defense purposes would receive fair payment as determined by the head of the department or agency in question.[14]

The initial contracts signed by ranchers included several stipulations. Under the lease and suspension agreements, they received payment for property as well as interests in state-leased grazing lands. Through suspension agreements they received payment for federal grazing permits either deferred for the duration of the lease or terminated altogether. In the 1970 renegotiation of lease contracts the federal government reduced its payments by suspending compensation distributed under the rules of section 315q. Most of the ranchers rejected those new terms.[15]

Landholders responded by creating the White Sands Missile Range Ranchers, a group joined by the New Mexico Cattle Growers Association (an organization whose board included some of the largest landowners in the state of New Mexico, including for a time Representative Joseph Skeen). At the organizational meeting ranchers recognized that the Army Corps of Engineers, who assessed new lease figures, had lowered overall payments on state lands to "an acreage price" with grazing leases on federal lands completely subtracted. Many felt the federal government was not dealing fairly with the ranchers. Thus the newly created organization turned to the possibility of using the regulations established under section 315q as a means to compel what they saw as the equitable negotiation of new leases. On the other hand the army argued that ranchers had received, over the terms of their lease, adequate compensation for suspended grazing permits issued by the federal government.[16]

White Sands Missile Range Ranchers was no ineffectual organization. Members assembled a powerful community-based grassroots movement with the intention of taking on their own government. When the Missile Range Ranchers' committee met in May 1970 they came to several decisions about the organization's future plans for action. First they hired an attorney and set to gathering funds to pay legal fees. The committee encouraged members to sign nothing until they spoke with one of the principal intermediaries about the documents they received from the federal government. The group connected with legislators, national livestock organizations, and relevant financial institutions in an effort to compel the Department of Defense to reconsider the leases as "complete ranch units."[17]

Importantly, White Sands Ranchers encouraged all landholders to file applications for grazing licenses on their former landholdings as protest to the new lease agreements. As in the case of Quatro Amigos Cattle Company, several ranchers eventually filed grazing applications with the Bureau of Land Management (BLM). Not surprisingly, Quatro's owners found that because of the company's ongoing dispute with the Corps of Engineers, the bureau had forwarded their case to a BLM District Advisory Board, which had the authorization to forward them to "higher authorities." Subsequently, the bureau denied their application.[18]

In 1970 it seemed as though a monetary solution was in sight. By the first week of June Secretary of Defense Melvin Laird had agreed to buy ranches outright at "fair market value" and on a total ranch basis. Yet before the DOD could acquire those lands, they would have to get prior funding from Congress. For many ranchers the potential purchase of their lands acted as little consolation. Yet, at least one individual recognized that they possessed little chance of returning to former homesteads. As rancher Phil Harvey lamented in a letter to the White Sands Missile Range Ranchers, "I realize that many of you do not wish to sell your ranches. They are your homes and you want only to return to them and continue ranching. In my opinion, there would be no chance of this for many years, if ever, due to the importance of the range to the government."[19]

Two weeks later at a White Sands Missile Range Ranchers committee meeting U.S. marshals served several members with complaints of condemnation. The complaints sought new leases similar to those initially offered at the expiration of the former twenty-year contracts. Payments under the new agreements, seen by many ranchers as below market value, would continue for a period of no more than ten years or until the DOD acquired the land by purchase. Most ranchers sought a sixty-day extension to answer the complaint, which the District Court for the State of New Mexico granted. In the interim the missile range ranchers considered alternative solutions in the event that Congress did not earmark funds for the outright purchase of their lands. Of those, they considered a co-use agreement with restoration of prior improvements on the land and a guarantee from the federal government that the DOD would not bid to acquire privately held state grazing leases.[20]

Necessary congressional appropriations for the purchase of private landholdings did not appear immediately. As a result the White Sands Ranchers turned to litigation to halt continued leases on their property. They sought to have the ongoing proceedings dismissed on the grounds that the federal government's contractual obligation under the original lease and suspension agreements obstructed their right to file such litigation. In particular, original leases stated: "Provided that in the event any government property is located on the demised premises at the termination date, the rental will continue until such property is removed, restoration completed as provided for in Article 10 hereof, or cash settlement and possession tendered to the grantor."[21] Despite that language the district court denied the ranchers' motion for dismissal. Through 1975 condemnation hearings went forward. Rather than go to trial several ranchers represented by a Roswell, New Mexico, law firm accepted final agreements on leases as a measure to avoid a prolonged trial period. Payment for improvements upon land was crucial to those negotiations. Initially refusing to pay for housing, bunkhouses, barns, pump houses, or livestock feed sheds in disrepair, the Army Corps of Engineers, which assayed improvements, agreed to work with the owners to find reasonable sums for restoration damages.[22]

As renegotiation of leases continued, Congress finally passed appropriate legislation to acquire ranchlands in fee simple. Passed in late 1973, Military Construction and Reserve Forces Facilities Authorization Acts and the Military Construction Act offered the financial resources for acquisition of titles to private property and state lands. The 1980

Military Construction Appropriation Act offered additional funds. By 1983 the army had acquired almost seventy-two thousand privately owned acres through voluntary arrangements or through the process of condemnation proceedings.[23]

Many ranchers challenged the appraisals of their land. As in the case of the Quatro Amigos Cattle Company, those landholders who did not reach prior agreements with the Department of Defense faced condemnation hearings. In March 1975 the company had initially received an offer of $490,000, an offer seen by landowners as significantly less than the $800,000 desired for sale. The company took issue with the Army Corps of Engineers' failure to consider state-leased lands or water resources in the appraisal of the property. The corps turned down the counteroffer. On June 30 a delivery of possession filed in U.S. district court set the value of the Quatro Amigos ranch at $490,000.[24]

The White Sands Missile Range Ranchers sought recognition of a right to define the values of former homesteads and grazing rights and in the process looked to prove that White Sands answered to them as rightful owners of missile range property, not the other way around. Despite calls for détente during the Nixon, Ford, and Carter administrations, defense spending remained high. In 1975 White Sands Missile Range tested 1,843 projectiles. By the early 1980s President Reagan's strong anticommunist outlook had led to a chill in relations with the Soviet Union just as the legal battle over White Sands heated up. From 1981 to 1986 the Pentagon budget had doubled. There remained little chance that ranchers would return to their lands so long as a communist threat existed. Knowing this, ranchers increasingly sought to acquire greater, and sometimes seemingly imbalanced, payments for the lands lost to an enduring Cold War national security state.[25]

SECTION 315Q

While Quatro Amigos reached agreement on payment, many of the other landholders faced both litigation for the extension of federal leaseholds on their property and also the continued promise of eventual condemnation proceedings. By 1981 all but nine of the original White

Sands Missile Range Ranchers either agreed to sell their lands to the DOD or lost them through condemnation in fee simple hearings. Again, those agreements did not take into account the suspension of grazing permits issued and extended by the federal government and initially compensated for under section 315q of the Taylor Grazing Act. The federal government argued that payments over the course of the suspension agreements acted as total and just compensation. The battle to define the value of landholdings on White Sands Missile Range carried into the federal court system, as ranchers sought to cobble together a total land value from a patchwork of private property and interest in public lands.[26]

In 1976 the White Sands Missile Range Ranchers advocated for fair payment before the U.S. Court of Claims. In *D. I. Z. Livestock Co. et al. v. United States* a number of ranchers brought suit on two grounds. First, they argued that the original lease agreements promised, at the time of a contract's termination, either restoration of lands to their previous conditions or payment for private ranches and all improvements. The plaintiffs believed the federal government had breached that agreement by seeking extended contracts. They also reasoned that section 315q stipulated payment in lieu of canceled federal grazing leases. While they had already received payments under lease and suspension agreements, ranchers used the call for greater remuneration as a measure of protest to what they saw as a sleight of hand by the federal government in compensating landowners.[27]

The court found problems with both arguments put forth by the plaintiffs. First, the court agreed that the government's failure to restore lands or tender payment as stipulated by the original lease agreements did translate to a breach of contract. But because the plaintiffs had suffered no damages, a remedy did not exist. Since the federal government had in 1970 condemned ranchers property for an additional ten-year period, the court "could not say that plaintiffs have been harmed by the Government's failure to restore plaintiffs for the few seconds it would take to satisfy the 'lease and suspension' agreement provisions." Condemnation proceedings, explained the court, would best remedy those concerns. On the second point, the court argued that plaintiffs did not establish how the federal government's refusal to pay additional compensation as stipulated under section 315q had caused injury to landowners. Nor, explained the court, did the plaintiffs show that an abuse of discretion occurred in how the federal government determined payments for suspended grazing rights. In other words, the ranchers had no evidence to suggest that the government acted unfairly in determining the value of those permits in similar purchases of lands for military purposes.[28]

While ranchers lost their case, they continued to press for remuneration based upon the total value of their landholdings, including state and federal grazing leases. The courts again would play a role in deciding the value of ranches. The fact that private landholders demanded compensation for interests in permits on lands not owned by them remains the central paradox of the White Sands Missile Range Ranchers' call for an equitable settlement to their case. They expected the federal government to determine the potential yearly value of a tacit livestock population grazing on a dynamic environment. As we shall see, evidence later presented on behalf of the ranchers during congressional hearings presumed to offer such numbers.

In the meantime litigation initiated by the state of New Mexico offered the ranchers' their most salient chance for remuneration on suspended grazing permits. In the 1981 case *Lex J. Armijo et al. v. United States* the state of New Mexico sued the federal government, claiming inverse condemnation on state lands. The DOD had utilized temporary year-to-year leases to retain control of state lands incorporated in the missile range. In an argument later used by ranchers, the court explained that "the landowner is not put in as good a position as if the property were not taken, so far as money can do it. He could, with a unitary award, invest it in similar property and deal with that as owner." Thus the DOD had not offered New Mexico "just compensation" through temporary takings of state lands.[29]

While the case was remanded for further proceedings, in 1987 the court finally awarded the state of New Mexico more than $20 million in compensation for the surface rights to state grazing lands. (In 1988 the two parties settled subsurface interests.) At the behest of New Mexico state land commissioner Bill Humphries, ranchers received more than $3 million to compensate for the loss of value in state grazing permits on lands that became White Sands Missile Range. In a public ceremony Humphries alongside Representative Skeen presented a check to several former landholders. P. F. Sanders, who had owned land near Lake Lucero, exclaimed, "getting this money from them is a bigger surprise to me than it was when they told me to get off my land." While many of the older ranchers had died, most at the ceremony saw federal remuneration for state leases as a bona fide victory. Not all would benefit.[30]

Challenging the federal government's interpretation of total market value for ranches, many White Sands Missile Range Ranchers continued to demand compensation for their interests in federal grazing permits. New Mexico's congressional representatives sympathized with the ranchers and used every legislative path available to equalize the situation in south-central New Mexico. Between 1980 and 1995, Representatives Joe Skeen, Bill Richardson, and Steve Schiff, alongside Senators Harrison Schmitt and Pete Domenici, sought congressional appropriations to compensate displaced ranchers. Collectively the congressional attaché and the ranchers set out to gain additional payment for their financial interests in federal grazing leases.

One more court battle remained. In June 1984 Senator Domenici introduced a bill that ordered the secretary of the Treasury to pay an unfixed sum to ranchers as just compensation. The same day Domenici introduced another bill, which directed the U.S. Court of Claims to review continued requests for compensation. In the 1988 case *White Sands Ranchers of New Mexico v. United States* the court was asked to inform Congress whether the proposed bill would fulfill a reasonable claim for remuneration as stipulated by the claimants or act as mere "gratuity" on payments already made by the federal government.[31]

The court found that in most cases ranchers had also sought compensation under the *Armijo* litigation. Because that suit set the date of taking as July 1, 1976, most plaintiffs in the *White Sands* proceedings had failed to satisfy the court's six-year statute of limitations. Moreover, because the finding of the court in the *D. I. Z. Livestock* case acted as binding under the rules of res judicata (once a case is adjudicated and a final decision made, a court could not rehear that particular case), those ranchers who sought remuneration under that suit could not also seek compensation in the *White Sands* proceedings. All others faced a similar outcome under the doctrine of stare decisis, which compelled the U.S. Court of Claims to honor as precedent past decisions made by the same court unless modified by the U.S. Court of Appeals or the Supreme Court.[32]

However, as an equitable claim proceeding, the case survived under the rules of congressional reference hearings. Recognizing that the long delay in litigation had not prejudiced the government's case, the court proceeded to hear the complaint. As in the *D. I. Z. Livestock* case, the claimants argued that while grazing permits did not represent property according to the rules for taking under eminent domain, those lands taken under section 315q of the Taylor Grazing Act met a different standard. Having not considered interest in federal lands taken during World War II, the government had failed to render payment based on a total ranch unit basis.[33]

In part, the court agreed. Clearly section 315q set out to pay ranchers for lands ceded during the war and after. However, it did not stipulate that payment would be made on a total ranch unit basis. Instead, it argued for payment based merely upon what the taking department or agency saw as "fair and reasonable." The Department of Defense argued that leasehold payments prior to 1970 met those obligations. Yet more generally, the court found that because ranchers held no "enforceable property rights in the public domain to start with," they had no legal entitlement to further compensation.[34]

The claimants' final argument hinged upon whether the federal government equitably administered section 315q (a line of reasoning the plaintiffs failed to make in the *D. I. Z. Livestock* case). The plaintiffs pointed to the ranch unit purchasing price for lands on McGregor Range (now part of Fort Bliss) on a ranch unit basis as evidence of the federal government's inconsistency in following the law. On this final point the court again disagreed. The judges pointed to the per-acre value differential between 1956, when the government acquired lands for McGregor Range, and those in 1980, a year prior to the *Armijo* proceedings. The court found that when adjusted for inflation the per-acre value as related to the two cases differed by a mere eighty-three cents. Thus little evidence suggested that the federal government had haphazardly applied rule 315q in compensating the property owners at White Sands. Indeed, further payment would act as mere "gratuity."[35]

Ranchers were appalled. Howard Wood explained: "they took our lives from us. They just said get off and fend for yourself." G. B. Oliver's father, who had half of his 1,280 acres taken from him during the 1940s, had explained to his son "that it was like watching a snake swallow a rabbit. They wrapped around us until they got us in a position where we couldn't do anything, then they slobbered all over us and then they finished us off." Why so many waited for the military to clear out before moving on with their lives may not make sense to many readers. But most of these ranchers had ties to their community, their land, and the image of a once vibrant livestock economy in south-central New Mexico. As important, the lease and suspension agreements tied them to the missile range.[36]

IMAGINED ECONOMIES

The defeat in *White Sands Ranchers of New Mexico v. United States* acted as a last chance in the court system to compel the DOD to provide remuneration on the total ranch unit basis. Yet while ranchers had received compensation over the life of their leases for interests in state grazing lands, under condemnation cases or through settlements with the government, they remained determined to receive payments for interest in public lands. Having lost any chance to return to their homesteads, they ultimately raised protests through their congressional representatives.[37]

Dave and Mary McDonald's occupation of their family's former homestead six years before the *White Sands Ranchers* case acted as both a rallying cry for landholders and a powerful political moment. While the McDonalds' actions had compelled Senator Domenici to demand a U.S. Court of Claims review of the case, it also set in motion a series of measures that brought congressional representatives together with ranchers in seeking what they perceived as a fair outcome to the taking of property in south-central New Mexico. They wanted compensation not only for private property but also for the value lost in suspended grazing permits and the lapsed production from idle ranch units. Relying on land assayers, the White Sands Ranchers imagined a thriving livestock economy in south-central New Mexico during the years that missile testing dominated south-central New Mexico. What followed was an extraordinary effort to create a livestock economy that never really existed.

The White Sands Missile Range Ranchers were not a fringe group at the margins of Cold War America. The alliance between ranchers and their congressional representatives echoed a federal backlash among many rural westerners in the years after environmental legislation passed by the Kennedy, Johnson, and Nixon administrations expanded the role of the federal government in managing not only wilderness but also agricultural and militarized landscapes. During his first three years in office Ronald Reagan's environmental policies, namely the 12 percent slash in the EPA's budget and general reduction in the agency's regulatory power, reflected the growing influence of anti-environmentalist sentiment among conservatives in the United States.[38]

While Reagan never followed either movement to its logical extreme, both the Sagebrush Rebellion and Wise Use movement acted as the most overt push to rescind New Deal and Great Society style federal regulation of public lands.

The ranchers still in business in the areas surrounding the missile range would engage in land-use battles reflective of earlier Wise Use protests against the Forest Service and the Bureau of Land Management. However, property owners displaced at White Sands faced a fundamental contradiction of Reagan conservatism: a support for Wise Use ideas but never before national security.[39]

It was in conservative New Mexico politicians, including Domenici and Skeen (both of whom relied on rural New Mexico for reelection) that ranchers found their most important allies. While the ranchers recognized that White Sands would never again exist as ranchlands, remuneration would continue to act as the focus of their fight against White Sands Missile Range. In 1983 the General Accounting Office published a report on the White Sands Ranchers at the request of Representative Skeen and Senator Schmitt. The report revealed the long process of condemnation and the subsequent legal cases to determine the value of ranchlands surrendered to White Sands Missile Range. Yet because several cases remained in the courts, the GAO offered no resolution to the dispute. Determined to bring the issue to Congress, in September of the same year Skeen introduced a bill in the House of Representatives that ordered the secretary of the treasury to appropriate funds to compensate those ranchers who had surrendered their property to the military during and immediately after World War II. The bill died in committee before the House had the opportunity to vote on it.[40]

One month later Senator Domenici initiated oversight hearings before the Subcommittee on Public Lands and Reserved Water within the Committee on Energy and Natural Resources. He hoped the hearing would settle issues related to fair compensation for both private holdings and public domain grazing interests, whether assessors had accurately measured the values of former ranches, and how private interests in federal and state lands (namely grazing permits) would factor into compensation. Because some claims remained in the courts (including the *Armijo* case), the committee saw the hearings as less an opportunity to define the perimeters of possible relief and more as an occasion for parties to testify to the issue of appropriate remuneration. Representative Skeen and Senator Jeff Bingaman of New Mexico both spoke before the committee on behalf of the ranchers. Skeen appropriately asserted the position of New Mexico's congressional representatives when he explained "we have held these people's lives up for some 40 years, because we have captured their collateral and have not let them have access to their own property or to make decisions and have never told them go make another life for yourself . . . we have kept them captive for all of this time." Having held their land for so long, the federal government had deceived ranchers and in the process disallowed them from moving forward with their business elsewhere.[41]

Importantly, the hearings allowed former ranchers to speak about their long relationship with the missile range. Most citied the unacceptable compensation for leases and the unexpected change in payment for suspended grazing permits. All testified that the creation of the missile range had upended their means of survival. Dolly Helms of Oscura, New Mexico, lamented: "I am very bitter. The Government took away my ranch, which was my only livelihood, on [two] weeks notice. My cattle had to be sold for a fraction of their value. I had to work at any job I could find to support my family and get back in the cattle business." G. B. Oliver of Alamogordo recalled: "We, as a family, sank every penny we could scrape up to buy what is now known as White Sands Ranch. This really placed us in a financial bind. We were still paying for the total ranch and figuring very closely to do so. Then to have half of it taken out of operation made it very hard to make payments on the whole." Dave McDonald echoed his fellow rancher's feelings, saying: "the problem was that the ranch was my livelihood and the sole support for my family. If I was going to exist I had to find a new ranch promptly and move my cattle to it." Unable to find suitable pasture at the time of eviction, he sold two-thirds of his livestock at one-third the price. In 1943 a lack of on-hand capital led McDonald to sell off the rest of his herd. The loss of his homestead had forced him to live "hand to mouth, supporting my family with any job I could get," which included time working as a security guard and laundryman, doing yard work, and digging ditches. What ranchers did with the money garnered over the twenty-year lease and suspension agreements remains mere speculation.[42]

To evaluate the case for further payments, the subcommittee enlisted the support of the Range Improvement Task Force within New Mexico State University's Agricultural Experiment Station, Cooperative Extension Service to consider what the value of idle ranches may have looked like over the term of lease and suspension agreements. Using a leasehold value approach that set per animal unit prices at $1,654.00, the task force determined that fair compensation for a ranch on White

Sands Missile Range carrying 992 animal units would have warranted a final payment of $1,640,000. They also recognized that most payments under condemnation in fee simple hearings had not used the standard western ranch appraisal method of leasehold value based upon per animal unit. The squabbles over the minutiae of how a ranch might work if allowed to over the course of lease and suspension agreements was clearly an attempt by ranchers to acquire as much remuneration as possible from the federal government. Ranchers tied their passing way of life not to local mismanagement of desert grasslands some one hundred years earlier, but to the federal government, which had emerged as the power broker of land use politics in the region. With ranchers not taking into account their role in the federalization of south-central New Mexico, what they conjured as just payment from the government looked punitive.[43]

During the hearings, the Office of the Chief of Engineers in the Department of the Army argued to the Subcommittee on Public Lands and Reserved Water that ranchers had received a total of more than $17 million in payments through lease agreements, compensation for damage to improvements, and the total sums paid for acquisition of private lands. They explained that while full compensation per landholder varied by private acreage, demonstrated damage to improvements, and the total sum of leasehold payments, all had received fair payment for their land. Foretelling the decision in *White Sands Ranchers of New Mexico v. United States*, the chief of engineers also argued that permits issued under the Taylor Grazing Act "confer a mere privilege to graze livestock which can be withdrawn by the United States without payment of compensation." Moreover, section 315q offered no language that defined how to measure compensation for federal grazing permits. As later argued by the federal government, the decision to make payments to the McGregor Range ranchers on a "cow-year-long" valuation for ranch units occurred at the "discretion" of the secretary of the army. So too were payments measured at White Sands. Either way, those grazing lands belonged to the federal government, and the assumption of payment for an envisaged past income hardly held water among Army Corps officials.[44]

Before the hearings McDonald remained cautiously optimistic about the possibility of final resolution to the dispute with the Department of Defense. But while the courts continued to adjudicate cases, federal hearings were disappointing. Several years passed with little action. At a meeting with ranchers in April 1989, both Domenici and Skeen emphasized that they sympathized with the group. Yet many former landholders had lost faith in the system. Following the McDonalds' lead, a former landowner called for direct action tactics. "Each one I talk to say the only way you'll get anything to move is to demonstrate," she explained. "I don't think White Sands people would shoot us if we moved onto the range." Some of the crowd agreed with utterances of "let's go." Mary McDonald presented what she called her "death list." The sheet included the names of seventeen former ranchers who had died since the seizure of their land during the Second World War. Time for the White Sands ranchers was running out.[45]

Skeen and Domenici attempted to assuage the crowd by promising a renewed fight in Congress. In October 1989 the congressmen introduced fair compensation legislation. The language of the Senate bill followed closely that introduced in the House. Together the two pieces of legislation directed the Department of the Interior to create a commission with the primary goal of determining reasonable compensation for ranchers (and those denied payment for mining claims). Both authorized $17.5 million, a figure supported by assessments that estimated the total value of seventy-six former ranches at more than $27 million. Neither bill would pass.[46]

The following spring Skeen launched hearings before the Subcommittee on Administrative Law and Governmental Relations within the Committee of the Judiciary in the House of Representatives. Moving away from justification for payment under section 315q, Skeen pointed to Public Law 100-383, which directed Congress to authorize funds to repay Aleutian Island inhabitants displaced from their homes during World War II. He explained: "if this same standard were applied to the case of the White Sands ranchers and miners, it would allow them to be compensated for public domain lands included in the ranch and mining units . . . what was taken from them is a business unit, not just particular pieces and parcels of private property."[47]

Former ranchers followed Skeen's lead by saying that payments needed to reflect the total operational value of ranches taken under condemnation proceedings. Former landowners had long argued for remuneration based upon the total value of their operations. Yet only during the 1989 hearings did it seem so clear. Prior litigation leaned on the value of grazing permits, the significance of improvements in adjudicating payment, and the discrepancies between purchases made at White Sands versus those at McGregor Range.

Priscilla Baca Ortiz, heir to the Baca Ranch, recalled her father saying, "The lease money was way below the amount he would have received from the sale of cattle, and retiring earlier than he had planned would necessitate his complete dependence on his life savings for a living." Through condemnation proceedings the Department of Defense acquired the San Augustine Ranch, owned by the J. W. Cox family, for a "take it or leave it deal" of $53,600 (90 percent of the land value and 87 percent of the grazing leases), far below what they saw as the correct market value for the early 1950s. Relatives Alice and Hal Cox met a similar fate. They held a co-use lease with the army before 1950, and the Corps of Engineers forced the family from their lands during the same year, which led them to sell off livestock because they had no place to pasture the animals. When they lost their home in condemnation litigation, the government paid less than half the value of improvements, paid a third of the worth of mineral claims, and refused to pay altogether for income lost because of the closure of their dude ranch (a business listed with American Airlines and the Santa Fe and Rock Island Railroads).[48]

Former residents of lands taken for nearby Holloman Air Force Base also felt insulted by the federal government. According to his family, Luther Boles had developed two wells to irrigate his small farming venture. During 1947 he offered to provide the necessary amount of water to salve the needs of the growing Alamogordo Army Air Field. Less than ten years later, the government cancelled the contract and gave him thirty days to vacate his property. Boles's family explained that he received a "token settlement" of just over $41,000. The appraised value of the land not including water rights amounted to as much as $95,000. During the hearings the family asked for additional payment to meet the real value of the farm, lost wages and earnings, the capital value lost from the time of property seizure, as well as punitive damages.[49]

Within the government most agreed that the White Sands ranchers had no right to additional compensation. Myles Flint, deputy assistant attorney general of the Environment and Natural Resources Division within the Department of Justice, argued that in the *D. I. Z. Livestock* and *White Sands Ranchers* cases the U.S. Court of Claims had clearly denied further payment to displaced ranchers. The proposed bill acted as "redetermination" by an administrative commission for claims already settled. Furthermore, the bill merely suggested payment based on "established precedents," without actually defining the standard for monetary payment. Either way, by Department of Justice calculations "payment of additional monies to those individuals whose property was taken and who have already received just compensation for those property interests, it should regard such payments as gratuities, not legal obligations of the United States." Both the Senate and House bills died in committee as a result of questions about presumed incomes presented by the congressional allies of ranchers.[50]

In the wake of the 1988 Court of Claims decision McDonald promised to once again take back his property. With no legal recourse, he assured the media that his family would protect their land by force. "I may get shot and I might have to shoot somebody," he explained. "But I'll take no more promises. They're either going to pay me for my land, or there's going to be some bloodshed." On June 6, 1993, McDonald passed away before making good on his promise. An op-ed piece said he, like other ranchers, "died with fist clenched, cursing the big boys right up to the end." With praise perhaps best reserved for individuals who actually fought and died during World War II, the writer extolled McDonald and his compatriots as "heroes, heroes one and all—not for giving up their land, but fighting to save their homes."[51]

A community faded away. Reality had set in. As the Cold War passed, the vast majority of south-central New Mexico remained in the hands of the Department of Defense. White Sands Missile Range, Holloman Air Force Base, and Fort Bliss remained active, and there was little sense they would close anytime soon. In 1992 a tally counted fewer than 30 of the original 110 White Sands ranchers as still living.[52]

Those White Sands ranchers still alive in the early 1990s believed they would never receive just compensation for lands taken during World War II. Rancher Bob Jones lamented, "we're pretty discouraged about it because it's gone on and on and on, we always hope something will come of it." The New Mexico Cattle Growers Association remained on their side. In a resolution the organization stated that "patriotic ranchers" had failed to receive compensation as a result of the "cold-blooded attitude of an ungrateful government using every subterfuge to avoid fair treatment to this persecuted minority." For the cost of a "test vehicle or two" the federal government could finally do right by a whole community upended during and after the war. Seeking to establish their domain over land leased for the missile range, ranchers still cast themselves as landlords to an unthankful DOD.[53]

Well in to the 1990s New Mexico's congressional representatives continued to advocate for legislative funding with the sole purpose of repaying the White Sands ranchers. In 1991 Domenici and Bingaman introduced legislation in the Senate while Skeen along with Representatives Bill Richardson and Steve Schiff introduced similar legislation in the House. In both cases the language sought land appraisals based upon "established precedents for the valuation of similar real estate in New Mexico," a thinly veiled reference to the McGregor Range cases. Again, the bill failed to make it out of committee. In 1995 both parties reintroduced similarly worded bills, but this time stating that based upon the McGregor case, ranchers had not received just compensation for the total value of their ranches. Once more, both the House and Senate bills failed to make it to a vote.[54]

Even as New Mexico congressional representatives pushed for payment, in 1991 the George H. W. Bush administration argued that because the U.S. Court of Claims had twice rejected the assertions made by ranchers, they had no right to further payments. The Bureau of Land Management followed suit, suggesting that "merely staking a mining claim or holding grazing privileges does not and should not establish a compensable property right in public lands." The ranchers failed to make the government see things from their perspective. With the exception of payment at the behest of the state land commissioner in the wake of the *Armijo* case, they had failed on all accounts.[55]

The White Sands ranchers had lost their fight for compensation on leased lands. Yet in a way they had achieved a symbolic political victory in their stand for western property rights. McDonald was a folk hero of sorts. He had the backing of the New Mexico Cattle Growers Association and their New Mexico congressional representatives. He made national news. While the growing American military presence around the world shaped a new land-use ethic in south-central New Mexico, protest against federal confiscation of private property helped to bolster the ranchers' claims.

At the end of their lives, most ranchers cared deeply about the loss of their homes. In some sense McDonald's passing was a sad end to a more ugly history. Jim Eckles, former public affairs officer for White Sands, often took displaced property owners out to see their land. Some asked the military to allow internment at their former ranches once they died. While the military would not permit those burials because it implied ownership of property, it did allow several former residents to have their ashes spread on the missile range.[56]

Lease and suspension agreements tied ranchers to militarized landscapes. In paying to use the land, rather than condemning it from the beginning, the War Department and Department of Defense found themselves wrestling with the politics of the old and new West. White Sands was not only a weapons testing facility. As late as 1990 ranchers remained, and so did their economies and environmental legacy. The missile range would soon find itself at the middle of a conflict to reintroduce an endangered species that the very same livestock community had reduced to a few animals some sixty years earlier.

6

Natural Security States

In February 1988 a small crowd convened in a dimly lit lecture hall on the University of New Mexico campus. As part of "Lobo Week," the group assembled to discuss the proposed, and decidedly contested, reintroduction of the endangered Mexican gray wolf (*Canis lupus baileyi)* to lands inhabited by White Sands Missile Range. The audience, generally sympathetic to the wolf, heard a series of opening comments from a roundtable that included a spokesperson for the powerful New Mexico Cattle Growers Association, members of the New Mexico Department of Game and Fish, representatives of the U.S. Fish and Wildlife Service, the key wildlife biologist in the wolf recovery program, environmental activists, and missile range personnel. Their remarks ranged from outright opposition from the Cattle Growers Association and the army to discussions among environmentalists and Game and Fish agents about the viability of the missile range, given its primary mission as a weapons testing facility, to support recovery efforts there. After a question and answer session with mud slinging from both sides, the meeting concluded with a collective howl from the large cadre of audience members who supported Mexican wolf reintroduction.[1]

Although it may seem counterintuitive, environmentalists and wildlife scientists in the room overwhelmingly supported wolf recovery on the missile range. In fact, like local ranchers they did not classify White Sands as a ruined environment. They found an ecological value in the

12. Mexican gray wolf. Author's collection.

massive open landscapes created by the federal weapons industry. In the process they cast the Department of Defense as a crucial participant in the protection of endangered species. In the wake of battles over wolves at White Sands, the missile range would play an integral role in protecting the endangered desert bighorn sheep and the Northern Aplomado falcon. Making once private ranches and public grazing lands into a largely empty site secure from public use allowed wolf advocates and wildlife scientists to envisage White Sands as a protected habitat. As the missile range had an environmental impact beyond the landscape that it physically occupied, it ironically became the preeminent site for future wolf protection, forever altering the meaning of environments on the missile range and for militarized landscapes across the West.

While Cold War national security stifled local challenges to the presence of White Sands Missile Range in the first twenty years of its existence, it had become an openly contested site with the political turn of the 1960s. Through public debate and the litigation of federal environmental legislation, the increasingly powerful American environmental movement cast the national security state as defenders of wildlife. In the process environmentalists had emerged as peculiar Cold War actors. They came to have a voice in defining land stewardship on military-scientific sites across the United States. Wolf recovery at White Sands was at the vanguard of a broader reinterpretation of habitats on North American militarized landscapes during the late Cold War. In the mid-1990s the Dare County Air Force Range on the eastern coast of North Carolina, a weapons testing site shared by the navy and air force, was recognized for its role in the successful reintroduction of the endangered red wolf (*Canis rufus*) to the region (although it faces threats from poachers). During the same period Tyndall Air Force Base southwest of Tallahassee, Florida, on the Gulf of Mexico played a part in protecting endangered loggerhead sea turtles. In the 1980s and 1990s similar programs were initiated in the American West. Camp Pendleton, north of Oceanside, California, has sought to protect the dwindling Least Bell's vireo population (a small bird species with a historic range from the Baja to northern California). In the Mojave Desert, Edwards Air Force Base and China Lake Naval Weapons Center have recently set aside sixty thousand and two hundred thousand acres, respectively, for the protection of the endangered desert tortoise.[2]

National security came not only to define protecting the nation-state, but also the evolving natural state of south-central New Mexico and other North American militarized environments. Military personnel attempted to block the wolf program at White Sands by arguing it would interfere with missile testing. At the same time, displaced ranchers who continued to fight for both a return of and payment for lands taken in the process of militarization intensely opposed the program on economic grounds. Water once utilized for revitalizing forage to feed cattle now provided for growing military communities in Alamogordo, Las Cruces, and on the missile range itself. Many ranchers with lands around White Sands saw their powerful lobby challenged by environmentalists. For the southern New Mexican cattlewomen and men who fought to keep wolves from the region, the Mexican wolf recovery effort became a symbol of how an urban-based cultural and environmental order in North America had projected its economic and land use values onto the rural West.

Objections to wolf recovery programs across the West were reflective of the rural politics of the Sagebrush Rebellion and Wise Use politics in the New West. Rural westerners contested the proper role of the Bureau of Land Management, Forest Service, National Park Service, and U.S. Fish and Wildlife Service in managing public lands. They often saw those agencies as promoting biodiversity at the behest of environmentalists. During the mid-1990s plans to reintroduce wolves near the Arizona–New Mexico border and in Yellowstone National Park led to heated debates about the cultural and environmental value of wolf packs. Ranchers near Yellowstone showed their dismay at plans to reintroduce wolves by setting up a "Wolf Management Team," which distributed T-shirts inscribed with the anti-wolf slogan "Shoot, Shovel and Shut Up." Although the federal government had always played a role in western land use, wolves were symbolic reminders, however loosely, of the relationship between public lands agencies and urban environmentalists.[3]

In New Mexico the presence of the military-scientific apparatus put a new wrinkle into the conflict over wolf recovery. Environmentalists argued that the missile range was legally bound to the rules set out in the National Environmental Policy Act (NEPA) and the Endangered Species Act (ESA). But unlike Yellowstone, it was also a place ostensibly off limits to the public. As a federal entity White Sands was both at the center of securing the world from communism and now a part of the legal battle to protect endangered wildlife.

If introduced, wolves would not stay within the porous boundaries that separated the missile range from surrounding areas. Thus the most formidable foes to ranchers were not only environmentalists but also the environmental scientists who made studies of White Sands as wolf habitat. Led by James Bednarz, who completed the first study of wolves at White Sands, wildlife biologists emerged as the environmental brokers in the battle over wolf recovery on the missile range. They did not side with ranchers.

Following the passage of NEPA in 1969, the requirement that federal agencies complete environmental impact statements meant that all federal militarized landscapes became sites of environmental science. They were also bound to account for endangered species as required by the 1973 ESA. Wildlife biologists and pro-wolf environmentalists used science as a tool to cast White Sands as fertile ground for wolf recovery and in the process discredited the anti-wolf arguments set forth both by ranchers and military personnel.

While blaming environmentalists and federal land management officials, Wise Use advocates rarely acknowledged that historical failures in managing natural resources at the local level had encouraged increased federal regulation. The culture of locally controlled grazing commons and forests in the late nineteenth and early twentieth centuries had ultimately undermined the environmental viability of many western landscapes. In the years after the Dust Bowl the survival of western ranchers and farmers necessitated either a new economic and ecological order or federal regulation of an overextended capitalist culture. To quote the historian Richard White, "What Wise Use believes is that a nineteenth-century program that failed under nineteenth-century conditions will somehow succeed under twentieth-century economic conditions."[4]

Ranchers in south-central New Mexico likewise refused to concede that the push for recovery of the endangered Mexican wolf stemmed, at least in part, from their own extermination measures. While early twentieth-century ranchers saw predator control as vital to their economy, their descendants never saw it as a root cause in shaping modern calls for wolf protection or the taking of their private lands for a military reserve. In the growing post–World War II environmental movement the wolf found influential allies including the Sierra Club, Wilderness Society, and Environmental Defense Fund. What followed in the public sphere and federal courts was a battle that would define the trajectory of the missile range as a national and natural security state.

By natural security state I mean that militarized sites as secured from public access (or at least perceived as such) became useful to environmentalists in their advocacy for wildlife regeneration. Without NEPA and the ESA, environmentalists could not compel the de jure construction of natural security states by using the courts. Even as they won legal battles over wolf reintroduction, the program remained politicized in the media. At White Sands the natural security state remained contested. Ranchers created their own version of the idea. Local communities opposed to wolf recuperation saw the missile range as a natural buffer from environmentalists and their projects. Military personnel wanted nothing to do with conflict.

Advocacy for recovery at White Sands Missile Range and the subsequent struggles by ranchers, politicians, and military personnel to undermine the project emphasize the complex meanings bound up in the idea of a military-scientific reserve. While army personnel at the missile range argued that the mission of White Sands could potentially damage the program by harming wolves and the people who monitored pack movements, ranchers tied the same place to the fate of the livestock economy. Wolf recovery advocates suggested not only that the habitat was suitable for the wolf, but also that restricted public access to the military site would actually protect wolves from undue harm at the hands of people opposed to the program. White Sands had become more than a missile range. Its new mission as environmental steward and cultural broker reflected the complex environmental realities of the postwar rural West.

EXTIRPATION

Mexican wolf recovery efforts found their roots in turn-of-the-century endeavors to extirpate the predator from the southwestern United States and northern Mexico. Before 1890 several wolf species roamed the pinelands, pinyon-juniper forests, oak woodlands, ponderosa pine forests, and surrounding grasslands across Arizona, New Mexico, and northern Mexico. Wolf numbers remained particularly strong in the Sierra Madre Occidental across the Mexican states of Chihuahua, Durango, Sonora, and Zacatecas. In New Mexico wolves existed in large numbers across the Black Range and the San Mateo, Datil, Gallinas, Animas, and Sacramento Mountains. Importantly, wolves rarely were found in the Sonoran or Chihuahuan deserts because of the lack of water and protective foliar cover.[5]

Between the 1890s and 1940s, most efforts to control the Mexican wolf population came at the behest of cattle ranchers who sought to end attacks on their livestock. Control began with a number of practices including the use of double spring traps to catch wolves or through "denning" (the act of seeking out wolf dens during breeding season and killing litters). As a result of long-term economic volatility caused in part by prolonged drought at the end of the nineteenth century, state and federal trapping programs sought to hinder attacks on already precarious cattle and sheep herds. The Territorial Bounty Act of 1893, passed by the Arizona–New Mexico Territorial Legislature, permitted counties to pay bounties on any predatory species determined detrimental to livestock.[6]

By 1914 the United State Biological Survey took a primary responsibility for the control of all predators. Working in "control districts," J. Stokely Ligon supervised trappers in the Predatory Animal and Rodent Control division of the Biological Survey. The high demand for meat during World War I allowed Ligon and Aldo Leopold, among other federal and state wildlife officials, to utilize wartime economic conditions to push for the further elimination of predators. At the height of the war, Ligon suggested that wolves alone had caused $100,000 in damage to the livestock economy.[7]

In 1918 New Mexico's game and fish warden explained that despite the efforts of both federal and private trappers, "there still remains in this state a large number of predatory animals which are most destructive, not only to the cattle and sheep interests, but also to our wild game." Yet Vernon Bailey, senior biologist for the Bureau of Biological Investigations within the Bureau of Biological Survey, intimated that as early as 1906 only about one hundred wolves remained in the Gila Mountain Ranges across western New Mexico. The following year the newly created Forest Service killed seventy-two more. In the mid-1920s Ligon suggested that gray wolves "are no longer a menace since they are practically eliminated from New Mexico." Twenty years later the Division of Wildlife Research in the Biological Survey classified the Mexican wolf as virtually "extinguished" despite some sightings in parts of Mexico.[8]

By actively participating in extermination efforts and lobbying for federal control of predators, ranchers who sought to undermine a loss of stock played a vital role in the extirpation of the Mexican wolf from the southwestern United States and northern Mexico. The growth of the cattle and sheep industry during the second half of the nineteenth century had the effect of reducing wild prey key to the diet of southwestern wolves. Before the arrival of domestic livestock, wolves fed on white-tailed deer, mule deer, bighorn sheep, pronghorn, elk, rabbits, beaver, and other small prey. Many species sought by wolves declined in numbers because of a lack of forage caused by overgrazing or at the hands of hunters seeking to put food on the table. In turn, cattle and sheep herds incapable of utilizing flight to ward off attacks became the food of choice for wolf populations. As a result of the declines in wild prey and easy predation on livestock populations, wolf numbers actually increased for a time, creating an even greater demand among ranchers for control efforts.[9]

The subsequent human assault on a growing wolf population ultimately led to their overwhelming disappearance from the American Southwest. What remained of the dwindling population existed in the mountains of northern Mexico. In the extirpation of the species during the first half of the twentieth century, ranchers from south-central New Mexico had a hand in making the imminent battle between livestock owners and environmentalists over wolf protection. Recovery efforts during the 1980s and 1990s found their roots in a region where the livestock industry had dictated the ecological value of an animal species. Like the historical place of livestock in the Cold War era militarization of the region, ranching had played some role in creating the conditions for confrontation with wolf activists at White Sands.

Despite continued petitions from the livestock industry to control predators after World War II, wildlife sciences propelled an already growing wilderness and wildlife protection movement in North America. By the mid-1960s protection of endangered species emerged from a growing national environmental movement in the United States. Following weaker acts passed in 1966 and 1969, the Endangered Species Act of 1973, to quote the historian Thomas Dunlap, reflected the fact that "people wanted to save all species and to save them as part of a system. All, they argued, have a place and a purpose on earth." The environmental turn evinced by the popularity of Earth Day in April 1970 had brought questions of wildlife extinction to the fore of the American environmental consciousness. Yet, not all would join the crusade to save the Mexican wolf.[10]

For wolves in the Southwest, the legislation could not have come sooner. In 1973 no evidence showed that the species existed in any part of the southwestern United States. On April 28, 1976, the Mexican wolf was added to the list of endangered species by federal mandate. The Endangered Species Act made it unlawful to harass, harm, hunt, kill, or trap what remained of the Mexican wolf population. Texas (1977), New Mexico (1976), and Arizona (1973) had also designated the wolf as an endangered species. Importantly, the ESA required an official recovery plan that laid the groundwork for the eventual reintroduction of wolves to the wild.[11]

In the late 1970s the Fish and Wildlife Service commissioned professional trapper Roy T. McBride to determine what remained of the wild Mexican wolf population in Mexico. His report revealed that between 1972 and 1978 residents of Durango and Chihuahua had trapped, shot, tracked, or poisoned a total of fifty-three wolves. Although discouraging, McBride's findings offered initial hope that Mexican wolf populations endured in the mountainous terrain of Mexico. But by examining the stomach contents of wolves trapped between 1958 and 1968, he also explained that livestock overwhelmingly comprised the diets of Mexican wolves. Because of new anti-predator technology and increased control efforts within Mexico's livestock industry, McBride forecast the eventual disappearance of the wolf. What remained of the species faced "imminent extinction" in Mexico as "the reason for extermination is clear; the only ingredients lacking are expertise and control equipment." Appropriate funding for capture and breeding programs, he explained, acted as the only hope for a recuperation of the species.[12]

Since 1980 transnational projects in watershed protection and waterfowl management and attempts to combat wildlife habitat fragmentation as result of border fences, among other issues, have become important issues among environmentalists and wildlife scientists. Cooperative wolf recuperation ran deeper. In 1977 the United States and Mexico entered a mutual cooperation agreement to capture and breed Mexican wolves. At the United States–Mexico Joint Committee on Wildlife Conservation meeting during September 1980, the Fish and Wildlife Service and its Mexican counterpart, *Fauna Silvestre*, reiterated their call for capture as a measure of protection and recovery. The 1982 *Mexican Wolf Recovery Plan* became the first step toward recuperation of the wolf population. The study measured relationships between the wolf's calorie intake, adequate water sources, a reliable prey base, and the need for large recovery areas. It encouraged several tactics for captive breeding and a mating regiment that maintained the "sound genetic basis of the species." The plan also called for implementation schedules, although Fish and Wildlife Service set no expected release date. Importantly, because of "the uncertainties that exist now about the rate of progress of the captive propagation project," the report offered no clear site for release.[13]

A discourse had opened about potential areas for reintroduction programs. In a letter to the Region Two director of the Fish and Wild Service, Larry Woodard, the Bureau of Land Management director for the State of New Mexico, argued that general opposition in the mountainous area surrounding Roswell, New Mexico, hindered any release there. However, "within the Las Cruces District, there are larger tracts which may be suitable for future reintroductions." While federal agencies needed to complete further studies of potential livestock depredation, interaction with other endangered species, and the relationship between public and private lands, south-central New Mexico seemed a possible reintroduction site. The report did not mention White Sands Missile Range, but with its controlled landscape and suitable natural environment, it would become a primary site for Mexican wolf recovery only four years later.[14]

The wolf program at White Sands had antecedents. While some early nineteenth-century American conservationists promoted wolf destruction, namely in the name of better deer hunting, many also began to question the loss of the species. In his 1949 book *A Sand County Almanac*, Aldo Leopold, who had played a role in wolf extirpation in the Southwest, condemned the practice. He argued that people should "think like a mountain." Here he explained that the loss of a deer to a wolf pack was minor compared to the loss of the entire mountain due to the irruption of a deer population. Six years prior Adolph Murie completed his seminal study, *The Wolves of Mount McKinley*, which examined the precious relationship between Dall sheep and Alaskan wolves. He emphasized the importance of rethinking the central role of predators in dynamic environments. In the early 1950s Milton H. Stenlund completed aerial studies of wolves in the U.S.-Canada borderlands. He produced the 1955 Minnesota Department of Natural Resources Bulletin "A Field Study of the Wolf in the Superior National Forest" wherein he deduced that the timber wolf was essential to the "ecological community" of the forest. In the 1960s and 1970s wildlife biologist L. David Mech, author of *The Wolf: The Ecology and Behavior of an Endangered Species*, brought the plight of the species into the public sphere at the height of the environmental movement.[15]

The post-ESA years saw an amplification of wolf recuperation programs in Minnesota, the Pacific Northwest, and American Southwest, led by biologists including Mech and environmental organizations such as Defenders of Wildlife. The program at White Sands was the first major attempt to reintroduce wolves on a military site. In 1988 wildlife biologist James C. Bednarz completed *An Evaluation of the Ecological Potential of White Sands Missile Range to Support a Reintroduced Population of Mexican Wolves*. Under contract to carry out the study for the U.S. Fish and Wildlife Service, Bednarz felt that Arizona, Texas, and New Mexico had found no other appropriate site for release. The acceptable mountainous geography, defensive foliar cover, water sources, prey base, and "low level of human and other types of disturbance" made the missile range an ideal site for recovery. With most weapons testing relegated to the lower basin areas, the likelihood of wolf recovery efforts at higher elevations interfering with weapons testing remained minimal. Bednarz's study laid the foundational scientific elements for creating a natural security state at White Sands. He gave scientific backing to the environmentalists who sought to both compel the Department of Defense to cooperate with the program and also to undermine the claim that wolves would endemically kill livestock.[16]

Bednarz's examination of wolves at White Sands acted as the first significant study to interpret militarized landscapes as sites of recovery and in the process make the Department of Defense a central actor in protecting endangered species. Bednarz paid special attention to those middle and higher elevations across the missile range capable of sustaining the Mexican wolf. Recognizing that steep and difficult mountainous terrain hindered wolf predation, he argued that moderate gradation on northern portions of the San Andres and most of the Oscura Mountain Ranges existed as suitable terrain for wolf populations. Moreover, the thin pinyon-juniper areas mixed with shrubs, high- and moderate-density pinyon-juniper woodlands, and verdant grassland meadows offered the necessary cover for hunting prey and defensive positioning. While the missile range controlled the Tularosa Basin and the San Andres and Oscura Mountains, Bednarz defined the military reserve's moderate and higher elevations not as wastelands but as landscapes capable of supporting a wolf population.[17]

Not surprisingly, water acted as a crucial concern in examining the potential of the missile range to support wolf recovery. In arid climates wolves need consistent hydration both for thermoregulation and as a measure to offset high bodily evaporation. Their ability to easily traverse large distances in short amounts of time allow wolf species to find numerous sources of water when needed. Prey also act as a source for rehydration because water generally makes up between 50 and 75 percent of tissues consumed by wolves. The process of nursing newborns amplifies the need for water.[18]

Proving the presence of significant sources of water would strengthen the argument for survival at White Sands. Admitting that data on water sources remained "sketchy" at best, Bednarz found that at least fifty permanent, year-round water sources existed. Another thirty-three had sporadic flows. He showed that more than one hundred natural springs (although less reliable) would also act as potential places to find water. Interestingly, the built environment could also offer sites for wolves to water. If properly maintained, wells, water catchments, dirt tanks, and windmills offered places to rehydrate.[19]

The need for a large prey base was critical in measuring the ability of the missile range environment to support Mexican wolf recovery efforts without disrupting ranching in the area. Spatial requirements for wolves vary, but at the greatest prey density (fifteen deer for about every square mile) an area of thirty square miles can support about four wolves. Wolves find, kill, and consume prey at irregular intervals. In between feedings they turn to catabolism (or the breakdown and decomposition of sources of metabolic energy) to survive. When they do find food, wolves can consume as much as 19 percent of their total body weight. Understanding the need for wild sources of food, Bednarz had to show that a large enough prey base existed to keep the reintroduced wolf population from feeding on domestic cattle and sheep herds at the edges of the missile range. On average, energy requirements reach about 3.25 kilograms per wolf per day. No studies had adequately measured the prey base for the missile range, but a "relatively stable" mule deer population would offer the key wild sustenance for wolves. Based upon data models, Bednarz concluded that regional mule deer numbers fluctuated between 3,414 in May, when the population reached its nadir, and 5,202 in the summer, after the birth of most fawns. Other possible prey included pronghorn, endangered bighorn sheep, feral horses, and the African oryx. However, because of little habitat overlap most of those species would act as either supplementary nourishment or a rare kill (the latter species seems less likely either way because of the animal's size, aggressive demeanor, and herd numbers).[20]

Despite his findings, domestic animals remained particularly vulnerable because, beyond flight, they had few defense mechanisms to ward off attack. Less physically vigorous prey remained even more susceptible to wolf predation. Wolves will stalk and kill animals in their adolescence or old age and also will seek those hindered by disease, injury, or malnutrition. By the turn of the twentieth century, wolves in the Southwest eagerly declined wild game in favor of domestic livestock. "Once set," says Wildlife Biologist David Brown, "this table was too good to resist." Nonetheless, Bednarz argued that while wolves would indeed take cattle and sheep, "they never take great numbers of livestock." This differed greatly from McBride's suggestion that livestock would remain the key portion of wolf diets. Using studies done in Minnesota and Canada, Bednarz explained that depredation rates varied from one cow per fifty-two wolves to as little as one cow per ninety-three wolves. Because wolves could more easily kill them, the rate of depredation on sheep remained higher.[21]

Based upon that data, Bednarz estimated that if the Fish and Wildlife Service introduced forty wolves, recovery program administrators could potentially see only one cow and two sheep as the expected rate of livestock depredation per year for the White Sands area. He recognized that clear differences existed between the environments of Canada, Minnesota, and New Mexico. Yet proper management would keep depredation at a "negligible level." Importantly such an assumption did not reflect the dynamics that dictated the relationship between wolves, environment, and wild prey. If the mule deer population changed due to drought, livestock would become a more likely target for wolves. Either way, it was clear that with the growth and dispersal of wolf populations along south-central New Mexico, packs would inevitably move beyond the permeable boundaries of White Sands and target cattle and sheep in greater numbers.[22]

By naming the Mexican wolf an experimental, non-essential endangered species under the Endangered Species Act, recovery personnel could introduce them outside their natural habitats and with fewer protective measures. Thus the experimental non-essential designation accepted the possibility of accidental death (vital for their reintroduction on the missile range) and allowed for the legal killing of wolves due to predation on livestock or threat to human life. Bednarz could safely conclude that along with ideal environmental conditions the isolation and protection provided by the military site made it "one of the best refuges possible for an isolated population of wolves in the United States." Moreover, "released wolves within the missile range are almost guaranteed safety from illegal shooting, trapping, and automobile accidents." In the end, considering ecological and biological factors, White Sands Missile Range could support a population of at least thirty-two wolves. Including additional wild prey beyond the mule deer, a population of as many as forty did not seem unreasonable. Through the lens of wildlife science the missile range would come to hold new meaning as a viable environment and secure place for wolf recovery.[23]

IMAGINING WOLVES

In September 1987, before Bednarz could submit the final draft of his study, missile range commander General Joe Owens had sent a letter to the Fish and Wildlife Service withdrawing the missile range as a possible site for wolf reintroduction. He based his decision on the assumption that wolf recovery would interfere with the mission of White Sands and that missile testing could potentially harm human monitors of the wolf population there.[24]

During the Lobo Week panel missile range representative Colonel Edward Williams reiterated that reintroduction would conflict with the mission of White Sands. Yet as the wolf controversy heated up, the missile range increasingly took a neutral position among public audiences, hoping that neither side would cast it as an antagonist. Little support for recovery plans from local, federal, and state game officials was a much larger problem. By the end of 1988 the Fish and Wildlife Service had effectively killed Mexican wolf reintroduction. Regional director Michael Spear suggested that with the removal of White Sands, "we have no sites, the wolf reintroduction program, as of now, is terminated." During the panel discussion, Harold Olsen, director of the New Mexico Department of Game and Fish, voiced opposition to implementation of the program. He argued that he could not support the recovery efforts unless both the State Game

Commission and the Department of Game and Fish guaranteed that wolf reintroduction would not affect other endangered species (including the desert bighorn sheep at the San Andres National Wildlife Refuge).[25]

Olson explained further that the wolf issue had gotten "too emotional too fast." Wildlife biologists needed to complete further studies on the interactions between the wolf, other indigenous species, and proposed recovery areas. Similarly, Keith Russell, deputy assistant regional director of wildlife enhancement for the Fish and Wildlife Service suggested that some things took longer than others. In the case of wolf recovery the program required time to reconcile "diverse interests, values, and priorities," something the missile range had come to discover through battles with the White Sands Missile Range Ranchers during the 1970s and 1980s. Only when all parties addressed the interests of those affected by the program would wolf recovery succeed.[26]

Ranchers, county governments, and the New Mexico Cattle Growers Association voiced the greatest resistance to wolf recovery efforts at White Sands. In 1982 Norma Ames, leader of the Mexican Wolf Recovery Team for the New Mexico Department of Game and Fish, addressed an already growing opposition to the possibility of reviving what remained of the wolf population. She explained that "resistance to the idea of wolves in the wild stems mainly from the fact that the wolf is an efficient competitor with man for use of livestock and game." Comments made by rancher Phil Harvey Jr. in talking to CBS reporters in 1990 suggest that Ames was right. With his ranch near White Sands Missile Range, Harvey used the language of anthropomorphism to argue that "people don't realize that they're really an ornery kind of creature . . . they want to go out and kill livestock."[27]

Others corroborated Harvey's feelings. Rob Cox, who ran cattle on the eastern slope of the Organ Mountain Range argued that the loss of property in livestock, worth as much as $800 per head, acted as a logical reason to oppose the reintroduction of wolves on the missile range. He explained of recovery efforts: "it makes as much sense to me as getting all the murderers out of prison in Huntsville, Texas, and letting them out in downtown Dallas." In 1987 the Otero County Board of Commissioners passed a resolution in support of the missile range's opposition to possible recovery there. During the same year the commission wrote a letter to Joe Skeen, the congressional representative for the second district of the state of New Mexico, explaining "we are very much opposed to the possibility of the Mexican gray wolf being released onto the White Sands Missile Range, and public lands in Otero County, therefore we respectfully request your assistance in preventing this from happening."[28]

By pitting livestock against imagined wolf packs, ranchers shaped a competing vision for the natural security state at White Sands, one that sought to use the missile range as a buffer zone to the environmental movement. Their aspirations fit well into the prevailing political atmosphere of the postwar rural West. Wolf opposition was not fleeting. It reflected greater protests over the federal control of rural landscapes in the region. Between 1987 and 1993 the total number of grazing permits dropped from 35,175 to 34,661 in Catron County alone. But continued public land constrictions acted as a major reason for ire toward federal land management organizations in rural New Mexico and across the greater West. Ranchers near White Sands had experienced the loss of near two million acres of public grazing lands and private ranches in the first twenty years after World War II. Despite the promise of reimbursement for livestock killed by reintroduced wolf populations, ranchers continued to see the wolf recovery program as bad for business and an assault on their political sphere of influence. As one wolf supporter argued, "I think the wolf issue is sort of a symbol for ranchers . . . it's a symbol of loss of power."[29]

White Sands area ranchers were organized in resistance to the wolf program and had established a base of support from farm organizations and state politicians. A rancher himself, Skeen gave important support to their cause. In a radio address he explained that he understood the solemn history of the wolf and remained concerned about its preservation and protection. However, he also offered a key rationale behind regional opposition to the recovery program. Skeen believed "the introduction of any predator poses a risk to livestock, which in turn, would damage our already depressed economy."[30]

Cox and other ranchers also gained valuable support from the state Farm and Ranch Bureau and the New Mexico Cattle Growers Association. During the Lobo Week panel Cattle Growers Association spokesperson Denny Gentry explained to an audience member that the organization would not recommend an alternative plan to the proposed release at the missile range and, in fact, opposed reintroduction altogether. His response to the conflict reflected how the broader ranching community understood the politics of wolf reintroduction. Gentry later recalled that even before he stepped into the lecture hall he felt that "from a sense of fair play" it was a "concocted deal." The meeting was on a university campus where the mascot was the Lobo and among an urban population that sympathized with wolf recovery.[31]

Farm Bureau spokesperson Erik Ness explained: "I don't think it's the government's place to go around playing savior of humanity. These are tax dollars that a hell of a lot of people don't agree should be spent this way." In a letter to Skeen, Farm Bureau president William E. McIlhaney suggested that ranchers "already have tremendous predator problems in this area of the country and are constantly fighting to remain economically viable in the face of continued depredation of our livestock." The battle over wolf recovery set the value of the livestock economy against a program that as I show later was overwhelmingly supported by most New Mexicans.[32]

McIlhaney's comments confirmed a crucial aspect of the battle over recovery at White Sands. In the end, whose existence would have more meaning in the local and national consciousness, wolves or ranchers? In 1992 Harvey reflected on those fears, explaining: "We live in a civilized society, which is supposed to guarantee safety for people. And when their livelihood and way of life is threatened, that's not very civilized." Ranchers found that they still had some political support to oppose recovery. Yet the overwhelming demand for the protection of wilderness and wild species during the post 1960s-era had become a powerful counterforce. In 1992 environmental lawyer and pro-wolf advocate Grove T. Burnett suggested: "For 100 years, the rancher has dictated every decision about our public lands. But now their power is being eroded.

They see (reintroduction) as an erosion of their control of public land."
Despite holding fast, by the beginning of the 1990s ranchers saw the
balance of power tip overwhelmingly in favor of reintroduction.[33]

For supporters of recovery the time had come to return the wolf
to the wild. They had organizing power, a federal mandate, and public
opinion on their side. Mexican wolf supporters organized the panel during Lobo Week. Alongside James Bednarz, pro-wolf panelists included
David Henderson of the Mexican Wolf Coalition and Doug Meiklejohn
of the Environmental Law Center based in Santa Fe. Both Henderson
and Meiklejohn pointed to the fact that Bednarz's study had fallen on
deaf ears within the regional office of the Fish and Wildlife Service
despite the completion of the Mexican Wolf Recovery Plan six years
earlier. Henderson revealed that not even twelve thousand signatures
in support of recovery had encouraged reintroduction efforts among
state and federal game officials. Most importantly, Meiklejohn argued
that the Endangered Species Act had required the swift revival of endangered species, regardless of their popularity. Whether ranchers liked it
or not, all federal agencies, including the Department of Defense, had
to comply.[34]

With recovery at White Sands stalled, environmentalists sued the
federal government in an effort to jumpstart the program. In 1990 *Wolf
Action Group et al. v. the United States* brought the Mexican Wolf Coalition,
National Audubon Society, Environmental Defense Fund, Sierra Club,
Wilderness Society, and the ad hoc Wolf Action Group together in an
effort to "compel the Secretary of the Interior [Manual Lujan], through
the United States Fish and Wildlife Service, to implement the Mexican
wolf Recovery Plan." It also called upon Secretary of Defense Richard
Cheney to cooperate with the Fish and Wildlife Service in executing
wolf recovery at White Sands Missile Range.[35]

The Wolf Action Group claimed that Michael Spear, regional director for the Fish and Wildlife Service, capriciously allowed state officials
and local land managers to veto suggested reintroduction sites. That
decision "unreasonably constrained" the search for a suitable location.
The slow pace of the program also put the Fish and Wildlife Service

in violation of the Administrative Procedures Act. Importantly, the claimants argued that the withdrawal of White Sands Missile Range by the Department of Defense as a possible recovery site before the completion of James Bednarz's study further violated the ESA, which maintains that all federal agencies must "utilize their authorities in furtherance of the purposes of this Act by carrying out programs for the conservation of endangered species." They also believed that it breached the section of the act that requires federal agencies to consult with the Fish and Wildlife Service when any action taken may put at risk endangered or threatened species. The Wolf Action Group called for a mandatory injunction to compel Secretary Lujan to carry out wolf recovery efforts.[36]

The defendants disagreed on several points. Because the Fish and Wildlife Service had recently reconsidered the value of the missile range as a site for wolf recovery, they argued that "there is no actual controversy for the court to decide, and the defendants are already pursuing an administrative process designed to provide the relief that the plaintiffs request." Furthermore, they claimed that the secretary of defense had not violated the Endangered Species Act. In particular, they argued that army personnel had agreed to grant the Fish and Wildlife Service "reasonable access" to White Sands Missile Range. Attorneys also suggested that because the wolf did not necessarily reside on the range at the time of the complaint the Department of Defense did not have to follow ESA requirements for interagency consultation in the protection of endangered species.[37]

Despite the defendants' demands for dismissal, the case remained in the court system for three more years. In 1993 all parties reached an agreement on the future of wolf recovery efforts on the missile range. The settlement unconditionally supported the arguments established by proponents of the program. It required the Fish and Wildlife Service to "expeditiously" implement the Mexican Wolf Recovery Plan, achieve a return of the wolf to the wild, hire a full-time wolf recovery coordinator, complete an environmental impact study on the proposed program, and find and designate feasible sites for reintroduction. It also required expansion of captive breeding and the creation of an oversight committee (including members named in the complaint). By making the missile range a wolf habitat, environmentalists and their brethren in the scientific community emerged as proven agents in defining the perimeters of a natural security state in the American West.[38]

After the settlement of the case, proponents of wolf recovery found public opinion on their side. In an op-ed piece for the *Las Cruces Sun-News*, an angry resident explained: "Conservationists are armed with the facts, ranchers armed with folklore. Conservationists [are] willing to compromise, ranchers [are] against any compromise. It's no wonder the industry is on a decline. Arrogance is bad business. . . . Never mind the fact that ranchers are subsidized by being allowed grazing on public lands at extremely low fees. That we pay for their roads, cattleguards, fences, waterholes, pipelines, etc. That they don't have to restore damaged fish and wildlife habitat or polluted watersheds. Its time to give something back."[39] In more subdued terms Roger Kennedy, head of the National Park Service, explained that by allowing certain species to die off humans had demonstrated "astonishing ignorance about what other living things have done and can do for us." Moreover all wild species maintained important values significant in sustaining human life. He went further, intimating that "in the human drama, some hunter's grandchild may die unnecessarily because of something that was heedlessly eliminated."[40]

As a general rule more New Mexicans supported than opposed reintroduction of the Mexican wolf. A survey done in 1995 suggested that 70 percent of residents statewide voiced in favor of recovery efforts; 60 percent of residents living in the vicinity of White Sands Missile Range also supported the program. The strongest backing came from people under the age of forty-five. Residents of cities and those with college or trade school training also voiced a stronger voice in support of recovery: 74 percent agreed with the statement "although I may never see a Mexican wolf in the wild, it is important to know they exist in New Mexico." It probably didn't hurt that the Lobo was the mascot of the state's flagship university.[41]

With public support, binding federal legislation, and the settlement agreement, recovery plans went forward as stipulated. In November 1996 the Fish and Wildlife Service approved the final environmental impact statement for the reintroduction of the Mexican gray wolf. In the wake of its release, ranchers and governmental bodies near the missile range continued to overwhelmingly oppose the program. For ranchers across the West it was basic economics. In terms very similar to those used at White Sands, rancher Frank Rigler discussed reintroduction at Yellowstone: "I think the government has got a lot more problems to solve in the United States today than reintroducing wolves in Yellowstone Park, It's just another way to waste people's money. It's going to put the cattleman out of business. People don't count any-more." Questions of economic survival and property rights also drove opposition to any wolf release at White Sands.[42]

The Otero County Board of Commissioners, "strongly opposed" to recovery, argued that wolf reintroduction would negatively influence the local economy. In a letter to the Fish and Wildlife Service they explained "endangered species have stopped economic growth in the Western States for the past 10 years, never taking into account the impact it had on human life or economic impact." Similarly, the Sierra County Commission maintained that the final environmental impact study did not satisfactorily measure the effects of reintroduction on sites within the region. The Fish and Wildlife Service had not calculated the influence of wolf reintroduction on the county's recreational, hunting, and livestock industries. The commission called for a reexamination of the economic and ecological data presented in the plan.[43]

While there may be a tendency to assume that Native Americans outright supported reintroduction of wolves, such a notion plays into the idea of the "Ecological Indian." The anthropologist Shepard Krech III sees this as the misguided deduction of disparate cultures to benign ecologists and conservationists. Such a notion has plagued American understandings of Indian land use before and after contact with Europeans. In fact, just like their historical relationship to the predator, support for wolf reintroduction varies by culture. For example, in the Southwest, Apaches hold little affinity for wolves and have often opposed reintroduction, but in Idaho the Nez Perces held spiritual ties to wolves and looked favorably upon plans to rehabilitate the species. Factors such as age and class complicate these issues.[44]

It should come as little surprise then that the Mescalero Apache, who in part relied on pastoral endeavors, opposed the program at White Sands. The group equated recovery efforts at the missile range to "the introduction of an exotic species with numerous untold ramifications." Wolves in the region would both alter the floral and faunal makeup of the landscape while struggling in a harsh desert environment. "Change has occurred, and nature has compensated," explained Thora Walsh-Padilla of the Mescalero Office of Environmental Protection. "To attempt to play 'God' and interfere at this point will wreak havoc with a system that has already equalized." The Bureau of Indian Affairs supported the Mescalero Apaches' claim, arguing that designation of an endangered species near or on reservation property would hinder "their ability to manage their lands as they see fit." The bureau's argument stemmed from the proposed Mexican wolf experimental population rule, which limited the conditions for harassing or destroying Mexican wolves off the missile range to incidents of wolf attacks on livestock or when necessary to protect human life.[45]

Despite opposition, in 1995 the secure White Sands Missile Range (designated as White Sands Wolf Recovery Area and expanded to include Holloman Air Force Base, White Sands National Monument, the San Andres National Wildlife Refuge, and lands adjoining the refuge and nearby Jornada Experimental Range) was still a site for reintroduction. Yet something had changed. The final environmental impact statement named the Blue Range Wolf Recovery Area in the Apache National Forest as the primary site for reintroduction. Spanning across the south-central region of the New Mexico–Arizona state border, the Blue Range offered a suitable seven-thousand-square-mile, federally controlled habitat. The region also had a broad prey base that included white tailed deer, mule deer, elk, and javelina. It had plentiful sources of water. Importantly, the fact that wolves had historically populated the Blue Range region played a central role in the decision to make the area the primary release site.[46]

Considering the prolonged struggle to get the wolf onto the missile range, why did the Fish and Wildlife Service suddenly move wolf recovery efforts to the Blue Range? First, conflicts over the missile range as a site for reintroduction made the process increasingly cumbersome. White Sands was secured from poachers. Environmentalists had won in the courts. But because the missile range remained active, recovery teams would face "management constraints" not favorable to wolf recuperation.[47]

Second, in characterizing Mexican wolves as analogous to an exotic species, the Mescalero Apache Tribal Government made an important point about White Sands Wolf Recovery Area. Despite Bednarz's study, little evidence suggested that the species had ever continuously inhabited the Oscura and San Andres Mountain Ranges. The Fish and Wildlife Service acknowledged that by some indications wolves most likely traversed the regional landscape in search of water or prey, but "it was probably not prime wolf habitat." The regional climate was dry, hot, and vulnerable to drought. Revealing the shortfall in Bednarz's study, the Fish and Wildlife Service argued that the degree to which a self-supporting wolf population could actually survive there remained mere speculation. The agency said that the San Andres and Oscura Mountain Ranges did not meet the environmental conditions to support recovery objectives initially set forth by Fish and Wildlife Service personnel. At just over four thousand square miles, the reintroduction area could not sustain the proposed one hundred wolves seen as vital to the long-term perseverance of the species.[48]

Finally, environmental conditions had played a role in the removal of White Sands as the primary site for recovery. Between 1993 and 1995 a major drought hit Texas and New Mexico. It caused a decline in mule deer numbers in south-central New Mexico. The growth of the oryx population on the missile range likely contributed to the dwindling mule deer population by competing for food and spreading disease. As a result wildlife biologists estimated that the primary prey species for an introduced Mexican wolf population numbered only about 5,300, less than desirable for recovery efforts at the numbers stipulated for long-term survival. Bednarz had not accounted for a similar environmental shift.[49]

In the end the Mexican wolf never came to the missile range. By 2001 the interplay between an ambitious scientific study, political opposition, and the environmental limits of a drought-ridden region led the Fish and Wildlife Service to reconsider White Sands as a site for release. Published in 2003, the three-year review of the program reemphasized that geographical restrictions meant White Sands Wolf Recovery Area could support a mere twenty to thirty wolves. Furthermore, the sixty-two mile stretch between White Sands and the Blue Range Wolf Recovery Area included Interstate 25. If wolves attempted to reach the closest viable regional habitat, they would face large human populations along the heavily traveled interstate corridor.[50] In 2005 the program's five-year review reiterated those findings. It also added that "although wolves might eventually disperse to WSMR [from other recovery areas], neither the habitat (prey base) nor the management constraints of that site (i.e. national defense and Homeland Security issues) would be conducive to establishing a significant population segment or to contributing toward wolf recovery on a rangewide basis."[51] In the end, program officials chose to remove the White Sands Wolf Recovery Area as the principal place for reintroduction.

Efforts to impede wolf recovery did not cease. In 1998 the Fish and Wildlife Service released the first Mexican wolves into the Blue Range Wolf Recovery Area. In 2000 it translocated wolves to the Gila National Wilderness in western New Mexico. Two years earlier, the New Mexico Cattle Growers Association brought legal suit claiming the Fish and Wildlife Service had violated the National Environmental Policy Act, the Endangered Species Act, and the Administrative Procedures Act. Courts dismissed the case. In Catron County, New Mexico, near the Blue Range Wolf Recovery Area, New Mexico rancher Hugh McKeen created a stir when he suggested recovery efforts could cause civil war. "You can go into any country that tends to go toward a fascist or a total government-control thing, and people are going to overthrow it," he explained. "If the government keeps pushing us, something like that is going to happen." In 1998 it came as no surprise that of the eleven wolves reintroduced to the Gila, four died due to gunshot wounds. One need not ponder whether Mexican wolves would have met a similar fate near the missile range.[52]

It would be easy to dismiss the wolf program at White Sands as an ultimate failure. But to do so veils the new role environmentalists and wildlife scientists had in dictating environmental policy on militarized landscapes. While opposition from ranchers and missile range personnel acted as resistance to recovery on the missile range, the push for the protection of an endangered species overwhelmingly remade White Sands as part of a broader late twentieth-century natural security state. The activities of the environmental office on White Sands speak to this new land ethic. Wolf recovery went forward at the Blue Range Recovery Area despite continued protests from regional ranchers and the New Mexico Cattle Growers Association. But as of 2010 the missile range remained a legally sanctioned site for Mexican gray wolf recovery if issues arose at the primary site of reintroduction.[53]

In the first struggle to define how the National Environmental Policy Act and Endangered Species Act would dictate the relationship between rural western economies, the Department of Defense, and environmentalists, ranchers failed to see the historical ties between wolf eradication and wolf recovery. From biodiversity to the cultural significance of wolves in New Mexico, there were many reasons environmentalists promoted the program. But perhaps more than any other, historically wolves were a part of the southwestern landscape.

Ranchers had valid reasons to stake claim to south-central New Mexico. For more than one hundred years they had lived and worked in the region. They had created ties to the land. Into the 1930s they had managed the grazing commons. Rather than some relic of a western past they continued to adapt to the conditions of the post-1960s political landscape by using grassroots organization and neoliberal notions of individual property rights to push their agenda. They may have been the losers in the legal battles over White Sands as a natural security state, but they altered the trajectory of Mexican wolf recuperation in the region.

Yet their role in the whole conflict has deeper origins. In promoting predator control efforts the livestock industry in the late nineteenth and early twentieth centuries had established the roots of future calls for wolf protection. Rural westerners conveniently ignored that ranching historically played a central part in eradicating wolves from western North America. In protesting the program, ranchers hoped to use the wolf issue to reaffirm a nineteenth-century land ethic that could not possibly survive in the twentieth century.[54]

At the same time, environmentalists overreached in making the missile range a wolf habitat. While wolves crossed the Tularosa Basin and surrounding mountains in search of prey and water, it could be argued that the landscape did not fit within the species' premier historical range. Moreover, while Bednarz's study made the case for wolf recovery on the secure missile range, the nature of drought would transform how wolves used the regional ecosystem. Without the mule deer, livestock would become premier fodder for the wolf. Protest, science, and environmental change collided to undo the recovery program in south-central New Mexico.

Yet the actions of environmentalists signified a shift in how the military did business in the American West. In the wake of the environmental turn of the 1960s and 1970s, military sites had another mission: saving America's wildlife. While ranchers tied White Sands to the legacy of a deep-seated pastoral economy, environmentalists and wildlife biologists saw the missile range not as destroyed by weapons testing but as a secure place for reintroduction of the endangered Mexican gray wolf. Both ranchers and environmentalists sought to establish their authority in redefining the value of a Cold War landscape, but it was wolf proponents and wildlife scientists who became de facto environmental agents of the Cold War military-scientific apparatus. Missile testing was not erased from the region's postwar environmental history. But the removal of the livestock economy to make a massive militarized landscape had created new ways of knowing nature in south-central New Mexico. As the contentious roundtable at the University of New Mexico suggests, the encounters with the missile range landscape were often imagined contests between rivaling land-use ideals. White Sands was not only the dominion of the national security state but also the province of environmentalists, ranchers, and, perhaps in the future, wolves.

Conclusion

At the same time that drought and political conflict moved the wolf recovery program off the missile range, a new storm brewed at White Sands. On July 6, 1994, military personnel led by missile range wildlife biologist Patrick Morrow found more than 100 wild horses dead or dying near a small water source at Mound Springs at the northern end of the missile range. Drought and overpopulation had left the herd of 400 emaciated and with little hope for survival (in total some 1,400 feral horses had at one time roamed the missile range). Many had died of their own accord, but the military shot 49 out of mercy.[1]

The condition of the horses incensed animal rights activists. Unlike other wild horses in the West, the herds at White Sands did not fall under the protective measures of the 1971 Wild Free-Roaming Horses and Burros Act because they were on military lands. The Fund for Animals had offered help to White Sands, which missile range commander Brigadier General Jerry Laws declined. Heidi Prescott, national director for the organization, showed her frustration in a letter to Laws. She explained that members were "infuriated that reporters, other organizations, and even sport hunters have been allowed on White Sands Missile Range, yet The Fund for Animals, a group with extensive rescue experience that is offering to help the horses is being denied access." In the end what remained of the herd found homes in greener pastures with help from the International Society for the Protection of Wild Horses and Burros.

By 1999 an adoption program created in cooperation with White Sands sent the last thirty-six horses to a private ranch in South Dakota.[2]

Even as environmentalists cast White Sands as perfect for wolf recovery, the Fund for Animals and the International Society for the Protection of Wild Horses and Burros saw the missile range as a death trap for a wild animal with roots in the nineteenth-century West. The feral horses were indeed a remnant of the pastoral Tularosa Basin. Some believed the horses might have belonged to former lawman Patrick Garrett, who briefly made a home in the region. Garrett was murdered in February 1908, and his horses, which he bred for racing, went free. He was not the only one of his generation to have horses. The militarization of the area forced cattle out and opened the landscape to the feral horse herds, which competed with oryx and native ungulate populations for fodder. In turn they became a part of the unexpected environmental history of militarized landscapes in south-central New Mexico.[3]

In July 1995 the missile range celebrated its fifty-year anniversary; it had existed over a period of time that matched the era when cattle ruled the desert. Yet the quarrel over wild horses at White Sands signaled how the area's ranching past continued to shape debates about the nature of White Sands Missile Range. The memory of a livestock culture in this region never totally disappeared. Since 1940 the cattle kingdom of south-central New Mexico had played a role in both the making of the missile range and the competing perceptions of the missile range. Ranchers shaped a narrative around White Sands that reflected the loss of community. In the 1980s and 1990s ranchers tried to assert the importance of a pastoral narrative but ultimately failed. In this sense the dying horse herds reflected a destroyed landscape; the missile range was a pastoral wasteland.

Like Forest Service lands or the National Park System, White Sands Missile Range was an invented landscape. Thus like large federal landscapes created for the purposes of resource management or public enjoyment, the missile range led people to make sense of its environment through their own beliefs and desires. It fulfilled the desires of tourists, big game hunters, and environmentalists. Science shaped those ideas.

In their ability to create competing environmental narratives ecologists, wildlife biologists, health physicists, and rocket scientists played a significant role in molding how everyday people perceived the missile range. Raising unique questions about security and containment on the Cold War home front, militarized landscapes were proving grounds not only for new weaponry but also for the American encounter with the national security state and the newfangled environmental spaces that it made. What emerged from the environmental contest over the missile range was profound and often unexpected.

It should thus come of little surprise that White Sands Missile Range won the 2007 Military Conservation Partner Award. The U.S. Fish and Wildlife service wove the premise of military conservation at White Sands that could have only emerged in the wake of the environmental shift of the 1960s and 1970s. Outwardly, conservation efforts seem sincere. Recognizing the painstaking process of wildlife management, Junior Kerns of the missile range's Environmental Stewardship Branch explained that "none of our (conservation projects) occurred overnight. Most have been ten years in the making." Teaming up with the U.S. Fish and Wildlife Service and the New Mexico Department of Game and Fish, White Sands figured not only in bat and falcon conservation but also in the management of other at-risk wildlife, including the pinyon jay, Colorado chipmunk, and gray vireo.[4]

It would be easy to mark missile range cooperation in the conservation and management of threatened and endangered species as "green washing." In awarding the military conservation award to White Sands, the Fish and Wildlife Service said nothing about missile testing. Today the missile range remains a fully operational weapons testing facility. In the summer of 2007 I stopped behind a long line of cars on U.S. 70 at the top of San Augustín Pass. I was caught in a military blockade with many other travelers. From there I watched a missile take off from the southern end of the testing site and head due north to impact at some flat area in the middle of the desert. There was something technologically sublime, to use the historian David Nye's words, in watching it buzz into the air, leaving only a contrail across the blue sky. It was,

13. Minor Scale explosion, White Sands Missile Range, June 1985. Courtesy of White Sands Missile Range Museum and Archives.

frankly, an astounding moment. I almost forget what I was watching and what it meant: What kind of missile was it? Why was it tested that day? How did it crash into the desert? Where in the world would the military deploy this type of weapon? Unfortunately, the answers to those questions remain obscured by the secrecy surrounding missile testing and its environmental impact at White Sands.[5]

To call White Sands Missile Range even a de facto wildlife preserve is, at the very least, misleading. As the historian Edmund Russell argues, "I suspect students of state building might attribute our surprise and delight at ironic conservation to a streak of naiveté. After all, both bases and preserves build and project state power over people, space, and nature. That is what states have always done, do now and will do in the future." The reimagination of militarized landscapes as sites of wildlife regeneration has made for a perplexing situation in studying the nature of military sites. Bases and testing facilities as conservation landscapes seems counterintuitive to what militaries do to nature in preparation for war.[6]

Thus the theme of an "ugly west" or "tainted desert" not only makes sense but also falls in line with how environmentalists think about military environments. Yet here it is important to return to Richard White's "just so story" or what the historian William Cronon calls the post hoc, ergo propter hoc fallacy in environmental history. To simply measure White Sands by what it does is to ignore how everyday peoples challenged the environmental designs of the national-security state. To this end militarized landscapes exist neither in a temporal nor geographical stasis. They are sites of military power that are always contested. White Sands experienced unexpected twists and turns in its everyday activities as a result of nonmilitary actors. It is worth reemphasizing that environmentalists never explicitly protested the mission of the missile range. Instead they cast White Sands as a site secure for reviving endangered species. Its secure borders offered them a place for wildlife conservation free from public interference.[7]

With this in mind, I found two important lessons in the environmental history of the missile range. First, White Sands shapes the places around it that are not technically militarized. Indeed most militarized landscapes are fluid rather than fixed in place. They change over time, and their effects defy any fixed geographical boundaries. The missile range has not only cratered the lands within its boundaries but has also colonized those around it. The deserts, forests, and cities of the U.S.-Mexico borderlands and the greater Southwest remain a part of White Sands.

Second, White Sands (like other militarized landscapes) exists in a place with real people, who have their own social, political, and economic agendas as well as environmental ideals. People not a part of White Sands have altered the meaning of (and therefore the environments within) the massive weapons testing facility. White Sands is a place with a past, a past with an environmental history made as much by the disparate peoples of the region as through the goings on of the military-scientific apparatus. This is not to press missile testing to the backburner, but to recognize and promote exploring nuances in the environmental history of militarized landscapes.

There is no doubt that weapons testing transformed the environment of south-central New Mexico. The Trinity Site, unexploded ordnance, and a cratered landscape mark the environmental legacy of the missile range. At the same time, the perceived emptiness and real enormity of White Sands led local and extra-local people not just to comprehend the economic and ecological implications of a missile range. It also led them to reimagine a militarized landscape to fit their interests and satisfy their desires in a changing economic, environmental, and social landscape. In the process they wove a more complicated environmental history of the Cold War American West.

Notes

INTRODUCTION

1. "White Sands Missile Range Receives Prestigious Award from Fish and Wildlife Service," 28 March 2008, http:// www.fws.gov/home/feature/2008 /MilitaryConservationAward.pdf (accessed 7 September 2013).

2. Sue Vorenberg, "Animals Find Refuge in Protected Government Sites," http:// www.abqtrib.com/news/2006/oct/17/animals-find-refuge-protected-government -sites/ (accessed 31 July 2008).

3. Boice, "Endangered Species Management," 7–9; J. Cohn, "New Defenders of Wildlife." On militarized landscapes and wildlife see Havlick, "Logics of Change"; Cohn, "New Defenders of Wildlife."

4. Havlick, "Logics of Change"; Pearson, Cole, and Coates, *Militarized Landscapes*, 113–70; Riebsame, Robb, et al., *Atlas of the New West*, for the "Ugly West," see 132–41; Kuletz, *Tainted Desert*; Davis, "Dead West."

5. Russell, "Afterword: Militarized Landscapes," 234.

6. Pinto, Lenko, and Johnson, *Final Environmental Impact Statement,* 1–1, 1–3; Vanderbilt, *Survival City*, 39.

7. Pinto, Lenko, and Johnson, *Final Environmental Impact Statement,* 4–64, 4–65, 4–66; Vanderbilt, *Survival City*, 42–43.

8. Jim Eckles, interview by author, 23 March 2011, Las Cruces, tape recording.

9. For an account of conflict at Hanford see Gerber, *On the Home Front.* On the Rocky Mountain Arsenal see Havlick, "Logics of Change."

10. For an account of the conflict between local communities and state and national parks see Spence, *Dispossessing the Wilderness*; Jacoby, *Crimes against Nature*; Kosek, *Understories.*

11. I take my cues here from Scott, *Seeing Like a State*; Craib, *Cartographic Mexico*; Casey, "How to Get from Space," 26, 27. Benedict Anderson offered important early analysis for rethinking the conceptualization and "imagined" nature of

the nation-state through the use of maps. See Anderson, *Imagined Communities*, esp. chapter 10.

12. On a culture of the Cold War see Boyer, *By the Bomb's Early Light*; Boyer, *Fallout*; Henriksen, *Dr. Strangelove's America*; Whitfield, *Culture of the Cold War*; Winkler, *Life under a Cloud*. On connections between economy and the Cold War see L. Cohen, *Consumer's Republic*; May, *Homeward Bound*; Jacobs, *Pocketbook Politics*. On environmental movements see Rome, *Bulldozer in the Countryside*. On defense dollars in the region see G. Nash, *American West in the Twentieth Century*, 217, 233–35, 238; Markusen et al., *Rise of the Gunbelt*, 12. Numbers for population growth can be found in Leonard, "Migrants, Immigrants, and Refugees." On World War II and the West see G. Nash, *American West Transformed*; M. Johnson, *Second Gold Rush*; Fryer, *Perimeters of Democracy*. See also G. Nash and Etulain, *Twentieth-Century West*, 1–30, 407–18; Findlay, *Magic Lands*, esp. chapter 3.

13. Limerick, *Legacy of Conquest*, 159, 163. On the history of perceptions of deserts see Limerick, *Desert Passages*. On the Atomic West see Hevly and Findlay, *Atomic West*; Ackland, *Making a Real Killing*; Admundson, *Yellowcake Towns*; Ringholz, *Uranium Frenzy*; Brugge, Benally, and Yazzie-Lewis, *Navajo People and Uranium Mining*; Masco, *Nuclear Borderlands*; Kosek, *Understories*, esp. chapter 6.

14. A good place to start with the myth of New Mexico is Wilson, *Myth of Santa Fe*; Johansen, *New Mexico's Urban*; John Burnett, "New Mexico Dairy Pollution Sparks 'Manure War,'" NPR News, http://www.npr.org/templates/story/story .php?storyId=121173780 (accessed 7 February 2013). On the counterculture in New Mexico see Rudnick, *Utopian Vistas*.

15. Kosek, *Understories*; Masco, *Nuclear Borderlands*; Anaya, *Bless Me Ultima*; Anaya, *Heart of Aztlan*; Price, *Orphaned Land*; DeBuys, *Enchantment and Exploitation*; Nichols, *Milagro Beanfield War*.

16. Lynch, *Image of the City*, 4, 8. Lynch's work has influenced urban planning, cultural geography, and political theory. The theory of "cognitive mapping" is one of the critical outcomes of his work. See Jameson, "Postmodernism." While never on the scale of places like White Sands, large military sites existed prior to World War II. See Lotchin, *Fortress California*.

17. R. White, "Environmental History."

1. SEEDS OF DISCONTENT

1. R. G. Walker to John J. Dempsey, 5 October 1942, Box 4, Folder 9, Governor John J. Dempsey Papers, New Mexico State Records Center and Archives, Santa Fe (hereafter New Mexico State Records).

2. Walker to Dempsey, 5 October 1942.

3. "Hardship on Ranchers," *Carlsbad Daily Current-Argus*, 12 September 1943, Folder 5816, Vol. 44, New Mexico Adjutant General Records, New Mexico State Records.

4. "Grazing Service Shows Much Land Used by Military," *Gallup Gazette*, 31 December 1942, Folder 5815, Vol. 43, New Mexico Adjutant General Records, New Mexico State Records.

5. Vanderbilt, *Survival City*, 27.

6. On conflict over federal land-use policies in the West see L. Warren, *Hunters Game*; Spence, *Dispossessing the Wilderness*; Jacoby, *Crimes against Nature*; Kosek, *Understories*. On conflict over militarization in places other than White Sands see Carr Childers, "Size of the Risk," chapter 4.

7. On the Wise Use movement see Turner, *Promise of Wilderness*.

8. Merrill, *Public Lands*, 66.

9. Davis, *Late Victorian Holocausts*, chapter 4.

10. Brown et al., "Acquisition of Land," 2–6, 2–7, 2–8, 2–9.

11. On deserts in western history see Limerick, *Desert Passages*.

12. Sonnichsen, *Tularosa*, 3, 4–8.

13. Fugate and Chambers, *White Sands Missile Range*, 1–5.

14. Fugate and Chambers, *White Sands Missile Range*, 20–21. Readings for ground water come from several studies done by the U.S. Geological Survey. Those focus on the missile range's Main Post area but also reflect broader trends across the region. See White Sands Missile Range, *Range-Wide Environmental Impact Statement*, 3–16, 3–17, 3–25, 3–26.

15. For the vegetation of New Mexico generally see Dick-Peddle, *New Mexico Vegetation*, 101–44.

16. The historian Dietmar Schneider-Hector has thoughtfully considered the natural history of White Sands National Monument and its floral and faunal characteristics. See Schneider-Hector, *White Sands*, 5–7; Langford, "Holocene History," 31–39.

17. Dick-Peddle, *New Mexico Vegetation*, 47–100.

18. White Sands Missile Range, *Range-Wide Environmental Impact Statement*, 3-84 to 3-93; Southwest Parks, *Checklist of Mammals*.

19. Irwin-Williams, "Post-Pleistocene Archaeology," 31–33; Sale and Gibbs, *Archaeological Survey*, 6–7.

20. MacNeish, *Origins of Agriculture*, 7–9. On the Chihuahua Tradition I take my cues from Irwin-Williams, "Post-Pleistocene Archaeology," 33; Sale and Gibbs, *Archaeological Survey*, 9–11.

21. Perry, *Apache Reservation*, 18, 29–30, 38–42; Cordell, *Ancient Pueblo Peoples*, 148.

22. Weber, *Spanish Frontier*, 116–17; Faunce, "Perception of Landscape, 24–36; Schneider-Hector, *White Sands*, 32, 38–40. On Comanches, Apaches, and New Mexico see esp. Hämäläinen, *Comanche Empire*; DeLay, *War of a Thousand Deserts*. On earlier encounters between Spanish and New Mexico indigenous cultures see Brooks, *Captives and Cousins*.

23. Weber, *Spanish Frontier*, 78–79; Faunce, "Perception of Landscape," 27–36. See also Hämäläinen, *Comanche Empire*. For more on the Mescelaros during Spanish control over New Mexico see Sonnichsen, *Mescalero Apaches*, 23–40. On Apaches in this period generally see Worcester, *Apaches*, 3–49. For more on the history of the Mesilla Valley see Mora, *Border Dilemmas*.

24. For more on the Apaches during the Mexican-American War see DeLay, *War of a Thousand Deserts*. For a more general discussion of New Mexico Indians and the Civil War see C. Roberts and S. Roberts, *New Mexico*, chapter 7. See also Mora, *Border Dilemmas*, 1–102.

25. Schneider-Hector, *White Sands*, 33, 42–44; Faunce, "Perception of Landscape," 54–55, 65–75, 83, 84, 97; Roberts and Roberts, *New Mexico*, 120–23.

26. Schneider-Hector, *White Sands*, 34–42; Faunce, "Perception of Landscape," 49–51.

27. Quoted in Hawthorne-Tagg, *Life Like No Other*, 31; U.S. Department of War, *Reports of Explorations*, 2:6, 24.

28. Faunce, "Perception of Landscape," 59–84.

29. Faunce, "Perception of Landscape," 65–75, 83, 84–97.

30. Faunce, "Perception of Landscape," 115; Hawthorne-Tagg, *Life Like No Other*, 30; Faunce, "Perception of Landscape," 115.

31. Sonnichsen, *Tularosa*, 19–21; Roberts and Roberts, *New Mexico*, 131–32.

32. Faunce, "Perception of Landscape," 123–30.

33. Schneider-Hector, *White Sands*, 44–45; Meinzer and Hare, *Geology and Water Resources*, 20–21, 80–81, 124–25, 134–36; W. Carlos Powell and C. G. Staley, *Report on an Investigation of the Geology and Water Resources of the Tularosa Basin, New Mexico* (1928), 30, 40, Box 54, Folder 1403, New Mexico State Engineer Records, New Mexico State Records Center and Archives; W. Carlos Powell, *Tularosa Basin Investigation* (1930), Box 54, Folder 1412, New Mexico State Engineer Records, New Mexico State Records.

34. Gibbens et al., "Vegetation Changes," 651, 656; Schneider-Hector, *White Sands*, 18; Hawthorne, *Life Like No Other*, 21–22.

35. Gibbens et al., "Vegetation Changes," 657–62.

36. Gibbens et al., "Vegetation Changes," 657–62; On regional desertification, see Huenneke et al., "Desertification Alters Patterns," 247, 262.

37. U.S. Department of Agriculture, *Climatological Data*; Hawthorne, *Life Like No Other*, 30–31.

38. Schneider-Hector, *White Sands*, 18; *Albuquerque Morning Democrat*, 13 January 1889, 2, Box 11, Folder 104, Work Projects Administration Collection, New Mexico State Records; Hawthorne-Tagg, *Life Like No Other*, 31; Dave Cushman, "Later Pioneer Recalls Major Drought of 1900," *Sierra County Sentinel*, 17 August 1967, Box 3, Folder 87, Lucien A. File Research Files, New Mexico State Records; Hawthorne-Tagg, *Life Like No Other*, 30–31.

39. Quoted in Hawthorne-Tagg, *Life Like No Other*, 31, 143; Walker and Lantow, *Preliminary Study*, 25.
40. Lantow and Cunningham, *Emergency Feeding of Livestock*, 1–6; Di Matteo, quoted in Eidenbach and Morgan, *Homes on the Range*, 9–11.
41. U.S. Department of Agriculture, *Climatological Data*; Hawthorne-Tagg, *Life Like No Other*, 31.
42. Bursum, quoted in Hawthorne-Tagg, *Life Like No Other*, 34; Holm Bursum, interview by Beth Morgan, 7 February 1994, Box 2, Folder 5, White Sands Missile Range Oral History Legacy Project, Rio Grande Historical Collections, New Mexico State University Library, Las Cruces (hereafter Rio Grande Historical Collections). The Rio Grande Historical Collections holds a significant number of interviews that tell the personal stories of ranching in south-central New Mexico before World War II. See also Eidenbach and Morgan, *Homes on the Range*.
43. Governor Richard Dillon to Arthur Hyde, Secretary of Agriculture, 16 September 1930, Box 3, Folder 117, Governor Richard C. Dillon Papers, New Mexico State Records.
44. For more on federal grazing policy and western ranchers see Merrill, *Public Lands*.
45. Fred Sherman, Secretary Treasurer, Southwestern Grazing District Number Three, to Hatchet Cattle Company, 16 October 1935, Box 14, Folder 8, Mahlon T. Everhart Papers, Archives and Special Collections, New Mexico State University Library; J. E. Stablein, Division of Grazing, Department of the Interior, to The Bursum Company, 16 May 1936, Box 11, Folder 10, Holm O. Bursum Papers, Archives and Special Collections Department, New Mexico State University Library; Grover and Musick, "Shrubland Encroachment," 310–12; Hawthorne-Tagg, *Life Like No Other*, 21–22.
46. Buffington and Herbel, "Vegetational Changes," 162; Gibbens et al., "Vegetation Changes," 664–66.
47. Department of Interior Bureau of Land Management, "Table of Public Land Orders, 1942–1950," http://www.blm.gov/pgdata/etc/medialib/blm/wo/MINERALS__REALTY__AND_RESOURCE_PROTECTION_/lands_and_realty/public_land_orders.Par.66612.File.dat/1942–50. (accessed 7 May 2008); Second War Powers Act, 27 March 1942, Title II, 56 Stat. 176, 177, 50 U.S.C. App. 632.
48. G. Nash, *American West Transformed*, vii, 218, 223; U.S. Department of Interior, "Table of Public Land Orders, 1942–1950," http://www.blm.gov/pgdata/etc/medialib/blm/wo/MINERALS__REALTY__AND_RESOURCE_PROTECTION_/lands_and_realty/public_land_orders.Par.66612.File.dat/1942–50.pdf (accessed 7 May 2008); U.S. Department of Commerce, *United States Census of Population, 1950*, 31–15.

49. Eidenbach, *Star Throwers*, 13; Executive Order 9029, *Federal Register* 7, no. 15 (January 22, 1942): 443, Hawthorne-Tagg, *Life Like No Other*, 160–61.

50. "Condemnation Suit Filed for Bomb Range," *Santa Fe New Mexican*, 19 May 1942, Folder 5833, Vol. 70, New Mexico Adjutant General Records, New Mexico State Records; "Bombing Range Bill Introduced," *Albuquerque Journal*, 17 June 1942, Folder 5833, Vol. 70, New Mexico Adjutant General Records, New Mexico State Records.

51. Henry Stimson, Secretary of War, to Governor John Dempsey, 8 January 1943, Box 4, Folder 9, Governor John J. Dempsey Papers, New Mexico State Records.

52. *Taylor Grazing Act, U.S. Code*, vol. 43, secs. 315–315r.

53. R. G. Walker, Chairman, Otero County Board of Commissioners, Mose Cauthen, President, Alamogordo Chamber of Commerce, E. D. McKinley, Mayor, Alamogordo, New Mexico, to Henry L. Stimson, Secretary of War, 30 October 1942, Folder 326, Box 9, Governor John E. Miles Papers, New Mexico Adjutant General Records, New Mexico State Records.

54. Hawthorne-Tagg, *Life Like No Other*, 164; New Mexico Cattle Growers Association, Resolution no. 1, 17 December 1941, Folder 109, Box 3, Governor John E. Miles Papers, New Mexico Adjutant General Records, New Mexico State Records; "No Ranges for Stockmen Facing Eviction by Army," *Hobbs Daily News-Sun*, 5 October 1943, Folder 5816, Vol. 44, New Mexico Adjutant General Records, New Mexico State Records.

55. Lewis N. Gillis, President, Alamogordo Chamber of Commerce, to El Paso, Texas, Chamber of Commerce, 18 August 1943, Box 4, Folder 9, Governor John J. Dempsey Papers, New Mexico State Records.

56. A. B. Cox quoted in "38 Ranchers Protests Gunnery Range Proposal in Southeast Otero County," *Carlsbad Daily Current-Argus*, 10 September 1943, Folder 5833, Vol. 70, New Mexico Adjutant General Records, New Mexico State Records; "State Press Comment," *Albuquerque Journal*, 15 September 1943, Folder 5833, Vol. 70, New Mexico Adjutant General Records, New Mexico State Records.

57. Quoted in Carr Childers, "Size of the Risk," 239, 242–43. See chapter 4 generally.

58. "38 Ranchers Protests"; "Hardship on Ranchers," *Carlsbad Daily Current-Argus*, 12 September 1943, Folder 5816, Vol. 44, New Mexico Adjutant General Records, New Mexico State Records; "Gunnery Range Order 'Awful,'" *Santa Fe New Mexican*, 30 September 1943, Folder 5833, Vol. 70, New Mexico Adjutant General Records, New Mexico State Records; "Bomb Missed Its Target, Started Large Grass Fire," *Tucumcari American*, 5 March 1945, Folder 5833, Vol. 70, New Mexico Adjutant General Records, New Mexico State Records; "Stray Bullets Menace Lives in Range Area," *Carlsbad Daily-Current Argus*, 5 December 1943, Folder 5833, Vol. 70, New Mexico Adjutant General Records, New Mexico State Records. On McCarran in Nevada see Carr Childers, "Size of the Risk," chap. 4.

59. Eidenbach, *Star Throwers*, 15–23; Brown et al., "Acquisition of Land," 2–8, 2–9.

60. Eunice Brown et al., "White Sands History, Range Beginnings and Early Missile Testing" (1959 Historical Report), 14–16. This document can be found in the WSMR Public Affairs Office, White Sands Missile Range. The Department of Interior also got wind of the plan. See Schneider-Hector, *White Sands*, 132–34, 213 note 4.

61. E. Brown et al., "White Sands History," 14–16; Brown et al., "Acquisition of Land," 2–6, 2–7, 2–1, 2–8, 2–9; Hawthorne-Tagg, *Life Like No Other*, 165–66.

62. Brown et al., "Acquisition of Land," 2–6, 2–7, 2–8, 2–9.

63. Brown et al., "Acquisition of Land," 2–9; "3,000-Mile Rocket Ground Asked; Missile of 500 Miles Likely in '49," *New York Times*, 15 February 1949, 1; Hanson Baldwin, "Fort Bliss Is Expanding, It and White Sands Proving Ground Are Turning Area into Great Military Center," *New York Times*, 30 January 1949, 13.

64. Brown et al., "Acquisition of Land," 2–1, 2–8, 2–9, 2–10; Public Land Order, "Withdrawing Public Lands for Use of Department of the Army for Military Purposes, Public Land Order 833," *Federal Register* 17 (27 May 1953): 4822–33.

65. Acquisition Tract Register/Project Ownership Map, Holloman Air Force Base and Bombing Range, 6 September 1951, White Sands Missile Range Oral History Legacy Project, 1981–1997, Oversize, Archives and Special Collections, New Mexico State University Library.

66. Harry F. Lee to Bruce King, Governor of New Mexico, 5 May 1971, Box 54, Folder 1303, Governor Bruce King Papers, 1st Term, New Mexico State Records; U.S. General Accounting Office, *Acquisitions of Properties*, 1, 2.

67. Faunce, *Fort Bliss Preacquisition Project*, 120–25.

68. J. H. McLaughlin, Chairman, Dona Ana County Commissioners, to John Dempsey, Governor of New Mexico, 21 April 1943, Box 4, Folder 9, Governor John J. Dempsey Papers, New Mexico State Records; E. L. Rawlings, President, Las Cruces Lions Club, to John Dempsey, Governor of New Mexico, 27 April 1945, Box 4, Folder 9, Governor John J. Dempsey Papers, New Mexico State Records; "State Highway Office Joins Protest against Bombing Range," *Albuquerque Journal*, 29 April 1945, Folder 5833, Vol. 70, New Mexico Adjutant General Records, New Mexico State Records.

69. Mrs. Beasely, quoted in Faunce, *Fort Bliss Preacquisition Project*, 121,122,123.

70. Colonel Robert Cron, Army Corps of Engineers, District Office, to Senator Dennis Chavez, 3 October 1956, Box 141, Folder 29, Dennis Chávez Papers, Center for Southwest Research, University Libraries, University of New Mexico, Albuquerque (hereafter Center for Southwest Research); Tom Bell to Senator Dennis Chavez, 26 September 1956, Box 141, Folder 29, Dennis Chávez Papers, Center for Southwest Research.

71. "Public Hearing on the 3¼ Million Acre Army Bombing Range," 3 July 1948, Box 5, Folder: General Files, Alamogordo, Record Group 49, Records of the Bureau

of Land Management, National Archives, Rocky Mountain Division, Denver (hereafter National Archives).

72. G. W. Evans, President, New Mexico Cattle Growers Association, to Members of the New Mexico Cattle Growers Association, 31 December 1948, Box 5, Folder: Alamogordo Bombing Range 2, Record Group 49, Records of the Bureau of Land Management, National Archives; E. R. Smith, Regional Administrator for New Mexico, to Roscoe E. Bell, Associate Director of the Bureau of Land Management, 26 January 1949, Box 5, Folder: Alamogordo Bombing Range 2, Record Group 49, Records of the Bureau of Land Management, National Archives.

73. Southeastern Grazing Association to Julius A. Krug, Secretary of the Interior, 11 December 1948, Box 1, Folder 3, Southeastern New Mexico Grazing Association Records, Ms 35, Rio Grande Historical Collections.

74. Roscoe E. Bell, Associate Director of the Bureau of Land Management, to Thomas A. Young, Legislative and Liaison Division, Department of the Army, 24 January 1949, Box 5, Folder: Alamogordo Bombing Range 2, Record Group 49, Records of the Bureau of Land Management, National Archives; E. R. Smith, Regional Administrator for New Mexico, to Roscoe E. Bell, Associate Director of the Bureau of Land Management, 24 January 1949, Box 5, Folder: Alamogordo Bombing Range 2, Record Group 49, Records of the Bureau of Land Management, National Archives.

75. Seth, quoted in "Cattlemen Will Fight, Says Seth," *Albuquerque Journal*, 16 February 1949, Box 5, Folder: Alamogordo Bombing Range 2, Record Group 49, Records of the Bureau of Land Management, National Archives.

76. Riss Bishop to Julius A. Krug, Secretary of Interior, 24 January 1949, Box 5, Folder: Alamogordo Bombing Range 2, Record Group 49, Records of the Bureau of Land Management, National Archives.

77. Quoted in Hawthorne-Tagg, *Life Like No Other*, 165–66. Numbers of those who lost lands vary by source and year. Numbers for 1945 are slightly lower than numbers given by historians for total lands taken in 1952. See Szasz, *Day the Sun Rose Twice*, 30; "White Sands Proving Ground Ledger Papers," 1945, Box-0524–1, Oversize, Rio Grande Historical Collections.

78. Faunce, *Fort Bliss Preacquisition Project*, 124–25; Sonnichsen, *Tularosa*, 285–91.

79. "Senator Chavez' Land Statement Amazes Walker," *Albuquerque Journal*, 26 April 1957, 46, Box 4, Folder: McGregor Range 1950–61, Record Group 49, Records of the Bureau of Land Management, National Archives.

80. Mayor Mike F. Apodoca, Las Cruces, to Senator Dennis Chavez, 28 December 1954, Box 192, Folder 6, Dennis Chávez Papers, Center for Southwest Research; White Sands Missile Range, Information Office, "Release No. 331," Box 192, Folder 6, Dennis Chávez Papers, Center for Southwest Research; U.S. Department of Commerce, *United States Census of Population, 1960*, 33–15.

2. ATOMIC ATTRACTIONS

1. "First Atomic Bomb Crater to Disappear," *Los Angeles Times*, 5 July 1953, 9.
2. A. P. Grider and Fritz Heilbronn to Hillory A. Tolson, Director of the National Park Service, 11 August 1945, Box 382, Folder L58, Record Group 79, National Park Service, Southwest Office, National Archives, Rocky Mountain Division (hereafter RG79, NPS, SWO, NARA-Denver).
3. U.S. Congress, House, "A Bill to Establish the Trinity Atomic National Monument at Trinity in the State of New Mexico, and for other purposes," Box 382, Folder L58 D, RG79, NPS, NARA-Denver (1947–1953); M. R. Tillotson to Regional Director, NPS, Memorandum, 12 March 1952, Box 382 Folder L58 D, RG79, NPS, SWO, NARA-Denver (1947–53). The firing records for the years 1945–77 are available at http://wsmr-history.org/History.htm (accessed 7 June 2008); a hardcopy version of those records is available in the White Sands Missile Range Museum Archives, document 03.003.001. For concerns about radioactivity see *Report of the Field Conference at Trinity Atomic Site* (Draft), 20 May 1952, Box 382, Folder L58 D, RG79, NPS, NARA-Denver (1947–53).
4. Szasz, *Day the Sun Rose Twice*, 3.
5. Kingsland, *Evolution of American Ecology*, 8, but also see chapter 6 more generally; Worster, *Nature's Economy*, 363–64.
6. Worster, *Nature's Economy*, 342, 343–44; see also Kingsland, *Evolution of American Ecology*.
7. Hevly and Findlay, *Atomic West*, 5–6; Kosek, *Understories*, 230.
8. Hevly and Findlay, *Atomic West*, 5. The Nevada Test Site Oral History Project at the University of Nevada at Las Vegas has recently engaged in the social and cultural history of the Nevada Test Site. See *Nevada Test Site Oral History Project*, 2008, http://digital.library.unlv.edu/ntsohp/ (accessed 24 January 2013).
9. Outside money was most notable in places like Las Vegas, but it also affected the relationship between local businesses and larger hotel chains and other businesses in places like Santa Fe. See Rothman, *Devil's Bargains*.
10. Gottdiener, Collins, and Dickens, *Las Vegas*, 79; Chas, *Picturing Las Vegas*, 36; Gladwin Hall, "Viewing the Atom Explosions," *New York Times*, 27 April 1952, X18. On Los Alamos and the Manhattan Project see Rhodes, *Making the Atomic Bomb*; Hunner, *Inventing Los Alamos*.
11. The best treatment of Trinity remains Szasz, *Day the Sun Rose Twice*.
12. Szasz, *Day the Sun Rose Twice*, 27–31.
13. Szasz, *Day the Sun Rose Twice*, 67–78, 87, 123; Hacker, *Dragon's Tail*, 87, 89, 93; Colonel Stafford Warren, Chief, Medical Section, Manhattan Engineer District, to Major General Leslie R. Groves, 16 May 1945, Ferenc Szasz Trinity Papers, Unprocessed Collection, Center for Southwest Research. A roentgen

is an internationally recognized measurement of ionizing radiation used in assaying exposure to gamma radiation or x-radiation.

14. L. Don Leet, quoted in Szasz, *Day the Sun Rose Twice*, 83, 87.

15. Hoffman, *Nuclear Explosion*, 6–8; Szasz, *Day the Sun Rose Twice*, 115.

16. Quoted in Hacker, *Dragon's Tail*, 163–64; Meinhold and Taschner, "Brief History of Radiation," 116–23.

17. Quoted in Hacker, *Dragon's Tail*, 103; Hoffman, *Nuclear Explosion*, 6–9, 10, 11; Hacker, *Dragon's Tail*, 99, 100–101, 103; Szasz, *Day the Sun Rose Twice*, 126.

18. Hoffman, *Nuclear Explosion*, 12.

19. Stafford L. Warren to Leslie Groves, 21 July 1945, Ferenc Szasz Trinity Papers, Unprocessed Collection, Center For Southwest Research.

20. Hoffman, *Nuclear Explosion*, 18, 28–32, 33; Szasz, *Day the Sun Rose Twice*, 127.

21. Hempelmann, *Nuclear Explosion*, 7, 6–9.

22. Szasz, *Day the Sun Rose Twice*, 132; Hempelmann, *Nuclear Explosion*, 15–18, 70–74, 82.

23. Hempelmann, *Nuclear Explosion*, 66–75; Szasz, *Day the Sun Rose Twice*, 131–32.

24. Hempelmann, *Nuclear Explosion*, 71–74, 82; Szasz, *Day the Sun Rose Twice*, 133–34.

25. Szasz, *Day the Sun Rose Twice*, 136–37.

26. *Trinity Survey Program*, 54, 59–60.

27. S. Warren, *1948 Radiological and Biological Survey*, 6–22.

28. Abersold and Moon, *July 16th Explosion*, 3–6; Larson et al., *Alpha Activity*, 7, 32, 34–35.

29. *Trinity Survey Program*, 1, 4, 12.

30. Larson et al., *Alpha Activity*, 11, 7, 13, 32, 40.

31. Larson et al., *1949 and 1950 Radiological Soils Survey*, 16–17, 20–21 27, 28, 35, 36. 77–78, 80–81, 43, 76, 36–43, 71, 78–79.

32. Otherwise unidentified newspaper article, "Dempsey Backs Plan for Bomb Site," n.d., Box 382, Folder L58, RG79, NPS, NARA-Denver (1945); Charles S. McCullom to Senator Carl Hatch, 16 August 1945, Box 382, Folder L58, RG79, NPS, NARA-Denver (1945).

33. Thomas Ewing Dabney, "Red Hair of Hereford Cattle in Region Surrounding Site of Atomic Bomb Test in New Mexico Turns White," *New Mexico Stockman*, November 1945, Ferenc Szasz Trinity Papers, Unprocessed Collection, Center For Southwest Research; "Believe Atomic Dust Responsible for Gray Cattle," *Santa Fe New Mexican*, 18 December 1945, Box 382, Folder L58, RG79, NPS, SWO, NARA-Denver (1945); "Cattle Change Color in Region of Alamo Atomic Bomb Test," *Alamogordo News*, 8 November 1945, Box 382, Folder L58, RG79, NPS, SWO, NARA-Denver (1945); "Will Test Atom-Blasted Cows," *Santa Fe New Mexican*, 12 December 1945, Box 382, Folder L58, RG79, NPS, SWO, NARA-Denver (1945); Peter Edson, "Desert Sand in New Mexico Turned into Glass by Heat of

A-Bomb," *Visalia Times-Delta*, ca. 19 September 1945, Box 382, Folder L58, RG79, NPS, SWO, NARA-Denver (1945).; G. Millard Hunsley, "Big Saucer-Like Crater Marks Site of Bomb Test," *Albuquerque Journal*, 12 September 1945, Box 382, Folder L58, RG79, NPS, SWO, NARA-Denver (1945). See also Scrapbook, Serial 5834, Vol. 71, Subseries 18.3.10, New Mexico Adjutant General Records, New Mexico State Records.

34. Abe Fortas, Acting Secretary of the Interior, to Senator Carl Hatch, 21 September 1945, Box 382, Folder L58, RG79, NPS, NARA-Denver (1945); Memorandum for the Commissioner, General Land Office, 31 October 1945, Box 382, Folder L58, RG79, NPS, SWO, NARA-Denver (1945).

35. Otherwise unidentified newspaper article, "Survey Delayed of Atomic Site," 26 September 1945, Box 382, Folder L58, RG79, NPS, NARA-Denver (1945); Newton Drury, Director, National Park Service, to John Dempsey, Governor of New Mexico, 31 October, 1945, Box 382, Folder L58, RG79, NPS, SWO, NARA-Denver (1945); E. T. Scoyen, Acting Regional Director, NPS, Region Three, to Carroll L. Tyler, Manager, AEC Project, 26 September 1947, Box 382, Folder L58 D, NARA-Denver (1947–53).

36. Harold Ickes, Secretary of Interior, to Robert Patterson, Secretary of War, 28 January 1946, Box 382, Folder L58, RG79, NPS, NARA-Denver (1946); Julius A. Krug, Secretary of the Interior, to Robert Patterson, ca. April 1946, Box 382, Folder L58, RG79, NPS, SWO, NARA-Denver (1946); U.S. Congress, Senate, "A Bill to Provide for the Reservation and Maintenance of the B-29 bomber from which an atomic bomb was dropped on the city of Hiroshima and for its eventually being displayed near Alamogordo, New Mexico, at the site of the detonation of the first Atomic Bomb," 79th Cong., 2nd sess., S. 2054, 11 April 1946, copy in Box 382, Folder L58, RG79, NPS, NARA-Denver (1946).

37. M. R. Tillotson, Regional Director, Region Three, NPS, Memorandum for the Director, 1 August 1946, Box 382, Folder L58, RG79, NPS, NARA-Denver (1946).

38. Julius A. Krug to Harry Truman, ca. 1946, Box 382, Folder L58, RG79, NPS, NARA-Denver (1946); Szasz, *Day the Sun Rose Twice*, 164; John E. Kell, Park Planner, NPS, to Milton J. McColm, Regional Chief, Land Division, Memorandum, 15 November 1950, Box 382, Folder L58 D, RG79, NPS, NARA-Denver (1947–53); E. T. Scoyen, Memorandum for the Director, NPS, 14 April 1947, Box 382, Folder L58 D, RG79, NPS, NARA-Denver (1947–53).

39. E. T. Scoyen to Carroll L. Tyler, Manager, AEC Project, 26 September 1947, Box 382, Folder L58 D, RG79, NPS, NARA-Denver (1947–53); Scoyen, Memorandum for the Director, 14 April 1947; Ronald Lee, Acting Director, NPS, to Regional Director, Region Three, ca. April 1947, Box 382, Folder L58 D, RG79, NPS, SWO, NARA-Denver (1947–53); Ronald Lee, Chief Historian, NPS, Memorandum for the Director, 7 October 1947, Box 382, Folder L58 D, RG79, NPS, SWO, NARA-Denver (1947–53).

40. Scoyen, Memorandum for the Director, 14 April 1947; Lee to Regional Director, ca. April 1947; Ronald Lee, Chief Historian, NPS, Memorandum for the Director, 7 October 1947, Box 382 Folder L58 D, RG79, NPS, SWO, NARA-Denver (1947–53); Scoyen to Tyler, 26 September 1947.

41. E. T. Scoyen, Acting Regional Director, NPS, to Arthur Demaray, Associate Director, 8 August 1946, Box 382, Folder L58 RG 79, NPS, SWO, NARA-Denver (1946); George Kraker, Deputy Manager, AEC, to P. P. Patraw, 24 October 1952, Box 382, Folder L58 D, RG79, NPS, SWO, NARA-Denver (1947–53); P. P. Patraw, Assistant Regional Director, National Park Service, to George P. Kraker, Deputy Manager, Atomic Energy Commission, 29 October 1952, Box 382 Folder L58 D, RG79, NPS, SWO, NARA-Denver (1947–53); P. P. Patraw to Superintendent, White Sands National Monument, 29 October 1952, Box 382, Folder L58 D, RG79, NPS, SWO, NARA-Denver (1947–53).

42. B. O. Wells, Director of Security, Holloman Air Force Base, to Commanding Officer, Holloman Air Force Base, ca. 1947, Box 382, Folder L58 D, RG79, NPS, SWO, NARA-Denver (1947–53); Albert Bellamy, Chief, Alamogordo Section, Atomic Energy Project to James Jensen, Assistant Director of Medicine and Biology, AEC, 6 October 1948, Ferenc Szasz Trinity Papers, Unprocessed Collection, Center For Southwest Research.

43. Lee, Memorandum for the Director, 7 October 1947.

44. Charles Porter III, Acting Chief Historian, NPS, to Director, 27 December 1951, Box 382, Folder L58 D, RG79, NPS, NARA-Denver (1947–53).

45. M. R. Tillotson to Regional Director, NPS, Memorandum, 12 March 1952, Box 382 Folder L58 D, RG79, NPS, SWO, NARA-Denver (1947–53); Jerome C. Miller, Regional Landscape Architect, NPS, to Assistant Regional Director, 20 March 1953, Box 382, Folder L58 D, RG79, NPS, NARA-Denver (1947–53); George P. Kraker, Deputy Manager, Santa Fe Operations Office, to Ralph P. Johnson, Deputy Director, Office of Engineering and Construction, 31 March 1953, Box 382, Folder L58 D, RG79, NPS, SWO, NARA-Denver (1947–53).

46. U.S. Congress, House, "A Bill to Establish the Trinity Atomic National Monument at Trinity in the State of New Mexico, and for other purposes," copy in Box 382, Folder L58 D, RG79, NPS, NARA-Denver (1947–53); Oscar Chapman, Secretary of the Interior, to John Murdock, Chairman, Committee on Interior and Insular Affairs, U.S. Congress, House of Representatives, June 1952, Box 382, Folder L58 D, RG79, NPS, NARA-Denver (1947–53).

47. Hugh Miller, Acting Regional Director, NPS, to Captain Carroll Tyler, Manager, Santa Fe Operations Office, AEC, 21 April 1952, Box 382, Folder L58 D, RG79, NPS, NARA-Denver (1947–53); Welsh, *Dunes and Dreams*, 298.

48. *Report of the Field Conference at Trinity Atomic Site* (Draft), 20 May 1952, Box 382, Folder L58 D, RG79, NPS, NARA-Denver (1947–53).

49. C. Edward Graves to NPS, 26 October 1946, Box 382, Folder L58, RG79, NPS, SWO, NARA-Denver (1946).

50. Colonel Homer D. Thomas to P. P. Patraw, Assistant Regional Director, NPS, 15 October 1952, Box 382 Folder L58 D, RG79, NPS, SWO, NARA-Denver (1947–53); Colonel Homer D. Thomas to P. P. Patraw, Acting Regional Director, NPS, 18 March 1953, Box 382 Folder L58 D, RG79, NPS, SWO, NARA-Denver (1947–53); "The First Atomic Bomb," *Wind and Sand*, 30 September 1966, Lucien A. File Research Files, New Mexico State Records.

51. William E. Brown to Jack Turney, Superintendent, White Sands National Monument (WSNM), 20 December 1967, WHSA/WSNM Vertical Files, Folder: Trinity Site Keyman Project, WSNM NM (hereafter Trinity Site Keyman Project).

52. "Draft Statement for forwarding memo or as detachable part of report on urgency of preservation (interim) and need for NPS presence at Trinity Site," ca. March 1968, WHSA/WSNM Vertical Files, Folder: Trinity Site Keyman Project.

53. Park Naturalist to Superintendent, WSNM, Memorandum: notes from trip to Trinity Site, 17 January 1967, WHSA/WSNM Vertical Files, Folder: Trinity Site Keyman Project; Welsh, *Dunes and Dreams*, 160.

54. Fey, *Health Physics Survey*, 1, 7; Hakonson and Johnson, "Distribution of Environmental Plutonium," 242, 244–47.

55. National Park Service, "A Master Plan for the Trinity National Historic Site," March 1970, NPS, WHSA Files, NPS Southwest Regional Office, 10, 4, 12–15.

56. Trinity was redesignated a National Historic Site in 1975.

57. Theodore S. Thompson, Director, Southwest Division, NPS, to Associate Director, Professional Services, WASO, 14 July 1973, WHSA/WSNM Vertical Files, Folder: Historic Site Correspondence, White Sands National Monument, New Mexico.

58. Bill Fischling, "America's Ground Zero: Trinity Opens for Atomic Anniversary," *Washington Post*, 16 July 1995, 4; Katherine Saltzstein, "Protester Spills 'Symbolic Blood' at A-bomb site," *Chicago Sun-Times*, 17 July 1995, 19.

59. Szasz, *Day the Sun Rose Twice*, 89; Fischling, "America's Ground Zero," 4; Saltzstein, "Protestor Spills 'Symbolic Blood,'" 19; "Thousands Gather at First A-Bomb Site, 50 Years On," *Advertiser* (Adelaide, South Australia), 18 July 1995. On *Enola Gay* vandalism, see "3 Guilty in Enola Gay Vandalism," *Washington Post*, 3 August 1995. The *Enola Gay* exhibition was one of the most controversial events at the Smithsonian's National Air and Space Museum as World War II veterans groups clashed with historians over interpretations of the use of nuclear weapons as triumphant or troubling. See Linenthal and Engelhardt, *History Wars*.

60. Ben MacIntyre, "Blood, Protest Mark A-Bomb's 50 Years," *Australian* (Sydney), 18 July 1995.

61. White Sands Missile Range, "Trinity Site, 1945–1995" (WSMR Brochure, 1995). The author retains a copy of this document.

62. See White Sands Missile Range History, "Firing Records," http://wsmr-history
.org/History.htm (accessed 7 June 2008).

3. BOUNDARIES

1. Hanson W. Baldwin, "Wild V-2 Rocket 'Invades' Mexico; Backtracks in a White
Sands Test," *New York Times*, 30 May 1947, 1; Hanson W. Baldwin, "Scientists
Track Wild V-2 Rocket as Crowds Visit Crater in Juarez," *New York Times*, 31
May 1947, 14; "Impact of 4.5-Ton Rocket Caused Panic in Juárez," *Albuquerque
Journal*, 1 June 1947.
2. Vargas, quoted in "Impact of 4.5-Ton Rocket"; "U.S. Sends Regrets to Mexican
Officials," *Albuquerque Journal*, 1 June 1947.
3. Vanderbilt, *Survival City*, 39.
4. On nuclear landscapes in the West see Makhijani, Hu, and Yih, *Nuclear Waste-
lands*; Ackland, *Making a Real Killing*; Kuletz, *Tainted Desert*; Amundson,
Yellowcake Towns; Eichstaedt and Haynes, *If You Poison Us*; Pasternak, *Yellow
Dirt*; Ringholz, *Uranium Frenzy*; Heefner, *Missile Next Door*; Hevly and Findlay,
Atomic West.
5. The firing records for the period from 1945 to 1977 can be found in Doc. 03.003.001,
White Sands Missile Range Museum and Archives; they are also available online
at http://www.wsmr-history.org/History.htm (accessed 1 March 2008). The
author holds his Freedom of Information Act request. For more on the history
of rocket and missile technology see Chun, *Thunder over the Horizon*; Emme,
History of Rocket Technology.
6. Other historians have offered a similar approach to rethinking the history of
earth photography and its ties to environmentalism. Maher, "On Shooting the
Moon"; Poole, *Earthrise*; Kirk, *Counterculture Green*.
7. Holliday, "Seeing the Earth." The Applied Physics Laboratory (APL) at Johns
Hopkins University, which played a central role in early earth photography, first
distributed "V-2 Rocket-Eye View from 60 Miles Up" in a souvenir pamphlet
titled "Columbus Was Right!" See Poole, *Earthrise*, 58–59.
8. The APL explained that the image was approximately eight hundred thousand
square miles. *National Geographic* published the number as one million square
miles. I have used the more conservative number. See the image itself and Holliday, "Seeing the Earth," 524.
9. Holliday, "Seeing the Earth," 524.
10. Holliday, "Seeing the Earth," 524.
11. Other clear images include a north-to-south image shot from an Aerobee Rocket
that accompanied "V-2 Rocket-Eye View from 60 Miles Up" in the *National
Geographic* article. See Holliday, "Seeing the Earth," 524–25.
12. DeVorkin, *Science with a Vengeance*, 144–45.

13. The story of the V-2 rocket scientists and Wernher Von Braun at White Sands can be found in Ward, *Dr. Space*; see chapters 7 and 8. For a broader discussion of the early history of missile testing at White Sands see Eidenbach, *Star Throwers*.

14. Ley, *Rockets, Missiles, and Space Travel*, 247–54; Richie, *Space Flight*, 30–31.

15. Information Office, White Sands Missile Range, Fact Sheet: "V-2 Story," June 1972, Doc. 97.007.003, White Sands Missile Range Museum and Archives.

16. "25 V-2 Rocket Flight Tests Set for White Sands," *Albuquerque Journal*, 1 April 1946, Box 5833, Serial 4972, New Mexico Adjutant General Records, New Mexico State Records; "Formal Testing of V-2 Rocket Due Tomorrow," *Santa Fe New Mexican*, 9 May 1946; Box 5833, Serial 4972, New Mexico Adjutant General Records, New Mexico State Records; Ordnance Department, "Army Ordnance Department Guided Missiles Program," 1 January 1948, Doc. 97.012, White Sands Missile Range Museum and Archives; "V-2's to Radio Data on 100-Mile Leap," *New York Times*, 1 April 1946, 14; "Machine Computes Rocket Fire Data," *New York Times*, 12 April 1946, 11; "V-2 Reaches 104 Miles," *New York Times*, 31 July 1946, 6; "Armed Forces Send V-2 Rocket 102 Mi. High in New Mexico, Attain Rate of 3,600 M.P.H.," *New York Times*, 11 October 1946, 3; "V-2 Reaches 102 Miles in 12th Test at WSPG," *Las Vegas Sun-News*, 10 October 1946, Box 5833, Serial 4972, New Mexico Adjutant General Records, New Mexico State Records; "Rocket Sent Up at 3,600 Miles per Hour," *Las Vegas Daily Optic*, 12 October 1946, Box 5833, Serial 4972, New Mexico Adjutant General Records, New Mexico State Records; "New Navy Rocket Hits 3,000 Miles an Hour at Height of 78 Miles, an American Record," *New York Times*, 7 March 1948, 3; Ley, *Rockets, Missiles, and Space Travel*, 253–89; Newell, *Beyond the Atmosphere*, 41–42.

17. Gladwin Hill, "Try to Hurl Rocket Slugs into Space, Free of Earth," *New York Times*, 18 December 1946, 1; Gladwin Hill, "Photos Trap Fire of V-2 in Outer Air," *New York Times*, 21 December 1946, 34; "Rocket Would Create Shooting Stars," *Santa Fe New Mexican*, 14 November 1946, Box 5833, Serial 4972, New Mexico Adjutant General Records, New Mexico State Records.

18. Ley, *Rockets, Missiles, and Space Travel*, 290–91.

19. Newell, *Beyond the Atmosphere*, 34, 36, 39–40; Ley, *Rockets, Missiles, and Space Travel*, 254.

20. Quoted in Poole, *Earthrise*, 56–58.

21. Applied Physics Laboratory, Johns Hopkins University, Press Release, 21 November 1946, Doc. 02.037.421, White Sands Missile Range Museum and Archives; Holliday, "Seeing the Earth," 511; "The Horizon as Photographed at an Altitude of 65 miles," Photograph, Doc. 04.072.002, White Sands Missile Range Museum and Archives; Poole, *Earthrise*, 56–63; "Rocket View of Earth," *Albuquerque Journal*, 23 November 1946, Box 5833, Serial 4972, New Mexico Adjutant General Records, New Mexico State Records.

22. T. A. Bergstralh, *Photography from the V-2 Rocket at Altitudes Ranging up to 160 Kilometers* (Washington DC: Naval Research Laboratory, 1947), Doc. 04.072.002, White Sands Missile Range Museum and Archives; Poole, *Earthrise*, 60–61; "Rocket View of the Earth," *New York Times*, 22 March 1947, 12; "Picture of the Week," *Life magazine*, 31 March 1947, 34, 35.

23. Holliday, "Seeing the Earth," 511–21.

24. Poole, *Earthrise*, 60–61; Holliday, "Seeing the Earth," 528.

25. Barnes, *National Geographic Society*, 261; Cosgrove, *Apollo's Eye*, 5.

26. On the promise of nuclear energy at the dawn of the Cold War see Boyer, *By the Bombs Early Light*, 107–30. On big science see generally Galison and Hevly, *Big Science*.

27. Poole, *Earthrise*, 61; Markusen, *Rise of the Gunbelt*.

28. Holliday, "Seeing the Earth," 524. On panoramic photography in the nineteenth-century United States see "A Brief History of Panoramic Photography," Library of Congress, American Memory, accessed 25 May 2012, http://memory.loc.gov /ammem/collections/panoramic_photo/pnhist1.html. An example of the construction of a cyclorama can be found in Boardman and Porch, *Battle of Gettysburg Cyclorama*. On Bierstadt and other western painters see Boime, *Magisterial Gaze*.

29. Nye, *American Technological Sublime*, see especially the introduction and chapter 9; Holliday, "Seeing the Earth," 512. By the mid-1950s scientists were using rockets to follow weather patterns.

30. Nye, *American Technological Sublime*, 255–56; Virilio, *Vision Machine*, 59–60. Aerial photography was used extensively during World War II. See Maslowski, *Armed with Cameras*; Colton, "How We Fight with Photographs," 257–80. Kodak had developed several versions of black-and-white infrared film prior to World War II and had created false-color infrared film during the war; the military used both. See Monmonier, *Spying with Maps*, 43–45; Lindgren, *Land Use Planning*, 16.

31. Holliday, "Seeing the Earth," 512.

32. Waldemar Kaempffert, "Rocket Outpost in Space, Like a Little Moon, Is Being Studied by the Armed Forces," *New York Times*, 2 January 1949, E9; "Scientists Working on 'Space Ship,' Forrestal Report Gives Hint of Satellite Program," *Reading (PA) Eagle*, 16 February 1949, 14; "Scientists Plan 'Space Ship' Capable of 10,000 M.P.H.," *Spokane (WA) Daily Chronicle*, 16 February 1949, 11; "Rocket Soars 250 Miles, Nearly Becomes Satellite," *Pittsburgh Press*, 26 February 1949, 1.

33. On the post-1960 desire to shoot Earth rather than things out there see Maher, "On Shooting the Moon," 526–31. On the abilities of post–World War II telescopes see Zirker, *Acre of Glass*, especially chapter 2 on the Hale Telescope and Palomar Observatory.

34. Holliday, "Seeing the Earth," 512.

35. On Bentham and the Panopticon see Foucault, *Discipline and Punish*, 195–230.

36. Foucault, *Discipline and Punish*, 204.

37. Holliday, "Seeing the Earth," 512.

38. Holliday, "Seeing the Earth," 513.

39. Hubert and Berg, "Rocket Portrait." See also Committee on Scientific Accomplishments, *Earth Observations from Space*; Poole, *Earthrise*, 61–62.

40. See the images in Welsh, *Dunes and Dreams*, 116, 118–19.

41. Pinto, Lenko, Johnson, *Final Environmental Impact Statement*, 76–91; Welsh, *Dunes and Dreams*, 145–47; Schneider-Hector, *White Sands*, 138–54.

42. Newell, *Beyond the Atmosphere*, 42; Memorandum from Johnwill Faris, Superintendent, White Sands National Monument, to General Superintendent, SWNM, 4 March 1953, Box 1, Fold 0–10, RG79, NPS, SWO, NARA-Denver.

43. "Nike-Hercules Hits Near Ranch House," *New York Times*, 21 February 1959, 43.

44. "Missile Escapes Control in the West," *New York Times*, 22 February 1957, 1.

45. *White Sands Missile Range Bulletin*, ca. 1964, File: Missile Mishaps, White Sands Missile Range, Public Affairs Office; "Runaway Army Missile Hits near Creede," *Rocky Mountain News*, 20 November 1964, File: Missile Mishaps, Public Affairs Office, White Sands Missile Range; Bruce Wilkinson, "Misguided Missile Hits Creede Area," *Pueblo Chieftan*, 20 November 1964, File: Missile Mishaps, Public Affairs Office, White Sands Missile Range; "Reward," File 360–5E, Pershing in Mexico, Public Affairs Office, White Sands Missile Range; "The Athena Story," Doc. 97.021.012, White Sands Missile Range Museum and Archives; U.S. Army Missile Command Press Release, File 360–5E, Pershing in Mexico, Public Affairs Office, White Sands Missile Range; "An Errant Missile Lands outside a Town in Texas," *New York Times*, 8 August 1965, 45.

46. "Emergency Parachute Descent Reveals Secret Test Program," *Sarasota (FL) Herald Tribune*, 7 August 1969, 3; "Shroud of Secrecy Envelops 'Firefly,'" *Victoria (TX) Advocate*, 6 August 1969, sec. C, 9.

47. Disposition Form, "Recovery of Second Stage Athena Motors," Public Affairs Office, White Sands Missile Range, 19 September 1979, File: Missile Mishaps, Public Affairs Office, White Sands Missile Range.

48. Disposition Form, "Recovery of Second Stage Athena Motors."

49. Hernández, *Migra!*, 101–217.

50. See Chávez, *"¡Mi Raza Primero!"*; Rosales, *Chicano!*

51. For more on John Pershing see Hurst, *Pancho Villa*.

52. Missile Fact Sheet, Doc. 97–093, n.d, White Sands Missile Range Museum and Archives; Press Release, 12 September 1967, Public Affairs Office, White Sands Missile Range, File 360–5E, Pershing in Mexico, Public Affairs Office, White Sands Missile Range.

53. "En Bosque Bonito el Cayó," *El Fronterizo*, ca. 19 September 1967; see also "Only Fragments Remain of the Rocket," and "The Pershing Fell in Bosque Bonito,"

both in File 360–5E, Pershing in Mexico, Public Affairs Office, White Sands Missile Range.

54. Jorge Mario Rojas Madrigal, "Preliminary Report Concerning the Search and Recovery Operations of the Pershing," 21 September 1967, Doc. 03.032.042, White Sands Missile Range Museum and Archives; Press Releases, Public Affairs Office, White Sands Missile Range, 21 and 22 September 1967, File 360–5E, Pershing in Mexico, Public Affairs Office, White Sands Missile Range.

55. Press Release, 22 September 1967; Press Release, Public Affairs Office, White Sands Missile Range, 23 September 1967, File 360–5E, Pershing in Mexico, Public Affairs Office, White Sands Missile Range; Rojas Madrigal, "Preliminary Report"; "Receipt of Parts Corresponding to the Pershing Missile," 03.032.043, n.d., White Sands Missile Range Museum and Archives.

56. Colonel Dearl Jones to Lieutenant Colonel Jorge Mario Rojas Madrigal, Doc. 03.032.044, n.d., White Sands Missile Range Museum and Archives; From Major General H. G. Davisson to U.S. Ambassador to Mexico, Fulton Freeman, 4 October 1967, Doc. 03.032.045, White Sands Missile Range Museum and Archives; Rojas Madrigal, "Preliminary Report Concerning the Search and Recovery Operations."

57. Guillermo Asunsolo, "Runaway Missile Fragments Found," *El Paso Herald Post*, 13 July 1970, File 360–5E, Public Affairs Office, White Sands Missile Range; "The Athena Story," White Sands Missile Range Museum and Archives, Doc. 97.021.012; "Athena," in "White Sands Missile Range History," White Sands Missile Range Museum and Archives, http://www.wsmr-history.org/History.htm (select by year under "Firing Records Summary"), accessed 27 October 2012.

58. Draft Press Release, Public Affairs Office, White Sands Missile Range, 12 July 1970, Doc. 03.032.073, White Sands Missile Range Museum and Archives; Guill-ermo Asunsolo, "Runaway Missile Fragments Found," *El Paso Herald Post*, 13 July 1970, File 360–5E, Public Affairs Office, White Sands Missile Range; Guillermo Asunsolo, "Expert Reports Cobalt 57 in the Wreckage," *El Paso Herald Post*, 14 July 1970, File 360–5E, Public Affairs Office, White Sands Missile Range.

59. Guillermo Asunsolo, "Expert Reports Cobalt 57"; "Mexicans Seek Lost U.S. Missile," *Washington Post*, 14 July 1970, File 360–5E, Public Affairs Office, White Sands Missile Range; Press Release, n.d., File 360–5E, Public Affairs Office, White Sands Missile Range.

60. Deal et al., "Locating the Lost Athena Missile," 95–98.

61. Deal et al., "Locating the Lost Athena Missile," 95–98.

62. "Personnel and Equipment for Recovery of ATHENA in Mexico," n.d., Doc 03.032.072, White Sands Missile Range Museum and Archives.

63. Memorandum of Telephone Call, Subject: Athena, Doc. 03.032.071, White Sands Missile Range Museum and Archives; Carlos Bustamante, Hand Written Notes

on Recovery of Athena, n.d., 03.032.099, White Sands Missile Range Museum and Archives.

64. Questions and Answer Sheet, n.d., File 360–5E, Public Affairs Office, White Sands Missile Range; "Personnel and Equipment for Recovery of ATHENA; "Mexico Requests WSMR Team Dig Radioactive Soil," *El Paso Times*, 24 September 1970, File 360–5E, Public Affairs Office, White Sands Missile Range.

65. Press Release, Athena-Sand Patch, 2 October 1970, File 360–5E, Public Affairs Office, White Sands Missile Range; Information Plan—Great Sand, File 360–5E, Public Affairs Office, White Sands Missile Range.

66. OCINFO Question Document, 24 September 1970, File 360–5E, Public Affairs Office, White Sands Missile Range.

67. "Radio Active Pieces of Rocket U.S. Lost Found by Mexicans," *New York Times*, 4 August 1970; Table 18 (PIO), File 360–5E, Public Affairs Office, White Sands Missile Range; Information Plan—Great Sand, File 360–5E, Public Affairs Office, White Sands Missile Range.

68. "Extraerán Tierra Contaminada del Lugar Donde Cayó Athena," *El Siglo de Torreón*, 19 August 1970, File 360–5E, Public Affairs Office, White Sands Missile Range; "Se Llevarán a EU la Tierra Contaminada por el Cohete Athena," *La Opinion* (Torreón), 19 August 1970, File 360–5E, Public Affairs Office, White Sands Missile Range; "It Is Rumored That Radioactivity Exists in the Zone of Durango, Mysterious Nasa Convoy Was Expected Last Night in This City," *Correo*, 21 September 1970, trans. Carlos Bustamante, File 360–5E, Public Affairs Office, White Sands Missile Range.

69. H. J. Moore, *Missile Impact Craters*, 6–24, 25, 31–34.

70. Test Directorate, HE Simulation Division, New Mexico Operations Office, Defense Nuclear Agency, *Minor Scale Event: Test Execution Report* (Kirtland Air Force Base, 1986), 1, 122, 276.

71. UXO Hazards and Munitions Management Team, *White Sands Missile Range*; Shearer, *WSMR Unexploded Ordnance*, 3, 9.

72. The New Mexico Progressive Alliance for Community Empowerment and the National Depleted Uranium Citizens' Network of the Military Toxics Project, "Friendly Fire: The Link between Depleted Uranium Munitions and Human Health Risks," prepared by Damacio Lopez, March 1995, 1–2, Box 4, Folder 10, Albuquerque Center for Peace and Justice Records, Center for Southwest Research.

73. Damacio Lopez to the Editor, *Socorro (NM) Defensor Chieftain*, 5 February 1990, 5, Box 6, Folder 17, Citizens for Alternatives to Radioactive Dumping Records, Center for Southwest Research; Joe Gardner Wessely, "Depleted Uranium Weapons and the New Mexico Connection," *Albuquerque Crosswinds Weekly*, 8–9; New Mexico Institute of Mining and Technology, "Handling, Use and Storage of Depleted

Uranium within the Industrial/Research Park and the TERA Test Facilities," March 1986, Box 6, Folder 17, Citizens for Alternatives to Radioactive Dumping Records, Center for Southwest Research. See also "Gulf War II: Propaganda and Mythology about Health Effects of Depleted Uranium," 22 February 2003, http://peaceaware.com/DU/index.htm (accessed 28 January 2008).

74. White Sands Missile Range, *Final Environmental Impact Statement*, 3–216; Van Etten and Purtymun, *Depleted Uranium Investigation*, 1–6; White Sands Missile Range, *Final Environmental Impact Statement*, 3–89.

75. Van Etten and Purtymun, *Depleted Uranium Investigation*, 1–6.

76. Vanderbilt, *Survival City*, 39.

4. A CONSUMER'S LANDSCAPE

1. New Mexico Department of Game and Fish, *Annual Report, 58th Fiscal Year* (1 July 1969–30 June 1970), 12, New Mexico State Library and Archives.

2. White Sands Missile Range, *Final Environmental Impact Statement*, 3–63.

3. Riebsame, Robb, et al., *Atlas of the New West*; for the "Ugly West" see 132–41. On militarized landscapes and wildlife see Havlick, "Logics of Change" Cohn, "New Defenders of Wildlife," 11–14. On "ironic nature" see Wills, "'Welcome to the Atomic Park.'"

4. On postwar leisure hunting see Herman, *Hunting and the American Imagination*, 270.

5. On ideas of ecology and environmental perception see Worster, *Nature's Economy*. On the significance of modern environmental science in shaping the environmental movement of the 1960s and 1970s see Dunlap, *Saving America's Wildlife*. On perceptions of arid landscapes in the West see Limerick, *Desert Passages*; Worster, *Rivers of Empire*; Tyrrell, *True Gardens*.

6. The irruption of introduced species has long influenced ecosystems in the Western Hemisphere. See Crosby, *Ecological Imperialism*; Melville, *Plague of Sheep*; D. Klein, "Introduction, Increase, and Crash."

7. Crosby, *Ecological Imperialism*, chapters 4 and 9; Melville, *Plague of Sheep*; Worster, *Dust Bowl*, 200; C. Young, *In the Absence of Predators*; Dunlap, *Saving America's Wildlife*, chapter 5; Leopold, *Sand County Almanac*, 129–32.

8. Towle, "Authored Ecosystems; Coates, "Improving on 'A Paradise of Game'"; D. Klein, "Introduction, Increase, and Crash."

9. Mungall and Sheffield, *Exotics on the Range*, 8–10, 25–26.

10. Huey, "New New Mexicans," 25–26, 29; "Javelina Released on White Sands Missile Range," *New Mexico Department of Game and Fish News*, 24 March 1970, 1; New Mexico Department of Game and Fish, *Annual Report, 55th Fiscal Year* (1 July 1966–30 June 1967), 16.

11. *The Lacey Act*, U.S. Code 16 (1900) sec. 701 and President, Executive Order, "Exotic Organisms," Executive Order 11987, *Federal Register* 42, no. 101 (25 May 1977), 116.

12. Kirschner Associates, *Study of Recreation and Tourism*, 11C, 16C, 21C; see also Kirkpatrick, *Economic and Social Values*, 64.

13. New Mexico Department of Game and Fish, *Annual Report, 51st Fiscal Year* (1 July 1962–30 June 1963), 5; Huey, "New New Mexicans," 25–26, 29.

14. New Mexico Department of Game and Fish, *Annual Report, 53rd Fiscal Year* (1 July 1964–30 June 1965), 17, and *60th Fiscal Year* (1 July 1971–30 June 1972), 18–19; Huey, "New New Mexicans," 25–26, 29.

15. These are all found in New Mexico Department of Game and Fish, Annual Reports, *51st Fiscal Year* (1 July 1962–30 June 1963), 5, *52nd Fiscal Year* (1 July 1963–30 June 1964), 7, *53rd Fiscal Year* (1 July 1964–30 June 1965); *New Mexico Wildlife Management* (Santa Fe, 1967), 209; NMGF-AR, *56th Fiscal Year* (1 July 1967–30 June 1968), 17; *58th Fiscal Year* (1 July 1969–30 June 1970), 12; Huey, "New New Mexicans," 26; Saiz, *Exotic Mammal Investigations*, 3.

16. Ladd Gordon to Frank Koski, 19 September 1969, National Park Service General Administration Files, 1968–70, folder N16, box 161, RG79, NPS, SWO, NARA-Denver; Tom Ela to Frank Koski, 18 September 1969, National Park Service General Administration Files, 1968–70, folder N16, box 161, RG79, NPS, SWO, NARA-Denver.

17. Charles Hillinger, "Home on the Range—With Ibex, Gembsbok," *Los Angeles Times*, 28 May 1971, 1; Huey, "Promise of Exotic Hunting," 8. Both found in folder 1068, box 42, Governor Bruce King Papers, 1st term, New Mexico State Records.

18. Unidentified newspaper article, "Zoo Director Raps Kudu Disposal," 18 June 1971, folder 1068, box 42, Governor Bruce King Papers, 1st term, New Mexico State Records; Ladd S. Gordon to Eldon Marr, 21 May 1973, folder 755, box 27, Governor Bruce King Papers, 1st term, folder 1068, box 42, New Mexico State Records Center and Archives; Ladd S. Gordon to David King, 11 April 1972, folder 755, box 27, Governor Bruce King Papers, 1st term, New Mexico State Records; Huey, "New New Mexicans," 26.

19. New Mexico Department of Game and Fish, *Annual Report, 58th Fiscal Year* (1 July 1969–30 June 1970), 12; Saiz, *Exotic Mammal Investigations*, 3.

20. Eckles, interview; Huey, "New New Mexicans," 26.

21. Huey, "New New Mexicans," 26; New Mexico Department of Game and Fish, "Position Statement on Exotic and Native Big Game Animal Programs," March 1972, folder 755, box 27, Governor Bruce King Papers, 1st term, New Mexico State Records; Welsh, *Dunes and Dreams*, 172; Matthews, *Where the Buffalo Roam*.

22. Huey, "New New Mexicans," 26; New Mexico Department of Game and Fish, "Position Statement on Exotic"; Thomas Cornish to Bruce King, 3 March 1972, folder 755, box 27, Governor Bruce King Papers, 1st term, New Mexico State Records.

23. New Mexico Department of Game and Fish, "Exotic Big Game Animal Program," 13 December 1971, folder 1068, box 42, Governor Bruce King Papers, 1st term, New Mexico State Records; New Mexico Department of Game and Fish, *Annual*

Report, 72nd Fiscal Year (1 July 1983–30 June 1984), 20. All license numbers collected here are based on the New Mexico Department of Game and Fish annual fiscal reports held at the New Mexico State Library and Archives; White Sands and Game and Fish, *Comprehensive Oryx Management Plan*, 6, 9.

24. White Sands and Game and Fish, *Comprehensive Oryx Management Plan*, 10. On the African safari experience see Herne, *White Hunters*; White Sands, *Final Environmental Impact Statement*, 3–63; Barbary Sheep, Oryx, and Persian Ibex License Application Requirements and Restrictions, *New Mexico Register* 20, no. 20, October 30, 2009.

25. Michael Hyatt, Santa Fe, New Mexico, interview by author, 17 July 2008, written transcription. Hyatt is a lawyer and avid big game hunter based in Santa Fe.

26. Hyatt, interview.

27. "New Mexico Department of Game and Fish Exotic Big Game Animal Program Management Plans," 13 December 1971, folder 1068, box 42, Governor Bruce King Papers, 1st term, New Mexico State Records; New Mexico Department of Game and Fish, *Annual Report, 64th Fiscal Year* (1 July 1975–30 June 1976), 18; *72nd Fiscal Year* (1 July 1983–30 June 1984), 20; Patrick R. Morrow, wildlife biologist, White Sands Missile range, interview by author, 29 March 2007, written transcription. Morrow started at the range in 1989.

28. Saiz, *Exotic Mammal Investigations*, 4; New Mexico Department of Game and Fish, *Annual Report, 80th and 81st Fiscal Years* (1 July 1991–30 June 1993), 9; White Sands and Game and Fish, *Comprehensive Oryx Management Plan*, 12; White Sands, *Final Environmental Impact Statement*, 3–63.

29. For more on oryx biology, see Kingdon, *Kingdon Field Guide*, 441–43; Stuart and Stuart, *Field Guide to the Mammals*, 196–97; Taylor, "Eland and the Oryx," 89–95; White Sands and Game and Fish, *Comprehensive Oryx Management Plan*, 6; Estes, *Behavior Guide*, 127–32.

30. Wood, White, and Durham, *Investigations Preliminary to the Release*, 23–27.

31. Wood, White, and Durham, *Investigations Preliminary to the Release*, 21–24.

32. Wood, White, and Durham, *Investigations Preliminary to the Release*, 21–24, 35–38, 48.

33. Wood, White, and Durham, *Investigations Preliminary to the Release*, 49; Saiz, *Ecology and Behavior*, 4–5.

34. Wood, White, and Durham, *Investigations Preliminary to the Release*, 3; Saiz, *Ecology and Behavior*, iv–v.

35. Saiz, *Ecology and Behavior*, 111–16.

36. Saiz, *Ecology and Behavior*, 91–98, 114; Fletcher, "Gemsbok Diets," v, 4, 13–18, 20–21; Saiz, *Ecology and Behavior*, 119, 6; White Sands and Game and Fish, *Comprehensive Oryx Management Plan*, 6.

37. Saiz, *Ecology and Behavior*, 102–6.

38. Wood, White, and Durham, *Investigations Preliminary to the Release*, 49; Saiz, *Ecology and Behavior*, iii; Saiz, *Evaluation of Exotic Mammals*, 1.

39. Huey, "Promise of Exotic Hunting," 44.

40. Saiz, *Exotic Mammal Investigations*, 1; New Mexico Department of Game and Fish, *Annual Report, 70th Fiscal Year* (1 July 1981–30 June 1982), 14; *71st Fiscal Year* (1 July 1982–30 June 1983), 18; Saiz, *Evaluation of Exotic Mammals*, 2, 7.

41. Saiz, *Evaluation of Exotic Mammals*, 2, 3.

42. Saiz, *Evaluation of Exotic Mammals*, 3.

43. Reid and Patrick, "Gemsbok (*Oryx gazella*)." 44. U.S. Department of Interior, *Environmental Assessment*; Robert Rowley, "A Graceful Gazelle Becomes a Pest," *High Country News*, 22 October 2001, http://www.hcn.org/issues/213/10797 (accessed 6 July 2006).

44. United States Department of Interior, National Park Service, White Sands National Monument, *Environmental Assessment/Assessment of Effect, Complete the Removal of African Oryx, White Sands National Monument* (White Sands NM, 2001), http://www.nps.gov/archive/whsa/oryx%20eA.htm (accessed 26 August 2006), and Rowley, "Graceful Gazelle."

45. C. Smith et al., "Diets of Native and Non-Native Ungulates, 165–66; Dye, "Gemsbok and Mule Deer Diets, 20, 24; see also White Sands and Game and Fish, *Comprehensive Oryx Management Plan*, 8.

46. There are many scientific examinations of brucellosis in Yellowstone. For a primer see Cheville, McCullough, and Paulson, *Brucellosis*; Bender et al., "Infectious Disease Survey," 772; Clark et al., "Malpais Spring Virus," 586, 588–89. See also Stephenson, Holecheck, and Kuykendall, "Drought Effect on Pronghorn."

47. Bender et al., "Infectious Disease Survey," 774–78.

48. President Bill Clinton, Executive Order, "Invasive Species, Executive Order 13112," *Federal Register* 64, no. 25 (8 February 1999). The order revoked E.O. 11987 signed under the Carter administration.

49. White Sands and Game and Fish, *Comprehensive Oryx Management Plan*, 8; Bender, *Population Demographics*.

50. Charles Petit, "African Antelope are at Home on New Mexico Missile range," *San Francisco Chronicle*, 11 June 1996, p. A4; Morrow, interview.

51. Morrow, interview; White Sands and Game and Fish, *Comprehensive Oryx Management Plan*, 10–11.

52. White Sands and Game and Fish, *Comprehensive Oryx Management Plan*, 22–29; New Mexico Game Commission, Meeting Minutes (12 December 2006), Agenda item no. 7, http://www.wildlife.state. nm.us/commission/minutes /documents/2006index.html (accessed 1 April 2007).

53. Tom Waddell, Armendaris ranch manager, interview by author, 12 April 2007, written transcription. Tom Waddell has served at the Armendaris for fourteen years.

54. Morrow, interview; White Sands and Game and Fish, *Comprehensive Oryx Management Plan*, 3; White Sands, *Final Environmental Impact Statement*, 3–63.

55. White Sands, *Final Environmental Impact Statement*, 3–63.

56. White Sands, *Final Environmental Impact Statement*, 3–63; Rowley, "Graceful Gazelle."

5. RANGE WARS

1. Fritz Thompson, "Rancher Retakes Home on the Range," *Albuquerque Journal*, 14 October 1982, Box 22, Folder 15, John L. Sinclair Papers, Center for Southwest Research; Fritz Thompson and Nancy Harbert, "McDonalds End Ranch Vigil," *Albuquerque Journal*, n.d., Box 22, Folder 15, John L. Sinclair Papers, Center for Southwest Research.

2. Denny Gentry, president of the Cattle Growers Association, interview by author, March 25, 2011, Albuquerque, tape recording.

3. Thompson, "Rancher Retakes Home on the Range"; Thompson and Harbert, "McDonalds End Ranch Vigil."

4. "Rancher Vows to Reoccupy Land," *Clovis News*, 8 March 1989, Box 16, Folder 19, Joseph R. Skeen Papers, Joseph R. Skeen Library, NM Tech, Socorro (hereafter Joseph R. Skeen Papers); "White Sand Landowners Seek Dollars, Not Promises," unidentified newspaper article, 9 March 1989, Box 16, Folder 19, Joseph R. Skeen Papers.

5. See, for example, Hawthorne-Tagg, *Life Like No Other*.

6. On the New Right in the West and Sunbelt see McGirr, *Suburban Warriors*; Lassiter, *Silent Majority*.

7. Turner, *Promise of Wilderness*, 227–38.

8. Turner, *Promise of Wilderness*, 249–55; R. White, "Current Weirdness in the West," 11–14.

9. Robbins, "In Search of Western Lands," 4, 16. Louis Warren has explored the complicated meaning of the common good at a point in the late nineteenth century when federal regulation superseded the locally controlled natural resource commons. See L. Warren, *Hunter's Game*; also see Merrill, *Public Lands*; T. Anderson and Hill, *Political Economy*.

10. U.S. President, Executive Order, "Withdrawing Public Lands for Use of the War Department As A General Bombing Range, Executive Order 9029," *Federal Register* 7, no. 15 (22 January 1942): 443; U.S. President, Executive Order, "Amending Certain Executive and Public Land Orders for Purposed Incident to the National Emergency and the Prosecution of the War," *Federal Register* 10, no. 44 (2 March 1945): 2423–24; U.S. President, Public Land Order, "Withdrawing Public Lands for Use of Department of the Army for Military Purposes, Public Land Order 833," *Federal Register* 17 (27 May 1953): 4822–33.

11. Hunner, *Inventing Los Alamos*, 15–17; Gerber, *On the Home Front*, 11, 22–23; "Richland Folks Fears Lessened," *Spokane Daily Chronicle*, 14 March 1943, 1; Jackson and Johnson, "Summer of '44," 233–34.

12. I am informed here by Karen Merrill, *Public Lands*.

13. Harry F. Lee to Governor Bruce King, 5 May 1971, Box 54, Folder 1303, Governor Bruce King Papers, 1st Term, New Mexico State Records; U.S. General Accounting Office, *Acquisitions of Properties*, 1, 2.

14. *Taylor Grazing Act, U.S. Code*, vol. 43, secs. 315–315r.

15. Lee to King, 5 May 1971; U.S. General Accounting Office, *Acquisitions of Properties*, 1, 2.

16. A. D. Brownfield to Truman Spencer, 6 May 1970, Box 2, Folder 10, Truman A. Spencer Family Ranching Records, Rio Grande Historical Collections; U.S. General Accounting Office, *Acquisitions of Properties*, 2–3.

17. Phil Harvey to White Sands Missile Range Ranchers, 13 May 1970, Box 2, Folder 10, Truman A. Spencer Family Ranching Records, Rio Grande Historical Collections.

18. Phil Harvey to White Sands Missile Range Ranchers, 13 May 1970, Box 2, Folder 10, Truman A. Spencer Family Ranching Records, Rio Grande Historical Collections; J. W. Young, District Manager, Bureau of Land Management to Quatro Amigos Cattle Company, 27 May 1970, Box 2, Folder 10, Truman A. Spencer Family Ranching Records, Rio Grande Historical Collections; Col. R. L. West, Army Corps of Engineers, 5 June 1970, Box 2, Folder 10, Truman A. Spencer Family Ranching Records, Rio Grande Historical Collections.

19. Phil Harvey to White Sands Missile Range Ranchers, 5 June 1970, Box 2, Folder 10, Truman A. Spencer Family Ranching Records, Rio Grande Historical Collections; William Montgomery, "Leasing Policies Changed," unidentified newspaper article, n.d., Box 2, Folder 10, Truman A. Spencer Family Ranching Records, Rio Grande Historical Collections.

20. Phil Harvey to White Sands Missile Range Ranchers, 19 June 1970, Box 2, Folder 10, Truman A. Spencer Family Ranching Records, Rio Grande Historical Collections; Phil Harvey to White Sands Missile Range Ranchers, 25 June 1970, Box 2, Folder 10, Truman A. Spencer Family Ranching Records, Rio Grande Historical Collections; Clarence Hinkle et al. to Senator Clinton Anderson, 11 May 1970, Box 2, Folder 11, Truman A. Spencer Family Ranching Records, Rio Grande Historical Collections; Phil Harvey to White Sands Missile Range Ranchers, 9 November 1970, Box 2, Folder 10, Truman A. Spencer Family Ranching Records, Rio Grande Historical Collections. Examples of the motions to extend time can be found in Box 2, Folder 10, Truman A. Spencer Family Ranching Records, Rio Grande Historical Collections.

21. Quoted in Hinkle et al. to Anderson, 11 May 1971.

22. Clarence Hinkle et al. to White Sands Missile Range Ranchers, 12 March 1971, Box 2, Folder 11, Truman A. Spencer Family Ranching Records, Rio Grande Historical Collections.

23. U.S. General Accounting Office, *Acquisitions of Properties*, 2–3; Sean Bersell and Bruce Donisthorpe to Senator Pete Domenici, Memorandum: Background on White Sands Ranchers, 17 April 1989, Box 16, Folder 20, Joseph R. Skeen Papers.

24. See *Right of Eminent Domain, U.S. Code*, vol. 40, sec. 257, as amended; *Declaration of Taking Act, U.S. Code*, vol. 40, sec. 258a; Clarence Hinkle to Bill Davenport, Acting Chief, Acquisition Branch, Army Corps of Engineers, 21 March 1975, Box 2, Folder 14, Truman A. Spencer Family Ranching Records, Rio Grande Historical Collections; Bill Davenport, Acting Chief, Acquisition Branch, Army Corps of Engineers to Clarence Hinkle, 22 April 1975, Box 2, Folder 14, Truman A. Spencer Family Ranching Records, Rio Grande Historical Collections; Hinkle et al. to Spencer et al. 23 April 1975, Box 2, Folder 14, Truman A. Spencer Family Ranching Records, Rio Grande Historical Collections; Hinkle et al. to Spencer et al., 28 January 1977, Box 2, Folder 14, Truman A. Spencer Family Ranching Records, Rio Grande Historical Collections; *Acquisition, U.S. Code*, vol. 10, sec. 2663; *United States v. Truman Spencer et al.*, Civ-75-353 (United States District Court for the District of New Mexico 1975), Box 2, Folder 14, Truman A. Spencer Family Ranching Records, Rio Grande Historical Collections.

25. Schulman, *Seventies*, 199–200, 226.

26. *United States v. Truman Spencer et al.* Civ-75-353 (United States District Court for the District of New Mexico 1975), Box 21, Folder 8, Mahlon T. Everhart Papers, Archives and Special Collections, New Mexico State University Library; U.S. General Accounting Office, *Acquisitions of Properties*, 2–3. Generally much of the condemnation legal documentation can be found in the Everhart and Spencer Papers in the Rio Grande Historical Collections at New Mexico State University.

27. *D. I. Z. Livestock Co. et al. v. United States*, No 95–75, 210 Ct. Cl. 708 (Court of Claims 1976); U.S. General Accounting Office, *Acquisitions of Properties*, 2–3.

28. *D. I. Z. Livestock Co. et al. v. United States*.

29. *Lex J. Armijo et al. v. United States*, No 94–79L, 229 Ct. Cl 34 (U.S. Court of Claims 1981). This case would later become *Baca v. U.S.* and finally be resolved as *Humphries v. U.S.*

30. "White Sands Dispute Nets State $20 Million," *Santa Fe New Mexican*, 9 July 1987, Box 16, Folder 19, Joseph R. Skeen Papers; Stacey Bush, "U.S. Pays for Land Handed to WSMR," *Albuquerque Journal*, 18 July 1987, Box 16, Folder 19, Joseph R. Skeen Papers; Joan Morris, "Ranchers Get More Than $3 Million in Dispute over White Sands Land," *El Paso Times*, 18 July 1987, Box 16, Folder 19, Joseph R. Skeen Papers; Evan Leland, "WSMR Ranchers Receive Government Checks," *Las Cruces Sun-News*, n.d., Box 16, Folder 19, Joseph R. Skeen Papers. Mineral

Rights for the state lands were settled in 1988. See Bersell and Donisthorpe to Domenici, 17 April 1989.

31. Bersell and Donisthorpe to Domenici, 17 April 1989; *White Sands Ranchers of New Mexico, on Behalf of Themselves and Others Similarly Situated v. United States*, No. 2–84, 14 Cl. Ct. 559 (U.S. Court of Claims 1988).

32. Bersell and Donisthorpe to Domenici, 17 April 1989; *White Sands Ranchers of New Mexico v. United States*.

33. *White Sands Ranchers of New Mexico v. United States*.

34. *White Sands Ranchers of New Mexico v. United States*.

35. *White Sands Ranchers of New Mexico v. United States*; Scott McCartney, "Decades Later, White Sands Ranchers Remain Bitter about Taking of Land," *Associated Press*, June 22, 1988.

36. McCartney, "Decades Later."

37. The ranchers lost their appeal in November 1988. See *White Sands Ranchers of New Mexico v. United States*.

38. Cahn, *Environmental Deceptions*, 37.

39. Turner, *Promise of Wilderness*, 227–329.

40. U.S. General Accounting Office, *Acquisitions of Properties*; U.S. Congress, House, *A Bill to Provide for Compensation of Certain Ranchers in New Mexico for Ranching Units Taken from Them by the Department of the Army for White Sands Missile Range New Mexico*, 98th Cong., 1st sess., H.R. 4022, *Congressional Record*, 28 September 1983; Bersell and Donisthorpe to Domenici, 17 April 1989.

41. U.S. Congress, Senate, Subcommittee on Public Lands and Reserved Water of the Committee on Energy and Natural Resources, *White Sands Missile Range, New Mexico: Hearing before the Subcommittee on Public Lands and Reserved Water of the Committee on Energy and Natural Resources*, 98th Cong., 1st sess., 15 November 1983, 2, 9–13.

42. Senate, Subcommittee on Public Lands, *White Sands Missile Range*, 102–3, 115–18, 132.

43. Senate, Subcommittee on Public Lands, *White Sands Missile Range*, 190–214, 215.

44. Senate, Subcommittee on Public Lands, *White Sands Missile Range*, 28–31.

45. UPI tear sheet, 28 October 1983, Folder 31, United Press International: Santa Fe Office Collection, Fray Angélico Chávez History Library, Santa Fe; Don McKinney, "Ranchers See Glimmer of Hope," *Alamogordo Daily News*, 23 April 1989; David Sheppard, "Evicted Ranchers Find Allies," *El Paso Times*, 8 April 1989; quoted in Catherine Lazorko, "White Sands Land Dispute," *El Paso Times*, 23 April 1989, Box 16, Folder 19, Joseph R. Skeen Papers.

46. U.S. Congress, House, *A Bill to Establish a Commission to Provide Compensation to Individuals Who Lost Their Land or Mining Claims to the United States Government for the Establishment of White Sands Missile Range*, 101st Cong., 1st sess., H.R.

3408, *Congressional Record* 135, no. 131 (4 October 1989); U.S. Congress, Senate, *A Bill to Establish a Commission to Provide Compensation to Individuals Who Lost Their Land or Mining Claims to the United States Government for the Establishment of White Sands Missile Range*, 101st Cong., 1st sess., S1725, *Congressional Record* 135, no. 131 (4 October 1989); U.S. Congress, House, Subcommittee on Administrative Law and Governmental Relations of the Committee on the Judiciary, *White Sands Compensation Act of 1989: Hearing before the Subcommittee on Administrative Law and Governmental Relations of the Committee on the Judiciary*, 101st Cong., 1st sess., 13 June 1990, 11–19.

47. House, Subcommittee on Administrative Law, *White Sands Compensation Act of 1989*, 9–11, 81, 84–85.

48. House, Subcommittee on Administrative Law, *White Sands Compensation Act of 1989*, 38–39, 50–51, 111–18.

49. House, Subcommittee on Administrative Law, *White Sands Compensation Act of 1989*, 29–30, 56, 62–63.

50. House, Subcommittee on Administrative Law, *White Sands Compensation Act of 1989*, 91–95, 96, 97.

51. Thompson, "Rancher Retakes Home on the Range"; Thompson and Harbert, "McDonalds End Ranch Vigil"; Associated Press, "Rancher Vows to Reoccupy Land," *Clovis News* (NM), 8 March 1989; quoted in "Long Wait Ends for McDonald," *El Defensor Chieftain* (Socorro), 12 June 1993.

52. Susan Schwartz, "Time Running Out for White Sands Ranchers," *Alamogordo Daily News*, 23 October 1992.

53. Quoted in "White Sands Ranchers Think They'll Never Get Paid," *Sierra County Sentinel* (Truth or Consequences), 14 November 1990; quoted in "White Sands Ranch Families Justly Cynical," unidentified newspaper editorial, 28 March 1991, Box 16 Folder 19; Joseph R. Skeen Papers.

54. Senate, *A Bill to Establish a Commission in the Department of the Interior to Provide Compensation to Individuals Who Lost Their Land or Mining Claims to the United States Government for the Establishment of White Sands Missile Range*, 102nd Cong., 1st sess., S. 867, *Congressional Record*; House, *A Bill to Establish a Commission in the Department of the Interior to Provide Compensation to Individuals Who Lost Their Land or Mining Claims to the United States Government for the Establishment of White Sands Missile Range*, 102nd Cong., 1st sess., H.R. 1954, *Congressional Record*; Senate, *A Bill to Ensure the Provision of Appropriate Compensation for the Real Property and Mining Claims Taken by the United States as a Result of the Establishment of the White Sand Missile Range, New Mexico*, 104th Cong., 1st sess., S. 339, *Congressional Record*; House, *A Bill to Ensure the Provision of Appropriate Compensation for the Real Property and Mining Claims Taken by the United States as a Result of the Establishment of the White Sand Missile Range, New Mexico*, 104th Cong., 1st sess., H.R. 806.

55. "New Mexico Lawmakers Resume White Sands Compensation Fight," Associated Press tear sheet, 21 June 1991, Box 16, Folder 19, Joseph R. Skeen Papers.
56. Eckles, interview.

6. NATURAL SECURITY STATES

1. "Panel Discussion of Proposed Re-Introduction of Mexican Grey [sic] Wolf at WSMR," 1 hour and 38 min., White Sands Missile Range Museum Archival Holdings, Doc. 97.041.033, 26 May 1988, DVD.
2. Boice, "Endangered Species Management," 7–9; Erin James, "Feds Investigate Killings of Endangered N.C. Red Wolves," *The Virginian–Pilot*, 10 October 2010, http://hamptonroads.com/2010/10/feds-investigate-killings-endangered-nc -red-wolves; Cohn, "New Defenders of Wildlife."
3. Quoted in Edie Pells, "Crying Wolf," *Portland Sunday Oregonian*, 22 October 1995, sec. A, 24; Ed Timms, "Revival of the Species; Ranchers, Environmentalists Still Fiercely at Odds on Wolf Program," *Dallas Morning News*, 18 March 1996, 1A. See also D. Smith and Ferguson, *Decade of the Wolf*; more generally see Turner, *Promise of Wilderness*, 141–373.
4. The idea of western pastoralism as a capitalist culture comes from Worster, *Dust Bowl*; R. White, "Current Weirdness in the West," 11, 12, 13. See Coleman, *Vicious*; Dunlap, *Saving America's Wildlife*; Isenberg, "Moral Ecology of Wildlife," 60.
5. D. Brown, *Wolf in the Southwest*, 19–29; Maer, Noss, and Larkin, *Large Mammal Restoration*, 172.
6. D. Brown, *Wolf in the Southwest*, 31–54.
7. D. Brown, *Wolf in the Southwest*, 54–71; Miller, "Predator Control—Circa 1915," 16–17.
8. "Report of the Game and Fish Warden of New Mexico, 1917–1918," 31, Box 1, New Mexico Department of Game and Fish Papers, New Mexico State Records and Archives; Bailey, *North American Fauna No. 53*, 305; Ligon, *Wildlife of New Mexico*, 52; S. Young and Goldman, *Wolves of North America*, 471.
9. Ranchers and small livestock holders across North America clearly had a role in wolf extermination. See Coleman, *Vicious*; Dunlap, *Saving America's Wildlife*, 48–61; Miller, "Predator Control," 16–17; Maer, *Large Mammal Restoration*, 172; D. Brown, *Wolf in the Southwest*, 133.
10. Dunlap, *Saving America's Wildlife*, 142–55.
11. *Endangered Species Act*, *U.S. Code*, Vol. 16, secs. 1531–1544 (1973); U.S. Fish and Wildlife Service, *Mexican Wolf Recovery Plan*, 10.
12. McBride, *Mexican Wolf*, 8, 19, 20–22, 33–34, 36.
13. See, for example, see López-Hoffman et al., *Conservation of Shared Environments*; McBride, *Mexican Wolf*, 34; U.S. Fish and Wildlife Service, *Mexican Wolf Recovery Plan*, 11–12, 14, 17–20, 41–57, 63, 79–85.

14. Larry L. Woodard, New Mexico State Director, Bureau of Land Management to Regional Director, Region 2, U.S. Fish and Wildlife Service, 21 April 1982, in U.S. Fish and Wildlife Service, *Mexican Wolf Recovery Plan*, 105.

15. Leopold, *Sand County Almanac*, 129–32; Murie, *Wolves of Mount McKinley*; quoted in Mech, "Wolf Research in Minnesota,", 40; Mech, *Wolf*.

16. On wolf conservation see Mech and Boitani, *Wolves*; Bednarz, *Evaluation of the Ecological Potential*, 1, 64–65.

17. Bednarz, *Evaluation of the Ecological Potential*, 21–27.

18. D. Brown, *Wolf in the Southwest*, 137–39; R. Peterson and Ciucci, "Wolf as Carnivore," 114–15.

19. Bednarz, *Evaluation of the Ecological Potential*, 34–42.

20. Fuller, Mech, and Cochrane, "Wolf Population Dynamics," 163; Peterson and Ciucci, "Wolf as Carnivore," 126–27; Kreeger, "Internal Wolf," 201. Most studies on the physiological and ecological needs of North American wolves remain limited to species found in Minnesota and Canada. This is due to the larger number of animals available for study. Bednarz, *Evaluation of the Ecological Potential*, 42–61.

21. Mech and Peterson, "Wolf-Prey Relations," 139–14; D. Brown, *Wolf in the Southwest*, 132–134; McBride, *Mexican Wolf*, 19–22; Bednarz, *Evaluation of the Ecological Potential*, 72–74.

22. Bednarz, *Evaluation of the Ecological Potential*, 72–74.

23. Bednarz, *Evaluation of the Ecological Potential*, i–ii, 64–65, 75.

24. Bednarz, *Evaluation of the Ecological Potential*, 1.

25. Eckles, interview; Spear, quoted in Mark Taylor, "Gray Wolf Still Has a Chance," unidentified newspaper article, 17 October 1987, United Press International: Santa Fe Office Collection, Fray Angélico Chávez History Library; "Panel Discussion of Proposed Re-Introduction of Mexican Grey Wolf at WSMR," 1 hour and 38 min., White Sands Missile Range Museum Archival Holdings, Doc. 97.041.033, 26 May 1988, DVD.

26. "Panel Discussion of Proposed Re-Introduction."

27. Ames, "Wolves in Our Woods," 10; *Mexican Wolf at WSMR*, CBS Evening News with Connie Chung, 2 min and 30 sec., White Sands Missile Range Museum and Archival Holdings, Doc. 97.041.014, 27 May 1990, DVD.

28. Cox, quoted in Susan Dowdney, "Wolf: Nature's Jewel or Wanton Killer?," *Las Cruces Sun-News*, 19 April 1992, Box 12, Folder 45, United Press International: Santa Fe Office Collection, Fray Angélico Chávez History Library; Otero County Board of Commissioners, State of New Mexico, *Resolution No. 76–19*, 21 December 1987, Box 15, Folder 11, Joseph R. Skeen Papers; Billie Pender, Board of County Commissioners Otero County, New Mexico to Representative Joe Skeen, 22 December 1987, Box 15, Folder 11, Joseph R. Skeen Papers.

29. Quoted in Pells, "Crying Wolf," sec. A, 24.
30. Representative Joseph Skeen, Radio Address, Box 15, Folder 8, Joseph R. Skeen Papers.
31. Denny Gentry, interview by author, 25 March 2011, Albuquerque, tape recording; "Panel Discussion of Proposed Re-Introduction."
32. Ness, quoted in Dowdney, "Wolf"; William McIlhaney, President, New Mexico Farm and Livestock Bureau, to Representative Joe Skeen, 14 December 1987, Box 15, Folder 15, Joseph R. Skeen Papers.
33. Harvey, quoted in Dowdney, "Wolf"; "Panel Discussion of Proposed Re-Introduction."
34. "Panel Discussion of Proposed Re-Introduction."
35. *Wolf Action Group et al. v. the United States*, Complaint, Civ-90-0390-HB (U.S. District Court for the State of New Mexico 1990).
36. *Wolf Action Group et al v. the United States*, Complaint.
37. *Wolf Action Group et al v. the United States*, Motion to Dismiss, Civ-90-0390-HB (U.S. District Court for the State of New Mexico 1990).
38. *Wolf Action Group et al v. the United States*, Stipulated Settlement Agreement, Civ-90-0390-HB (U.S. District Court for the State of New Mexico 1990); "Lawsuit over Mexican Gray Wolf Settled," *Silver City Daily Press*, 22 May 1993, 1.
39. William Clark, "The Classic Battle," *Las Cruces Sun-News*, 7 March, 1991, Box 15, Folder 19, Joseph R. Skeen Papers.
40. Kennedy, quoted in "Wolf Reintroduction a Possibility," unidentified newspaper article, 8 July 1973, Box 15, Folder 19, Joseph R. Skeen Papers.
41. Duda, Bissell, and Young, *Wildlife and the American Mind*, 223–28.
42. Fen Montaigne, "Wolves Set Off Howling Debate, They're Being Returned to Yellowstone. Many Ranchers See it as the West Gone Wrong," *Philadelphia Inquirer*, 10 November 1994, sec. A, 1.
43. U.S. Fish and Wildlife Service, *Reintroduction of the Mexican Wolf*, 5-74–5-75, 5-76. A large number of county and tribal governments across the Southwest opposed the program. Their individual correspondence with the Fish and Wildlife Service is reprinted in the environmental impact statement as a measure for the Mexican wolf recovery team to answer criticism about the program. See pp. 5-1–5-79.
44. Krech, *Ecological Indian*; Fritts, Stephenson, Hayes, and Boitani, "Wolves and Humans," 296.
45. U.S. Fish and Wildlife Service, *Reintroduction of the Mexican Wolf*, 5-21, 5-48; Pavlik, "San Carlos and White Mountain Apache," 134.
46. U.S. Fish and Wildlife Service, *Reintroduction of the Mexican Wolf*, 2-1–2-5.
47. Paquet et al. *Mexican Wolf Recovery*, 68; Adaptive Management Oversight Committee, *Mexican Wolf Blue Range Reintroduction*, A-19, A-20.

48. U.S. Fish and Wildlife Service, *Reintroduction of the Mexican Wolf*, 2-2, 2-5, 3-25.

49. Allen Myerson, "For Ranchers, a 'Bare, Get-By Year,'" *New York Times*, 3 October 1995, sec. A, 12; U.S. Fish and Wildlife Service, *Reintroduction of the Mexican Wolf*, 3-30. See also Morrow, *Population Estimates*; Morrow, wsmr *Prey Status Update*; Bender et al., "Infectious Disease Survey," 772, 774-78.

50. Paquet et al. *Mexican Wolf Recovery*, 68.

51. Paquet et al., *Mexican Wolf Recovery*, 68; Adaptive Management Oversight Committee, *Mexican Wolf Blue Range Reintroduction*, A-19, A-20.

52. *New Mexico Cattle Growers Association et al. v. the United States Fish and Wildlife Service*, Complaint, Civ-98-0275 (U.S. District Court for the State of New Mexico 1998); Pells, "Crying Wolf"; "Wolves Die; Sabotage Seen," *New York Times*, 17 November 1998, sec. F, 5.

53. See White Sands Missile Range, "Draft Environmental Impact Statement: For Development and Implementation of Range-Wide Mission and Major Capabilities at White Sands Missile Range, New Mexico (February 2009).

54. My cue here is Richard White's critique of the Wise Use movement. See R. White, "Current Weirdness in the West," 11, 12, 13.

CONCLUSION

1. "Drought Kills Wild Horses," *New York Times*, 17 July 1994, 14; "Animal Activists Denied Access to Starving Horses, N.M. Missile Range Officials Decline to Help Offer," *Denver Post*, 21 July 1994, n.p. The story of the rescue of feral horses at White Sands is told in Höglund, *Nobody's Horses*, 30, 32.

2. Prescott, quoted in "Animal Activists Denied Access"; Höglund, *Nobody's Horses*, 30, 32.

3. Höglund, *Nobody's Horses*, 91.

4. Kerns, quoted in "White Sands Missile Range Wildlife Conservation Recognized," *Las Cruces Sun-News*, 13 April 2008, sec. News.

5. Nye, *American Technological Sublime*.

6. Russell, "Afterword: Militarized Landscapes," 233.

7. Riebsame, Robb, et al., *Atlas of the New West*; for the "Ugly West" see 132–41; Kuletz, *Tainted Desert*; Radkau, *Nature and Power*, 3, 4, 5; Cronon, *Changes in the Land*, 9; R. White, "Environmental History," 1111–16.

BIBLIOGRAPHY

ARCHIVES

Center for Southwest Research. University Libraries. University of New Mexico. Albuquerque NM.

Fray Angélico Chávez History Library. Santa Fe NM.

Joseph R. Skeen Papers. Joseph R. Skeen Library. New Mexico Institute of Mining and Technology. Socorro NM.

National Archives. Rocky Mountain Division. Denver CO.

National Park Service. Southwest Regional Office Library. Santa Fe NM.

Nevada Field Office Photograph Library. National Nuclear Security Administration. U.S. Department of Energy. Las Vegas NV.

New Mexico State Records Center and Archives. Santa Fe NM.

New Mexico State University Library. Las Cruces NM.

Rio Grande Historical Collections. New Mexico State University Library. Las Cruces NM.

White Sands Missile Range Museum and Archival Holdings. White Sands Missile Range NM.

REPORTS AND PUBLISHED SOURCES

Abbey, Edward. *Fire on the Mountain*. Albuquerque: University of New Mexico Press, 1962.

Abbott, Carl. *The New Urban America: Growth and Politics in Sunbelt Cities*. Chapel Hill: University of North Carolina Press, 1987.

Abersold, Paul, and P. B. Moon. *July 16th Explosion: Radiation Survey of Trinity Site Four Weeks after Explosion*. LA Report 359. 19 September 1946.

Ackland, Len. *Making a Real Killing: Rocky Flats and the Nuclear West*. Albuquerque: University of New Mexico Press, 1999.

Adaptive Management Oversight Committee. *Mexican Wolf Blue Range Reintroduc-tion Project 5-Year Review*. Albuquerque NM: Adaptive Management Oversight Committee, 2005.

Adelman, Jeremy, and Stephen Aron. "From Borderlands to Borders: Empires, Nation-States, and the Peoples in between in North American History." *American Historical Review* 104 (June 1999): 814–41.

Ames, Norma. "Wolves in Our Woods." *New Mexico Wildlife Magazine* 27 (January–February 1982): 6–12.

Amundson, Michael. *Yellowcake Towns: Uranium Mining Communities in the West*. Boulder: University of Colorado Press, 2001.

Anaya, Rudolfo. *Bless Me Ultima*. New York: Warner Books, 1994.

———. *The Heart of Aztlan*. Berkeley CA: Justa, 1976.

Anderson, Benedict. *Imagined Communities: Reflections on the Origin and Spread of Nationalism*. London: Verso, 1983.

Anderson, Terry, and Peter Hill, *The Political Economy of the American West*. Lanham MD: Rowman and Littlefield, 1994.

Archer, Steve, David S. Schimel, and Elisabeth A. Holland. "Mechanisms of Shrubland Expansion: Land Use, Climate or CO_2?" *Climatic Change* 29 (January 1995): 91–99.

Atomic Energy Commission. *Trinity Survey Program*. UCLA-22. 11 November 1947.

Bailey, Lynn. *If You Take My Sheep: The Evolution and Conflicts of Navajo Pastoralism, 1630–1868*. Pasadena CA: Westernlore, 1980.

Bailey, Vernon. *North American Fauna No. 53: Mammals of New Mexico*. Washington DC: U.S. Department of Agriculture, 1931.

Balderrama, Francisco E., and Raymond Rodríguez. *Decade of Betrayal: Mexican Repatriation in the 1930s*. Albuquerque: University of New Mexico Press, 2006.

Barnes, Courtlandt Dixon. *The National Geographic Society: 100 Years of Adventure and Discovery*. New York: Harry N. Abrams, 1997.

Bednarz, James. *An Evaluation of the Ecological Potential of White Sands Missile Range to Support a Reintroduced Population of Mexican Wolves*. Albuquerque NM: U.S. Fish and Wildlife Service, 1989.

Bender, Louis C. *Population Demographics, Dynamics, and Movements of South African Oryx (Oryx Gazella Gazella) in South-Central New Mexico*. Las Cruces: U.S. Geological Survey, 2006.

Bender, Louis C., et al. "Infectious Disease Survey of Gemsbok in New Mexico." *Journal of Wildlife Diseases* 39 (October 2003): 772–78.

Blum, James Morton. *V Was for Victory: Politics and American Culture during World War II*. San Diego: Harcourt Brace, 1977.

Boardman, Sue, and Kathryn Porch. *The Battle of Gettysburg Cyclorama: A History and Guide*. Gettysburg PA: Thomas, 2008.

Boehm, William B. *From Barren Desert to Thriving Community: A Social History of White Sands Missile Range, 1945–1954*. Tularosa NM: Human Systems Research, 1997.

Boice, L. Peter. "Endangered Species Management on U.S. Air Force Lands." *Endangered Species Update* (School of Natural Resources and Environment, University of Michigan) 13, no. 9 (September 1996): 7–9.

Boime, Albert. *The Magisterial Gaze: Manifest Destiny and American Landscape Painting, 1830–1865*. Washington DC: Smithsonian Institution Press, 1991.

Botkin, Daniel B. *Discordant Harmonies: A New Ecology for the Twenty-First Century*. New York: Oxford University Press, 1990.

Boyer, Paul S. *By the Bomb's Early Light: American Thought and Culture at the Dawn of the Atomic Age*. New York: Pantheon, 1985.

———. *Fallout: A Historian Reflects on America's Half-Century Encounter with Nuclear Weapons*. Columbus: Ohio State University Press, 1998.

Brooks, James. *Captives and Cousins: Slavery, Kinship, and Community in the Southwest Borderlands*. Chapel Hill: University of North Carolina Press, 2002.

Brown et al. "Acquisition of Land for ORDCIT Project Range Facilities." In *Development of the Corporal: The Embryo of the Army Missile Program*, by James W. Bragg. *Historical Monograph* no. 4, vol. 2, appendix no. 2. Redstone Arsenal AL: Army Ballistic Missile Agency, 1961.

Brown, David E., ed. *The Wolf in the Southwest: The Making of an Endangered Species*. Tucson: University of Arizona Press, 1983.

Browning, Cody, Mark Sale, David T. Kirkpatrick, and Karl W. Laumbach. *MOTR Site: Excavation at Site LA 72859, an El Paso Structure on Fort Bliss, Otero County, New Mexico*. Report no. 8927. Las Cruces NM: Human Systems Research, 1992.

Brugge, Doug, Timothy Benally, and Esther Yazzie-Lewis, eds. *The Navajo People and Uranium Mining*. Albuquerque: University of New Mexico Press, 2007.

Buffington, Lee C., and Carlton H. Herbel. "Vegetational Changes on a Semidesert Grassland Range from 1858 to 1963." *Ecological Monographs* 35 (Spring 1965): 140–64.

Cahalan, James. *Edward Abbey: A Life*. Tucson: University of Arizona Press, 2001.

Cahn, Matthew Alan. *Environmental Deceptions: The Tension between Liberalism and Environmental Policymaking in the United States*. Albany: State University of New York Press, 1995.

Carr Childers, Leisl. "The Size of the Risk: An Environmental History of the Nuclear Great Basin." PhD diss., University of Nevada–Las Vegas, 2011.

Carson, Rachel. *Silent Spring*. New York: Mariner Books, 1962.

Casey, Edward S. "How to Get from Space to Place in a Fairly Short Stretch of Time: Phenomenological Prolegomena." In *Senses of Place*, edited by Steven Feld and Keith H. Basso, 13–52. Santa Fe NM: School of American Research Press, 1996.

Chas, Linda. *Picturing Las Vegas*. Layton UT: Gibbs Smith, 2009.

Chávez, Ernesto. *"¡Mi Raza Primero!" (My People First!): Nationalism, Identity, and Insurgency in the Chicano Movement in Los Angeles, 1966–1978.* Berkeley: University of California Press, 2002.

Checchi and Company. *The Potential Power of Tourism—Mescalero Reservation.* Washington DC: Checchi and Company, 1963.

Cheville, Norman F., Dale R. McCullough, and Lee R. Paulson. *Brucellosis in the Greater Yellowstone Area.* Washington DC: National Academy Press, 1998.

Chun, Clayton K. S. *Thunder over the Horizon: From V-2 Rockets to Ballistic Missiles.* Westport CT: Praeger Security International, 2006.

Clark, Gary, et al. "Malpais Spring Virus: A New Vesiculorvirus from Mosquitoes Collected in New Mexico and Evidence of Infected Indigenous and Exotic Ungulates." *American Journal of Tropical Medicine* 39 (1988): 586–92.

Coates, Peter. "Improving on 'A Paradise of Game': Ecological Impacts, Game Management, and Alaska's Buffalo Transplant." *Western Historical Quarterly* 28 (Summer 1997): 133–59.

Cohen, Lizabeth. *A Consumer's Republic: The Politics of Mass Consumption in Postwar America.* New York: Knopf, 2003.

Cohn, Jeffrey P. "New Defenders of Wildlife: Practicing Conservation and Protect ing Habitat Are Not Usually Considered Part of the Military's Job Description." *Bioscience* 46, no. 1 (January 1996): 11–14.

Coleman, Jon. *Vicious: Wolves and Men in America.* New Haven CT: Yale University Press, 2004.

Colton, F. Barrows. "How We Fight with Photographs." *National Geographic* 86 (September 1944): 257–80.

Committee on Scientific Accomplishments of Earth Observations from Space, National Research Council. *Earth Observations from Space: The First 50 Years of Scientific Achievements.* Washington DC: National Academic Press, 2008.

Cordell, Linda S. *Ancient Pueblo Peoples.* Washington DC: Smithsonian Institution, 1994.

Craib, Raymond. *Cartographic Mexico: A History of State Fixations and Fugitive Landscapes.* Durham NC: Duke University Press, 2004.

Cronon, William. *Changes in the Land: Indians, Colonists, and the Ecology of New England.* New York: Hill and Wang, 1983.

———. "Kennecott Journey: The Paths out of Town." In *Under an Open Sky: Rethinking America's Western Past,* edited by William Cronon, George Miles, and Jay Gitlin, 28–51. New York: W. W. Norton, 1992.

———. "Modes of Prophecy and Production: Placing Nature in History." *Journal of American History* 76 (March 1990): 1122–31.

Crosby, Alfred. *Ecological Imperialism: The Biological Expansion of Europe, 900–1900.* Cambridge: Cambridge University Press, 1986.

Cruz, R. R. *Annual Water Resources Review, White Sands Missile Range, New Mexico.* Albuquerque NM: U.S. Geological Survey, 1982.

Davis, Mike. "The Dead West: Ecocide in Marlboro Country." *New Left Review* 200 (July–August 1993): 49–73.

———. *Late Victorian Holocausts: El Niño Famines and the Making of the Third World.* New York: Verso, 2001.

Deal, L. J., et al. "Locating the Lost Athena Missile in Mexico by the Aerial Radiological Measuring System (ARMS)." *Health Physics* 23 (July 1972): 95–98.

DeBuys, William. *Enchantment and Exploitation: The Life and Hard Times of a New Mexico Mountain Range.* Albuquerque: University of New Mexico Press, 1985.

Delay, Brian. *War of a Thousand Deserts: Indian Raids and the U.S.-Mexican War.* New Haven CT: Yale University Press, 2009.

DeVorkin, David H. *Science with a Vengeance: How the Military Created the US Space Sciences after World War II.* New York: Springer-Verlag, 1992.

Dick-Peddie, William A. *New Mexico Vegetation: Past, Present, and Future.* Albuquerque: University of New Mexico Press, 2000.

Douglas, Richard. *Levels and Distribution of Environmental Plutonium around the Trinity Site.* Las Vegas: Office of Radiation Programs, Environmental Protection Agency, 1978.

Duda, Mark Damian, Steven J. Bissell, and Kira C. Young. *Wildlife and the American Mind: Public Opinion on and Attitudes toward Fish and Wildlife Management.* Harrisonburg VA: Responsive Management, 1998.

Dunlap, Thomas R. *Nature and the English Diaspora: Environment and History in the United States, Canada, Australia, and New Zealand.* New York: Cambridge University Press, 1999.

———. "Remaking the Land: The Acclimatization Movement and Anglo Ideas of Nature," *Journal of World History* 8 (Fall 1997): 303–19.

———. *Saving America's Wildlife.* Princeton NJ: Princeton University Press, 1988.

Durham, Jackson Laverne. "Preliminary Investigations to the Release of Exotic Ungulates in New Mexico." Master's thesis, New Mexico State University, 1969.

Dye, Jeanne Lynn. "Gemsbok and Mule Deer Diets in Southern New Mexico." Master's thesis, New Mexico State University, 1998.

Eichstaedt, Peter H., and Murrae Haynes. *If You Poison Us: Uranium and Native Americans.* Santa Fe NM: Red Crane Books, 1994.

Eidenbach, Peter L. *Star Throwers of the Tularosa: The Early Cold War Legacy of White Sands Missile Range.* Tularosa NM: Human Systems Research, 1996.

Eidenbach, Peter L., and Beth Morgan, *Homes on the Range: Oral Recollections of Early Ranch Life on the U.S. Army White Sands Missile Range, New Mexico.* Tularosa NM: Human Systems Research, 1994.

Elton, Charles S. *The Ecology of Invasions by Animals and Plants.* London: Methuen, 1958.

Emme, Eugene M., ed. *The History of Rocket Technology: Essays on Research, Development and Utility*. Detroit: Wayne State University Press, 1964.

Estes, Richard Despard. *The Behavior Guide to African Mammals: Including Hoofed Mammals, Carnivores, Primates*. Berkeley: University of California Press, 1991.

Ettinger, Patrick. "'We Sometimes Wonder What They Will Spring on Us Next': Immigrants and Border Enforcement in the American West, 1882–1930." *Western Historical Quarterly* 37 (Summer 2006): 159–82.

Faunce, Kenneth. *The Fort Bliss Preacquisition Project: A History of the Southern Tularosa Basin*. Fort Bliss TX: Conservation Division, Directorate of Environment, U.S. Army Air Defense Artillery Center and Fort Bliss, 1997.

———. "The Perception of Landscape in the Use and Settlement of the Tularosa Basin." PhD diss., University of Idaho, 2000.

Fernlund, Kevin, ed. *The Cold War American West, 1945–1989*. Albuquerque: University of New Mexico Press, 1998.

Fey, Frederic L. *Health Physics Survey of Trinity Site*. Los Alamos NM: Los Alamos Scientific Laboratory (LA-3719), 16 June 1967.

Ficken, Robert. "Grand Coulee and Hanford: The Atomic Bomb and the Development of the Columbia River." In *The Atomic West*, edited by Bruce Hevly and John Findlay. 21–38. Seattle: University of Washington Press, 1998.

Findlay, John. *Magic Lands: Western Cityscapes and American Culture after 1940*. Berkeley: University of California Press, 1992.

Fletcher, Tammy. "Gemsbok Diets in Creosote Shrubland and Great Basin Conifer Woodland in Southcentral New Mexico." Master's thesis, New Mexico State University, 2000.

Foucault, Michel. *Discipline and Punish: The Birth of the Prison*. New York: Vintage, 1995.

Fritts, Stephen, Robert O. Stephenson, Robert D. Hayes, and Luigi Boitani, "Wolves and Humans." In Mech and Boitani, *Wolves*, 289–316.

Fryer, Heather. *Perimeters of Democracy: Inverse Utopias and the Wartime Social Landscape in the American West*. Lincoln: University of Nebraska Press, 2010.

Fugate, George, and John Chambers. *White Sands Missile Range Climate Calendar*. White Sands Missile Range NM: Atmospheric Sciences Laboratory, n.d.

Fuller, Todd K., L. David Mech, and Jean Fitts Cochrane. "Wolf Population Dynamics." In Mech and Boitani, *Wolves*, 161–91.

Galison, Peter, and Bruce Hevly, eds. *Big Science: The Growth of Large Scale Research*. Stanford CA: Stanford University Press, 1992.

Garza, Sergio, and J. S. McLean. *Fresh-water Resources in the Southeastern Part of the Tularosa Basin*. New Mexico State Engineer Technical Report no. 40. Santa Fe, 1977.

Gerber, Michele Stenehjem. *On the Home Front: The Cold War Legacy of the Hanford Nuclear Site*. Lincoln: University of Nebraska Press, 2007.

Gibbens, R. P., et al. "Vegetation Changes in the Jornada Basin from 1858 to 1998." *Journal of Arid Environments* 61 (June 2005): 651–68.

Gilbert, Marc Jason. "Next Stop—Silicon Valley: The Cold War, Vietnam, and the Making of the California Economy." In *What's Going On? California and the Vietnam Era*, edited by Marcia Eymann and Charles Wollenberg, 23–41. Berkeley: University of California Press, 2004.

Glass, Matthew. "Air Force, Western Shoshone, and Mormon Rhetoric of Place and the MX Conflict." In Hevly and Findlay, *Atomic West*, 255–75.

Gleick, James. *Chaos: Making a New Science.* New York: Viking, 1987.

Gottdiener, Mark, Claudia C. Collins, and David R. Dickens. *Las Vegas: The Social Production of an All-American City.* Malden MA: Blackwell, 1999.

Gottlieb, Robert. *Forcing the Spring: The Transformation of the American Environmental Movement.* Washington DC: Island Press, 1993.

Grover, Herbert G., and H. Brad Musick. "Shrubland Encroachment in Southern New Mexico, U.S.A.: An Analysis of Desertification Processes in the American Southwest." *Climatic Change* 17 (December 1990): 305–30.

Hacker, Barton. *The Dragon's Tail: Radiation Safety in the Manhattan Project.* Berkeley: University of California Press, 1987.

———. "'Hotter Than a Two Dollar Pistol': Fallout, Sheep, and the Atomic Energy Commission." In Hevly and Findlay, *Atomic West*, 157–75.

Hakonson, Thomas E., and LeMar J. Johnson. "Distribution of Environmental Plutonium in the Trinity Site Ecosystem after 27 Years." *Proceedings of the Third International Congress of the Radiation Protection Association* (1973).

Hales, Peter Bacon. *Atomic Spaces: Life on the Manhattan Project.* Urbana: University of Illinois Press, 1997.

Hämäläinen, Pekka. *The Comanche Empire.* New Haven CT: Yale University Press, 2008.

Hardin, Garret. "The Tragedy of the Commons." *Science* 162 (13 December 1968): 1243–48.

Havlick, David. "Logics of Change for Military-to-Wildlife Conversions in the United States." *GeoJournal* 69 (July 2007): 151–64.

Hawthorne-Tagg, Lori S. *A Life Like No Other: Ranch Life on Lands Now Administered by Holloman Air Force Base.* Holloman Air Force Base NM: Air Combat Command, U.S. Air Force, U.S. Dept. of Defense, 1997.

Heefner, Gretchen. *The Missile Next Door: The Minuteman in the American Heartland.* Cambridge MA: Harvard University Press, 2012.

———. "Missiles and Memory: Dismantling South Dakota's Cold War." *Western Historical Quarterly* 38 (Summer 2007): 181–205.

Hempelmann, Louis. *Nuclear Explosion 16 July 1945: Health Physics Report on Radioactive Contamination throughout New Mexico, Part B: Biological Effects.* LA-638. Los Alamos NM: Los Alamos Scientific Laboratory, 3 July 1947.

Henriksen, Margot A. *Dr. Strangelove's America: Society and Culture in the Atomic Age.* Berkeley: University of California Press, 1997.

Herman, Daniel Justin. *Hunting and the American Imagination.* Washington DC: Smithsonian Institution Press, 2001.

Hernandez, Kelly Lytle. "The Crimes and Consequences of Illegal Immigration: A Cross-Border Examination of Operation Wetback, 1943 to 1954." *Western Historical Quarterly* 37 (Winter 2006): 421–44.

————.*Migra! A History of the U.S. Border Patrol.* Berkeley: University of California Press, 2010.

Herne, Brian. *White Hunters: The Golden Age of African Safaris.* New York: Holt, 1999.

Hevly, Bruce, and John Findlay, eds. *The Atomic West.* Seattle: University of Washington Press, 1998.

Hoffman, Joseph G. *Nuclear Explosion 16 July 1945: Health Physics Report on Radioactive Contamination throughout New Mexico Following the Nuclear Explosion, Part A: Physics.* LA-626. Los Alamos NM: Los Alamos Scientific Laboratory, 20 February 1947.

Höglund, Don. *Nobody's Horses: The Dramatic Rescue of the Wild Herd of White Sands.* New York: Free Press, 2006.

Holliday, Clyde T. "Seeing the Earth from 80 Miles Up." *National Geographic* 98, no. 4 (October 1950): 511–28.

Hubert, L. F., and Otto Berg. "A Rocket Portrait of a Tropical Storm." *Monthly Weather Review* 83 (June 1955): 119–24.

Huenneke, Laura F., et al. "Desertification Alters Patterns of Aboveground Production in Chihuahuan Ecosystems." *Global Change Biology* 8 (March 2002): 247–64.

Huey, William. "The New New Mexicans." *New Mexico Wildlife Magazine* 26 (September–October 1981): 25–26, 29.

————. "A Promise of Exotic Hunting." *National Sportsmen Digest,* September 1971, 39–44.

Hunner, Jon. *Inventing Los Alamos: The Growth of an Atomic Community.* Norman: University of Oklahoma Press, 2004.

Hunt, Linda. *Secret Agenda: The United States Government, Nazi Scientists, and Project Paperclip, 1945 to 1990.* New York: St. Martin's Press, 1991.

Hurst, James W. *Pancho Villa and Black Jack Pershing: The Punitive Expedition in Mexico.* Westport CT: Praeger, 2008.

Irwin-Williams, Cynthia. "Post-Pleistocene Archaeology, 7,000–2,000 B.C." In *Handbook of North American Indians* 9, edited by Alfonso Ortiz and William C. Sturtevant, 31–42. Washington DC: Smithsonian Institution, 1979.

Isenberg, Andrew. *Destruction of the Bison: An Ecological History, 1850–1920.* Cambridge: Cambridge University Press, 2000.

————. "The Moral Ecology of Wildlife." In *Representing Animals*, edited by Nigel Rothfels, 48–64. Bloomington: Indiana University Press, 2002.

Jackson, Charles O., and Charles W. Johnson. "The Summer of '44: Observations on Life in the Oak Ridge Community." *Tennessee Historical Quarterly* 32 (Fall 1973): 233–48.

Jacobs, Meg. *Pocketbook Politics: Economic Citizenship in Twentieth-Century America*. Princeton NJ: Princeton University Press, 2005.

Jacoby, Karl. *Crimes against Nature: Squatters, Poachers, Thieves, and the Hidden History of American Conservation*. Berkeley: University of California Press, 2003.

Jameson, Frederic. "Postmodernism, or The Cultural Logic of Late Capitalism." *New Left Review* 146 (July–August 1984): 53–92.

Janis, Eugenia Parry. "A Hot Iron Ball He Can Neither Swallow Nor Spit Out." In *Nuclear Enchantment*, photographs by Patrick Nagatani; essay by Eugenia Parry Janis. Albuquerque: University of New Mexico Press, 1991.

"Javelina Released on White Sands Missile Range." *New Mexico Department of Game and Fish News* 17 (24 March 1970): 1.

Johansen, Sigurd. *New Mexico's Urban and Rural Population*. Las Cruces: New Mexico State University, Agricultural Experiment Station and the U.S. Department of Agriculture, 1971.

Johnson, Benjamin Heber. *Revolution in Texas: How a Forgotten Rebellion and Its Bloody Suppression Turned Mexicans into Americans*. New Haven CT: Yale University Press, 2003.

Johnson, Marilynn S. *The Second Gold Rush: Oakland and the East Bay in World War II*. Berkeley: University of California Press, 1993.

Kingdon, Jonathan. *The Kingdon Field Guide to African Mammals*. New York: Harcourt Brace, 1997.

Kingsland, Sharon. *The Evolution of American Ecology, 1890–2000*. Baltimore: Johns Hopkins University Press, 2005.

Kirk, Andrew G. *Counterculture Green: The Whole Earth Catalog and American Environmentalism*. Lawrence: University Press of Kansas, 2007.

Kirkpatrick, Thomas O. *The Economic and Social Values of Hunting and Fishing in New Mexico*. Albuquerque: Bureau of Business Research, University of New Mexico, 1965.

Kirschner Associates. *Study of Recreation and Tourism in New Mexico*. Prepared for Marplan Division of Communications Affiliates, 1965.

Klein, David. "The Introduction, Increase, and Crash of Reindeer on St. Matthew Island." *Journal of Wildlife Management* 32 (April 1968): 350–67.

Klein, Kerwin Lee. "On the Emergence of *Memory* in Historical Discourse." *Representations* 69 (Winter 2000): 127–50.

Klingle, Matthew. *Emerald City: An Environmental History of Seattle*. New Haven CT: Yale University Press, 2007.

Kosek, Jake. *Understories: The Political Life of Forests in Northern New Mexico*. Durham NC: Duke University Press, 2006.

Krech, Shepard, III. *The Ecological Indian: Myth and History*. New York: W. W. Norton, 1999.

Kreeger, Terry L. "The Internal Wolf: Physiology, Pathology, and Pharmacology." In Mech and Boitani, *Wolves*, 192–217.

Kuletz, Valerie. *The Tainted Desert: Environmental Ruin in the American West*. New York: Routledge, 1998.

Langford, Richard P. "The Holocene History of the White Sands Dune Field and Influences on Eolian Deflation and Playa Lakes." *Quaternary International* 104 (2003): 31–39.

Lantow, J. L., and O. C. Cunningham. *Emergency Feeding of Livestock*. Bulletin no. 227. Las Cruces NM: Agricultural Experiment Station of the New Mexico College of Agriculture and Mechanic Arts, 1934.

Larson, K. H., et al. *Alpha Activity due to the 1945 Atomic Bomb Detonation at Trinity, Alamogordo, New Mexico*. UCLA-108. Los Angeles: University of California, Los Angeles, 5 February 1951.

————. *The 1949 and 1950 Radiological Soils Survey of Fission Product Contamination and Some Soil-Plant Interrelationships of Areas in New Mexico Affected by the First Atomic Bomb Detonation*. UCLA-140. Los Angeles: University of California, Los Angeles, 12 June 1951.

Lassiter, Matthew. *The Silent Majority: Suburban Politics in the Sunbelt South*. Princeton NJ: Princeton University Press, 2007.

Leonard, Kevin Allen. "Migrants, Immigrants, and Refugees: The Cold War Population Growth in the American West." In *The Cold War American West*, ed. Kevin Fernlund, 29-49. Albuquerque: University of New Mexico Press, 1998.

Leopold, Aldo. *A Sand County Almanac: And Sketches Here and There*. New York: Oxford University Press, 1949.

Leopold, Aldo, Lyle Sowls, and David Spencer, "A Survey of Over-Populated Deer Ranges in the United States." *Journal of Wildlife Management* 11 (April 1947): 162–77.

Ley, Willy. *Rockets, Missiles, and Space Travel*. New York: Viking Press, 1957.

Ligon, J. Stokely. *Wildlife of New Mexico: Its Conservation and Management: Being a Report on the Game Survey of the State 1926 and 1927*. Santa Fe: New Mexico State Game Commission, Department of Game and Fish, 1927.

Limerick, Patricia Nelson. *Desert Passages: Encounters with American Deserts*. Albuquerque: University of New Mexico Press, 1985.

————. *Legacy of Conquest: The Unbroken Past of the American West*. New York: W. W. Norton, 1987.

Lindgren, David T. *Land Use Planning and Remote Sensing*. Dordrecht, Netherlands: Martinus Nijhoff, 1985.

Linenthal, Edward T., and Tom Engelhardt. *History Wars: The Enola Gay and Other Battles for the American Past*. New York: Holt, 1996.

Lippard, Lucy. *The Lure of the Local: Sense of Place in a Multicentered Society*. New York: New Press, 1997.

López-Hoffman, Laura, et al., eds. *Conservation of Shared Environments: Learning from the United States and Mexico*. Tucson: University of Arizona Press, 2009.

Lotchin, Robert. *Fortress California, 1910–1961: From Warfare to Welfare*. Urbana: University of Illinois Press, 2002.

Lueth, Virgil, Katherine A. Giles, Spencer G. Lucas, Barry S. Kues, Robert G. Myers, and Dana Ulmer-Scholle, eds. *Geology of White Sands*. New Mexico Geological Society Fifty-Third Annual Field Conference, 3–5 October 2002. Socorro: New Mexico Geological Survey, 2002.

Lynch, Kevin. *The Image of the City*. Cambridge MA: MIT Press, 1960.

MacCameron, Robert. "Environmental Change in Colonial New Mexico." *Environmental History Review* 18 (Summer 1994): 17–39.

MacNeish, Richard. *The Origins of Agriculture and Settled Life*. Norman: University of Oklahoma Press, 1992.

Maer, David S., Reed F. Noss, and Jeffery Larkin. *Large Mammal Restoration: Ecological and Sociological Challenges in the 21st Century*. Washington DC: Island Press, 2001.

Maher, Neil. "On Shooting the Moon." *Environmental History* 9, no. 3 (July 2004): 526–31.

Makhijani, Arjun, Howard Hu, and Katherine Yih, eds. *Nuclear Wastelands: A Global Guide to Nuclear Weapons Production and Its Health and Environmental Effects*. Cambridge MA: MIT Press, 1995.

Markusen, Ann, et al. *The Rise of the Gunbelt: The Military Remapping of Industrial America*. New York: Oxford University Press, 1991.

Marshal, Jason P., Paul R. Krausman, Cernon C. Bleich, Warren B. Ballard, and Jane S. McKeever. "Rainfall, El Niño, and Dynamics of Mule Deer in the Sonoran Desert, California." *Journal of Wildlife Management* 66, no. 4 (October 2002): 1283–89.

Masco, Joseph. *The Nuclear Borderlands: The Manhattan Project in Post–Cold War New Mexico*. Princeton NJ: Princeton University Press, 2006.

Maslowski, Peter. *Armed with Cameras: The American Military Photographers of World War II*. New York: Free Press, 1993.

Matthews, Anne. *Where the Buffalo Roam: Restoring America's Great Plains*. Chicago: University of Chicago Press, 2002.

May, Elaine Tyler. *Homeward Bound: American Families in the Cold War Era*. New York: Basic Books, 1988.

McBride, Roy T. *The Mexican Wolf (Canis lupus baileyi): A Historical Review and Observations on Its Status and Distribution*. Albuquerque NM: U.S. Fish and Wildlife Service, 1980.

McEvoy, Arthur. *The Fisherman's Problem: Ecology and Law in the California Fisheries*. Cambridge UK: Cambridge University Press, 1986.

──────. "Towards an Interactive Theory of Nature And Culture." In *The Ends of the Earth: Perspectives on Modern Environmental History*, edited by Donald Worster, 211–29. Cambridge UK: Cambridge University Press, 1988.

McGirr, Lisa. *Suburban Warriors: The Origins of the New American Right*. Princeton NJ: Princeton University Press, 2001.

Mech, L. David. "Wolf Research in Minnesota." In *The Wolves of Minnesota: Howl in the Heartland*, edited by L. David Mech, 37–50. Stillwater MN: Voyageur Press, 2000.

──────. *The Wolf: The Ecology and Behavior of an Endangered Species*. Garden City NY: Natural History Press, 1970.

Mech, L. David, and Luigi Boitani, eds. *Wolves: Behavior, Ecology, and Conservation*. Chicago: University of Chicago Press, 2003.

Mech, L. David, and Rolf Peterson, "Wolf-Prey Relations." In Mech and Boitani, *Wolves*, 131–60.

Meinhold, Charles, and John Taschner. "A Brief History of Radiation," *Los Alamos Science* 23 (1995): 116–23.

Meinzer, O. E., and R. F. Hare. *Geology and Water Resources of Tularosa Basin, New Mexico*. Water Supply Paper no. 343. Washington DC: Government Printing Office, 1915.

Melville, Elinor G. K. *A Plague of Sheep: Environmental Consequences of the Conquest of Mexico*. New York: Cambridge University Press, 1994.

Merrill, Karen. *Public Lands and Political Meaning: Ranchers, the Government, and the Property between Them*. Berkeley: University of California Press, 2002.

Miller, Michael. "Predator Control—Circa 1915." *New Mexico Wildlife Magazine* 29 (January–February 1984): 14–18.

Monmonier, Mark. *Spying with Maps: Surveillance Technologies and the Future of Privacy*. Chicago: University of Chicago Press, 2002.

Montoya, Maria. "Landscapes of the Cold War West." In *The Cold War American West, 1945–1989*, edited by Kevin Fernlund, 9–27. Albuquerque: University of New Mexico Press, 1998.

Moore, H. J. *Missile Impact Craters (White Sands Missile Range, New Mexico) and Applications to Lunar Research*. Geological Position Paper no. 812-B. Washington DC: Department of the Interior, 1976.

Morrow, Patrick C. *Population Estimates for Ungulate Prey Species on White Sands Missile Range*. Unpublished report. White Sands NM: White Sands Missile Range, 1994.

———. *WSMR Prey Status Update*. Unpublished report. White Sands NM: White Sands Missile Range, 1996.

Mora, Anthony. *Border Dilemmas: Racial and National Uncertainties in New Mexico, 1848–1912*. Durham NC: Duke University Press, 2011.

Mungall, Elizabeth Cary, and William J. Sheffield. *Exotics on the Range: The Texas Example*. College Station: Texas A&M University Press, 1994.

Murie, Adolph. *The Wolves of Mount McKinley*. Seattle: University of Washington Press, 1985.

Nagatani, Patrick. *Nuclear Enchantment*. Albuquerque: University of New Mexico Press, 1991.

Nash, Gerald D. *The American West in the Twentieth Century: A Short History of an Urban Oasis*. Englewood Cliffs NJ: Prentice-Hall, 1973.

———. *The American West Transformed: The Impact of the Second World War*. Lincoln: University of Nebraska Press, 1985.

———. *World War II and the West: Reshaping the Economy*. Lincoln: University of Nebraska Press, 1990.

Nash, Gerald D., and Richard W. Etulain. *The Twentieth-Century West: Historical Interpretations*. Albuquerque: University of New Mexico Press, 1989.

Nash, Linda. *Inescapable Ecologies: A History of Environment, Disease, and Knowledge*. Berkeley: University of California Press, 2006.

National Park Service. *A Master Plan for Trinity National Historic Site*. Washington DC: National Park Service, 1970.

Newell, Homer E. *Beyond the Atmosphere: Early Years of Space Science*. Washington DC: Scientific and Technical Information Branch, National Aeronautics and Space Administration, 1980.

Nichols, John. *The Milagro Beanfield War*. New York: Ballantine Books, 1976.

Nora, Pierre. "Between Memory and History: *Les Lieux Mémoire*." *Representations* 26 (Spring 1989): 7–24.

Nye, David E. *American Technological Sublime*. Cambridge: Massachusetts Institute of Technology Press, 1994.

O'Neill, Dan. "Alaska and the Firecracker Boys: The Story of Project Chariot." In Hevly and Findlay, *Atomic West*, 179–99.

———. *The Firecracker Boys*. New York: St. Martin's Press, 1994.

Orr, Brennon R., and Robert G. Myers. *Water Resources in Basin Fill Deposits in the Tularosa Basin, New Mexico*. Albuquerque NM: U.S. Geological Survey, 1986.

Paquet, Paul C., et al. *Mexican Wolf Recovery: Three-Year Program Review and Assessment*. Prepared by the Conservation Breeding Specialist Group for the U.S. Fish and Wildlife Service, 2001.

Pasternak, Judy. *Yellow Dirt: An American Story of a Poisoned Land and People Betrayed.* New York: Free Press, 2010.

Pavlik, Steve. "San Carlos and White Mountain Apache Attitudes toward the Reintroduction of the Mexican Wolf to Its Historic Range in the American Southwest." *Wizcazo Sa Review* 14 (Spring 1999): 129–45.

Pearson, Chris, Tim Cole, and Peter Coates, eds. *Militarized Landscapes: From Gettysburg to Salisbury Plain.* London: Continuum, 2010.

Perry, Richard J. *Apache Reservation: Indigenous Peoples & the American State.* Austin: University of Texas Press, 1993.

Peterson, David, ed. *Postcards from Ed: Dispatches and Salvos from an American Iconoclast.* Minneapolis: Milkweed Editions, 2006.

Peterson, Rolf, and Paolo Ciucci. "The Wolf as Carnivore." In Mech and Boitani, *Wolves,* 104–30.

Pinto, Otis M., John M. Lenko, and Albert N. Johnson. *Final Environmental Impact Statement, White Sands Interaction with White Sands National Monument.* White Sands Missile Range NM: Department of the Army, U.S. Army White Sands Missile Range, February 1975.

Poole, Robert. *Earthrise: How Man First Saw the Earth.* New Haven CT: Yale University Press, 2008.

Price, V. B. *The Orphaned Land: New Mexico's Environment since the Manhattan Project.* New Mexico: University of New Mexico Press, 2011.

Raatz, William D. "A Stratigraphic History of the Tularosa Basin Area, South-Central New Mexico." In *Geology of White Sands,* edited by Virgil Lueth et al. New Mexico Geological Society Fifty-Third Annual Field Conference, 3–5 October 2002. Socorro: New Mexico Geological Survey, 2002.

Radkau, Joachim. *Nature and Power: A Global History of the Environment.* New York: Cambridge University Press, 2008.

Reid, W. H., and G. R. Patrick. "Gemsbok (*Oryx Gazella*) in White Sands National Monument." *Southwestern Naturalist* 28 (February 1983): 97–99.

Reisner, Mark. *Cadillac Desert: The American West and Its Disappearing Water.* New York: Penguin Books, 1993.

Rhodes, Richard. *Making the Atomic Bomb.* New York: Simon & Schuster, 1995.

Richie, Jason. *Space Flight: Crossing the Last Frontier.* Minneapolis: Oliver Press, 2002.

Riebsame, William, gen. ed., James J. Robb, director of cartography, et al. *The Atlas of the New West: Portrait of a Changing Region.* New York: W. W. Norton, 1997.

Ringholz, Raye C. *Uranium Frenzy: Saga of the Nuclear West.* Logan: Utah State University Press, 2002.

Risser, Dennis. *Simulated Water Level and Air Quality Changes in the Bolson-Fill Aquifer Post Headquarters Area, White Sands Missile Range, New Mexico.* Albuquerque NM: U.S. Geological Survey, 1988.

Roberts, Calvin A., and Susan A. Roberts. *New Mexico*. Albuquerque: University of New Mexico Press, 2006.

Robbins, William G. "In Search of Western Lands." In *Land in the American West: Private Claims and the Common Good*, edited by William G. Robbins and James C. Foster, 3–20. Seattle: University of Washington Press, 2000.

Robbins, William G., and James C. Foster. *Land In the American West: Private Claims and the Common Good*. Seattle: University of Washington Press, 2000.

Rome, Adam. *Bulldozer in the Countryside: Suburban Sprawl and the Rise of American Environmentalism*. New York: Cambridge University Press, 2001.

Rosales, F. Arturo. *Chicano! The History of the Mexican American Civil Rights Movement*. Houston: Arte Público Press, 1997.

Rothman, Hal. *Devil's Bargains: Tourism in the Twentieth-Century American West*. Lawrence: University Press of Kansas, 1998.

——. *On Rims and Ridges: The Los Alamos Area since 1880*. Lincoln: University of Nebraska Press, 1992.

Rudnick, Lois Palken. *Utopian Vistas: The Mabel Dodge Luhan House and the American Counterculture*. Albuquerque: University of New Mexico Press, 1996.

Russell, Edmund. "Afterword: Militarized Landscapes." In *Militarized Landscapes: From Gettysburg to Salisbury Plain*, edited by Chris Pearson, Peter Coates, and Tim Cole, 229–37. New York: Continuum, 2010.

Saiz, Richard B. *Ecology and Behavior of the Gemsbok on White Sands Missile Range*. Federal Aid Project W-111-R-8. Santa Fe: New Mexico Department of Game and Fish, March 1975. General Collection, New Mexico State University Library, Las Cruces.

——. *Evaluation of Exotic Mammals: Evaluation and Introduction of Exotic Mammals*. New Mexico: 1977.

——. *Exotic Mammal Investigations: Evaluation and Introduction of Exotic Mammals*. New Mexico: 1976.

Sale, Mark, and Victor Gibbs. *An Archaeological Survey of Approximately 220 Miles of Right-of-Way for the Test Support Network Fiber Optics Cable Backbone on White Sands Missile Range*. Miscellaneous Report of Investigations no. 86. Fort Worth TX: U.S. Army Corps of Engineers, Fort Worth District, 1995.

Schneider-Hector, Dietmar. *White Sands: The History of a National Monument*. Albuquerque: University of New Mexico Press, 1993.

Schulman, Bruce. *The Seventies: The Great Shift in American Culture, Society, and Politics*. Cambridge MA: De Capo Press, 2002.

Scott, James C. *Seeing Like a State: How Certain Schemes to Improve the Human Condition Have Failed*. New Haven CT: Yale University Press, 1998.

Shearer, David. *WSMR Unexploded Ordnance (UXO) Awareness Training*. Las Cruces NM: NMSU Safety Office, n.d.

Shulman, Seth. *The Threat at Home: Confronting the Toxic Legacy of the U.S. Military.* Boston: Beacon Press, 1992.

Smith, Christine, et al. "Diets of Native and Non-Native Ungulates in Southcentral New Mexico." *Southwestern Naturalist* 43 (June 1998): 163–69.

Smith, Douglas W., and Gary Ferguson. *Decade of the Wolf: Returning the Wild to Yellowstone.* Granville OH: McDonald and Woodward, 2008.

Sonnichsen, C. L. *The Mescalero Apaches.* Norman: University of Oklahoma Press, 1973.

————. *Tularosa: Last of the Frontier West.* Albuquerque: University of New Mexico Press, 1980.

Southwest Parks and Monuments Association. *A Checklist of Mammals, Reptiles, Amphibians, and Arthropods of White Sands National Monument.* Tucson AZ: Southwest Parks and Monuments Association, 1994.

Spence, Mark David. *Dispossessing the Wilderness: Indian Removal and the Making of the National Parks.* New York: Oxford University Press, 1999.

Stephenson, Thor E., Jerry L. Holecheck, and Charles B. Kuykendall. "Drought Effect on Pronghorn and Other Ungulate Diets." *Journal of Wildlife Management* 49 (1985): 146–51.

Stock, Catherine McNicol. *Rural Radicals: Righteous Rage in the American Grain.* Ithaca NY: Cornell University Press, 1996.

Stuart, Chris, and Tilde Stuart. *Field Guide to the Mammals of Southern Africa.* Sanibel Island FL: Ralph Curtis Books, 1993.

Sutter, Paul. *Driven Wild: How the Fight against Automobiles Launched the Modern Wilderness Movement.* Seattle: University of Washington Press, 2002.

Szasz, Ferenc Morton. *The Day the Sun Rose Twice: The Story of the Trinity Site Nuclear Explosion, July 16, 1945.* Albuquerque: University of New Mexico Press, 1984.

Taylor, C. R. "The Eland and the Oryx." *Scientific American* 220 (January 1969): 88–96.

Test Directorate, HE Simulation Division, New Mexico Operations Office, Defense Nuclear Agency. *Minor Scale Event: Test Execution Report.* Kirtland Air Force Base NM: Defense Nuclear Agency, 1986.

Theberge, John B., and David A. Gauthier. "Model of Wolf-Ungulate Relationships: When Is Wolf Control Justified?" *Wildlife Society Bulletin* 13 (Winter 1985): 449–58.

Thelen, David. "Memory and American History." *Journal of American History* 75 (March 1989): 1117–29.

Towle, Jerry. "Authored Ecosystems: Livingston Stone and the Transformation of California Fisheries." *Environmental History* 5 (January 2000): 54–74.

Truett, Samuel, and Elliott Young, eds. *Continental Crossroads: Remapping U.S.-Mexico Borderlands.* Durham NC: Duke University Press, 2004.

Tuan, Yi-Fu. *Space and Place: The Perspective of Experience.* Minneapolis: University of Minnesota Press, 1977.

———. *Topophilia: A Study of Environmental Perception, Attitudes, and Values*. Englewood Cliffs NJ: Prentice-Hall, 1974.

Turner, James Morton. *The Promise of Wilderness: American Environmental Politics since 1964*. Seattle: University of Washington Press, 2012.

———. "The Specter of Environmentalism: Wilderness, Environmental Politics, and the Evolution of the New Right." *Journal of American History* 96 (June 2009): 123–48.

Tyrrell, Ian. *True Gardens of the Gods: Californian-Australian Environmental Reform, 1860–1930*. Berkeley: University of California Press, 1999.

U.S. Department of Agriculture, Weather Bureau. *Climatological Data*. New Mexico Section 34. Santa Fe NM: 1930.

U.S. Department of Commerce, Bureau of the Census. *United States Census of Population, 1950, General Characteristics, New Mexico*. Washington DC: U.S. Department of Commerce, Bureau of the Census.

———. *United States Census of Population, 1960, New Mexico, General Population Characteristics*. Washington DC: U.S. Department of Commerce, Bureau of the Census, 1961.

———. *1970 Census of Population, General Population Characteristics, New Mexico*. Washington DC: U.S. Department. of Commerce, Bureau of the Census, 1971.

———. *1980 Census of Population, Characteristics of the Population, Number of Inhabitants, New Mexico*. Washington DC: U.S. Department of Commerce, Bureau of the Census, 1982.

———. *1990 Census of Population and Housing, Summary Social, Economic, and Housing Characteristics, New Mexico*. Washington DC: U.S. Department of Commerce, Economics and Statistics Administration, Bureau of the Census, 1992.

U.S. Department of Interior, National Park Service, White Sands National Monument. *Environmental Assessment/Assessment of Effect, Complete the Removal of African Oryx, White Sands National Monument*. White Sands NM: White Sands Missile Range, 2001.

U.S. Department of the Army. "Acquisition of Land for ORDCIT Project Range Facilities." U.S. Department of the Army, *Historical Monograph No. 4*. April 1961.

U.S. Department of War. *Reports of Explorations and Surveys to Ascertain the Most Practicable and Economical Route for a Railroad from the Mississippi River to the Pacific Ocean, 1853–54*. Vol. 2. Washington DC: Beverley Tucker, 1855.

U.S. Fish and Wildlife Service. *Mexican Wolf Recovery Plan*. Denver: U.S. Fish and Wildlife Service, Unit 1, 1982.

———. *Reintroduction of the Mexican Wolf within Its Historic Range in the Southwestern United States: Final Environmental Impact Statement*. Washington DC: U.S. Fish and Wildlife Service, 1996.

U.S. General Accounting Office. *Acquisitions of Properties and Settling of Claims on White Sands Missile Range, New Mexico*. Washington DC: GAO, 1983.

UXO Hazards and Munitions Management Team. *White Sands Missile Range Unexploded Ordnance Hazards and Munitions Management Plan and Implementation Guide*. White Sands NM: White Sands Missile Range, February 1999.

Valenčius, Conevery Bolton. *The Health of the Country: How American Settlers Understood Themselves and Their Land*. New York: Basic Books, 2002.

Vanderbilt, Tom. *Survival City: Adventures among the Ruins of Atomic America*. Chicago: University of Chicago Press, 2002.

Van Etten, D. M., and W. D. Purtymun. *Depleted Uranium Investigation at Missile Impact Sites in White Sands Missile Range*. Los Alamos NM: Los Alamos National Laboratories, 1994.

Virilio, Paul. *The Vision Machine*. Translated by Julie Rose. Bloomington: Indiana University Press, 1994.

Walker, A. L., and J. L. Lantow. *A Preliminary Study of 127 New Mexico Ranches in 1925*. Bulletin no. 159. Las Cruces NM: Agricultural Experiment Station of the New Mexico College of Agriculture and Mechanic Arts, 1927.

Ward, Bob. *Dr. Space: The Life of Wernher von Braun*. Annapolis MD: Naval Institute Press, 2005.

Warren, Louis. *The Hunter's Game: Poachers and Conservationists in Twentieth-Century America*. New Haven CT: Yale University Press, 1997.

Warren, Stafford L. *The 1948 Radiological and Biological Survey of Areas in New Mexico Affected by the First Atomic Bomb Detonation*. UCLA-32. Atomic Energy Project. University of California at Los Angeles. 17 November 1949.

Weber, David J. *The Spanish Frontier in North America*. New Haven CT: Yale University Press, 1992.

Welsh, Michael E. *Dunes and Dreams: A History of White Sands National Monument*. Santa Fe NM: Division of History, Intermountain Cultural Resource Center, Intermountain Field Area, National Park Service, Dept. of the Interior, 1995.

W. F. Turney and Associates. *Proposed Investigational Program for the Limited Development of the Water Sources in Tularosa Basin, New Mexico*. Santa Fe NM: W. F. Turney, October 1965.

White, Richard. "Are You an Environmentalist or Do You Work for Living?" In *Uncommon Ground: Rethinking the Human Place in Nature*, edited by William Cronon, 171–85. New York: W. W. Norton, 1996.

———. "Contested Terrain: The Business of Land in the American West." In *Land in the American West: Private Claims and the Common Good*, edited by William Robbins and James C. Foster, 190–206. Seattle: University of Washington Press, 2000.

———. "The Current Weirdness in the West." *Western Historical Quarterly* 28 (Spring 1997): 5–16.

———. "Environmental History, Ecology, and Meaning." *Journal of American History* 76 (March 1990): 1111–16.

———. *The Organic Machine: The Remaking of the Columbia River.* New York: Hill and Wang, 1996.

White Sands Missile Range, Directorate of Environment and Safety, Environmental Services Division. *Final Environmental Impact Statement for Development and Implementation of Range-Wide Mission and Major Capabilities at White Sands Missile Range, New Mexico.* 2 vols. White Sands Missile Range NM, November 2009.

———. *White Sands Missile Range Range-Wide Environmental Impact Statement, Final.* White Sands Missile Range NM, January 1998.

White Sands Missile Range and New Mexico Department of Game and Fish. *Comprehensive Oryx Management Plan.* White Sands Missile Range NM, 2000.

Whitfield, Stephen J. *The Culture of the Cold War.* Baltimore: Johns Hopkins University Press, 1991.

Wills, John. "'Welcome to the Atomic Park': American Nuclear Landscapes and the 'Unnaturally Natural.'" *Environment and History* 7 (November 2001): 449–72.

Wilson, C. A., and Robert G. Myers. *Ground-Water Resources of the Soledad Canyon Re-entrant and Adjacent Areas, White Sands Missile Range and Fort Bliss Military Reservation, Doña Ana County, New Mexico.* Albuquerque NM: U.S. Geological Survey, 1981.

Wilson, Chris. *The Myth of Santa Fe: Creating a Modern Regional Tradition.* Albuquerque: University of New Mexico Press, 1997.

Winkler, Allan M. *Life under a Cloud: American Anxiety about the Atom.* New York: Oxford University Press, 1993.

Wishart, David. *Encyclopedia of the Great Plains.* Lincoln: University of Nebraska Press, 2004.

Wood, John E., Ronald J. White, and Jackson L. Durham. *Investigations Preliminary to the Release of Exotic Ungulates in New Mexico.* Bulletin no. 13. Santa Fe: New Mexico Department of Game and Fish, 1970.

Worcester, Donald. *The Apaches: Eagles of the Southwest.* Norman: University of Oklahoma Press, 1979.

Worster, Donald. *Dust Bowl: The Southern Plains in the 1930s.* New York: Oxford University Press, 2004.

———. "The Ecology of Order and Chaos." *Environmental History Review* 14 (Spring–Summer 1990): 1–18.

———. *Nature's Economy: A History of Ecological Ideas.* 2nd ed. New York: Cambridge University Press, 1994.

———. *Rivers of Empire: Water, Aridity, and the Growth of the American West.* New York: Oxford University Press, 1992.

Wrobel, David M., and Patrick T. Long, eds. *Seeing and Being Seen: Tourism in the American West*. Lawrence: University Press of Kansas, 2001.

Wunder, John R., and Pekka Hämäläinen. "Of Lethal Places and Lethal Essays." *American Historical Review* 104 (October 1999): 1229–34.

Yoshida, Kayoko. "From Atomic Fragments to Memories of the Trinity Bomb: A Bridge of Oral History over the Pacific." *Oral History Review* 30 (Summer–Autumn 2003): 59–75.

Young, Christian C. *In the Absence of Predators: Conservation and Controversy on the Kaibab Plateau*. Lincoln: University of Nebraska Press, 2002.

Young, Stanley P., and Edward A. Goldman. *The Wolves of North America*. Washington DC: American Wildlife Institute, 1944.

Zirker, J. B. *An Acre of Glass: A History and Forecast of the Telescope*. Baltimore: Johns Hopkins University Press, 2005.

INDEX

Page numbers in italics refer to illustrations.

A-1 rocket, 91
A-2 rocket, 91
Abbey, Edward: *Fire on the Mountain*, 51
Abert, James W., 26
Abert, John James, 27
Administrative Procedures Act, 190, 195
Advisory Exotic Mammal Task Force, 127
AEC. *See* Atomic Energy Commission (AEC)
Aerial Radiological Measuring System (ARMS), 110–11
Aerobee rocket, 86, 91, 99
Air Force Missile Development Center, 52
Alamogordo Army Air Field, 20, 37, 40, 43, 46, 70, 151, 167
Alamogordo Bombing and Gunnery Range, 20, 38, 39, 41–43, 50, 52, 59
Alamogordo Chamber of Commerce, 40–41, 54, 69

Albuquerque Peace and Justice Center, 115
Allen, James Van, 92
American Meteorological Society (AMS), 99
Ames, Norma, 186
Anaya, Rudolfo, 11
Anderson, Clinton, 76
Antiquities Act (1906), 72
Apache National Forest, 193–94
Apaches. *See* Mescalero Apaches
APL. *See* Applied Physics Laboratory (APL)
aplomado falcon, 1, 161, 172, 201
Apodoca, Mike, 51
Applied Physics Laboratory (APL), 86, 89, 92–94, 218n8
Armendaris Ranch, 142
Army Corps of Engineers, 153–54
Army Search Light Station L-8, 62
Army Service Forces Circular 268, 42–43
Atchison, Topeka, and Santa Fe Railroad, 27
Athena missiles, 86, 102–3, 109–13

Atlantic Research Corporation, 109
atomic calves, 65
Atomic Energy Commission (AEC),
    2, 11, 53–58, 66–67, 72–75, 82, 85,
    110, 119
atomic tourism, 57–58, 70. *See also*
    tourism
atomic weapons testing. *See* nuclear
    weapons testing
"Atoms for Peace" speech, 95

Baca Ranch, 167
Bailey, Vernon, 177
Bainbridge, Kenneth T., 67
Barker, Elliott S., 123
Barnes, Gladeon Marcus, 19, 42–43, 90
bats, 1, 201
Beatty, Les, 35
Bednarz, James C., 174, 181–85, 189,
    195, 197; *An Evaluation of the Ecolog-
    ical Potential of White Sands Missile
    Range*, 181–82
Bell, Roscoe E., 48–49
Bell, Tom, 47
Bentham, Jeremy, 98
Berg, Otto, 99
Bergstralh, Thor A., 93
bighorn sheep. *See* desert bighorn
    sheep
Bingaman, Jeff, 163, 169
Bishop, Riss, 50
black grama grass, 32–33
Blue Marble, 86, 89
Blue Range Wolf Recovery Area,
    193–96
bluetongue fever, 139
Bockscar, 71
Boreto, Manuel Velasquez, 109–10
Bosque del Apache National Wildlife
    Refuge, 141

Bosque Redondo, 26, 30
bovine respiratory syntactical virus,
    139
Bracero Program, 105
Brown, David, 184
Brown, William, 76
Bureau of Biological Investigations,
    177
Bureau of Indian Affairs, 193
Bureau of Land Management, 19, 35,
    48, 52, 132, 141, 147, 152–53, 162,
    170, 174
Burks, Melvin, 81
Burnett, Grove T., 188–89
Bursum, Holm, III, 35, 66
Bursum Cattle Company, 66
Bush, George H. W., 169–70
Bustamante, Carlos, 108, 111

Campbell & Kay, 53
Camp Doña Ana, 26
Camp Pendleton, 173
Canadian River Canyon, 123
cancer, 66, 74, 85, 95, 115
Cannon Air Force Base, 10
Carleton, James Henry, 26
Carson, Kit, 26
Casey, Edward, 9
Castner Target Range, 43
catabolism, 183
Chapman, Oscar, 74
Chavez, Dennis, 47, 51
Chavez-Garcia, Felipe, 107–8, 107
Cheney, Richard, 189
Chess Site, 115–16
Chihuahuan Desert Range Research
    Center, 32
Chisum, John, 30
Chisum Trail, 30
Cities of the Plain (McCarthy), 51

Citizens for Alternatives to Radioactive Dumping, 115
Civil War, 26
Clark, Wilbur, 58
Clinton, Bill, 139
Cobalt-57, 109–12
Cobb, John, 47
cognitive mapping, 206n16
Coker, Ted, 66, 70
Cold War, 6–11, 14, 16, 44, 52, 56–57, 82, 84–85, 87, 94–97
Comanches, 18, 25
common good, 149–50, 228n9
communism, 9, 16, 57, 174
Community Service Organization, 105
Comprehensive Oryx Management Plan, 140–41
Condron Airfield, 5
contestation, definition of, 12
Cornish, Thomas, 128
Coronado, Francisco Vásquez de, 24
Cosgrove, Denis E., 95
co-use land agreements, 44, 46–51, 101, 155, 167
Cox, A. B., 41–42
Cox, Alice, 167
Cox, Hal, 167
Cox, J. W., 167
Cox, Rob, 186, 188
craters, missile, 2, 14, 53–55, 61, 62, 67–75, 83, 108, 112–14, 203–4
creosote bush, 19, 22, 32, 34, 36, 134
Cronon, William, 203
Cushman, Dave, 33

Dare County Air Force Range, 173
Davis, Mike, 2
Davisson, H. G., 108–9, 127
Dayton, Donald, 77–78
Dean, Fred, 108

DeBuys, William, 11–12
Defenders of Wildlife, 181
Demaray, Arthur, 72
Dempsey, John J., 15, 38, 42, 46
denning, 177
Department of Agriculture, 43, 45, 50, 125, 151–52
Department of Defense (DOD): and militarization of WSMR, 17; power of, in borderlands, 84; and protection of endangered species, 2, 172, 182, 189–90, 196; radiation concerns of, and tourism, 54, 56; and range wars with ranchers, 144, 149, 151, 154, 156, 160, 166–70; and Trinity test site monument, 71, 74–75; and wolf reintroduction, 172, 182, 189–90, 196; as WSMR administrator, 5, 8–9, 11–13
Department of Energy, 2, 57
Department of Interior, 19, 35–36, 38, 44–45, 47–48, 52, 71–72, 124, 151
Department of the Army, 44, 48–50
Department of War, 12, 17, 37, 43, 71
depredation permits, 142
desert bighorn sheep, 1, 23, 136, 139, 142, 172, 178, 183, 186
desert tortoise, 2, 173
Dillon, Richard C., 35
Di Matteo, Natalia Lucero, 33
Division of Grazing, 19, 35, 36
Division of Wildlife Research, 177–78
D. I. Z. Livestock Co. et al. v. United States, 157–58, 160, 168
DOD. See Department of Defense (DOD)
Domenici, Pete, 159, 161–62, 169
Doña Ana Target Range, 43, 46–47, 50
Dunlap, Thomas, 179
Durham, Jackson, 132–34

Earth Day, 179

Earth photos, 86–100, *88*, 218nn6–8, 218n11, 220n30

Earthrise, 86, 89

Eckles, Jim, 6, 170

Ecological Indian, 192

Eisenhower, Dwight, 95

Ela, Tom, 126

El Niño, 19

El Paso and Northeastern Railroad, 29

endangered species, 1–2, 13, 23, 122, 136, 139, 148, 201, 203

Endangered Species Act (1973), 2, 119, 124, 174–76, 179, 184, 189–90, 195–96

Energy Research and Development Administration, 57

Eniwetok Atoll, 56

Enola Gay, 71, 81, 217n59

Environmental Defense Fund, 175, 189

environmental image, 12

environmental impact statements, 101, 115, 124, 175, 192–93

Environmental Law Center, 189

Environmental Stewardship Branch, 201

errant missiles, 83–84, 100–114, *104*

ESA. *See* Endangered Species Act (1973)

An Evaluation of the Ecological Potential of White Sands Missile Range (Bednarz), 181–82

Evans, G. W., 48

Executive Order 9029, 37, 150

Executive Order 11987, 124

Executive Order 13112, 139–40

exotic fish species, 124

exotic game at WSMR: adaptation and survival strategies of, 131–36; establishment of, 123–31;

introduction of, 118–23; irruption of, 136–43, 224n6

Explorer II, 93

fallout, radioactive. *See* radioactivity

Faris, Johnwill, 100–101

Fauna Silvestre, 180

Fermi, Enrico, 59

Fernandez, Antonio, 54, 74

Fey, Frederick L., Jr., 77

"A Field Study of the Wolf in the Superior National Forest" (Stenlund), 181

Findlay, John, 57

Firefly Program, 102

Fire on the Mountain (Abbey), 51

First National Chicano Liberation Youth Conference, 105

Flint, Miles, 168

Forest Service, 17, 148, 162, 174, 177, 200

Forrestal, James, 98

Fortas, Abe, 70–71

Fort Bliss, 6, 10, 20, 42–43, 48, 90, 106, 160, 169

Fort Fillmore, 26

Fort Selden, 26

Fort Stanton, 26

Fort Sumner, 26

Fort Wingate Launch Complex, 6, 100, 102–3

Foucault, Michel, 98

Fountain, Albert Jennings, 30

Fund for Animals, 199–200

Gadsden Purchase, 26

Garrett, Patrick, 200

Gatanas, Harry D., 114

gemsbok. *See* oryx

Gentry, Denny, 145–46, 188

Gila National Wilderness, 195

Gilliland, Dick, 45
Goddard, Robert H., 90
Goldwater, Barry, 147
Gonzales, Oved, 108
Goodnight, Charles, 29–30
Goodnight-Loving Trail, 29–30
Gordon, Ladd, 128
Grant, Ulysses S., 26
Grapevine Horse Camp, 30–31
Grazing Service, 16, 19–20, 38, 41, 43, 52, 152
Great Depression, 35, 37, 105
Green River Launch Complex, 6, 100, 102–3, 106, 109
Grider, Jim, 141
Groves, Leslie R., 58, 151
Guadalupe Aerial Gunnery Range, 40
Guggenheim, Harry, 90
gypsum dunes, 6, 22, 100, 134, 137

HAFB. See Holloman Air Force Base (HAFB)
Hall, H. Dale, 1
Hanford WA, 7, 10, 58, 85, 151
Hare, R. F., 31
Harvey, Phil, 154
Harvey, Phil, Jr., 186, 188
Harvey Cattle Company, 66
Hatch, Carl, 71
Hatch, Orrin, 148
health physics, 60
Helms, Dolly, 164
Hempelmann, Louis, 60, 64–66
Henderson, David, 189
Hermes B rocket, 91
Hermes Project, 91–92
Hevly, Bruce, 57
Hibben, Frank, 123, 125–26, 131, 142
Hirschfelder, Joseph, 62
Hoffman, Joseph G., 64

Holliday, Clyde T., 89, 93–99, 117
Holloman Air Force Base (HAFB): economic benefits of, 51–52; establishment of, 20; location of, 6, 10; and Luther Boles, 167–68; size of, 45; and Trinity test site monument, 70–72; and use of WSMR for test firings, 86; and wolf reintroduction, 193–95; and WSNM, 100. See also Alamogordo Army Air Field
Holloman Air Force Development Center, 102
Holm Bursum and Company, 36
Homer, John L., 48
Homestead Act, 149
Hopper, Dennis, 11
horses, feral, 183, 199–200
Hubbard, Jack, 60–61
Hubert, L. F., 99
Huey, William, 126, 136
Humphries, Bill, 159
hunters and hunting, 118–28, 130–34, 136–37, 140–43, 199–200
hunting licenses, 118, 125, 128, 141
Hyde, Arthur M., 35

ibex, 125–27, 133
Ickes, Harold, 71
International Society for the Protection of Wild Horses and Burros, 199–200
Invasive Species Council, 140

Jantzen, Robert, 126
Johnson, Otto, 43
Jones, Alton, 40–41
Jones, Bob, 145, 169
Jornada del Muerto (Jornada Basin), 6, 19, 21, 27, 59, 67

Jornada Experimental Range, 32, 34, 44–45, 193
Jornada Mogollon people, 24

Kawakami, Saburo, 81
Kearney, Stephen, 26
Kearns, Thomas, 112
Kennedy, Roger, 191
Kerns, Junior, 201
King, Bruce, 127–28
Kingsland, Sharon, 56
Kirtland Air Force Base, 10
Kosek, Jake, 11, 57
Koski, Frank, 126
Krech, Shepard, 192
Krug, Julius A., 48, 50, 72
kudu, 125, 127

Lacey Act (1900), 124
Laird, Melvin, 154
Lake Otero, 21
La Luz, 26
La Mesilla, 26
La Niña, 19
LANL. *See* Los Alamos National Laboratories (LANL)
Lantow, J. L., 33
Larson, Henry, 102
Las Cruces, 11, 26, 37, 43, 46–49, 51–52, 173
Las Cruces Lions Club, 47
Las Vegas Chamber of Commerce, 58
Launch Complex 33, 91
Lawrence, George, 92–93
Laws, Jerry, 199
lease and suspension agreements, 17, 45–47, 146–47, 149, 151–53, 155, 157, 161, 164–65
Least Bell's vireo, 173
Lee, Charles, 101–2

Lee, Oliver, 30–31
Lee, Ronald, 72–73
Leopold, Aldo, 122, 177; *A Sand County Almanac*, 181
Lex J. Armijo et al. v. United States, 158–59, 163
Ligon, J. Stokely, 177
Limerick, Patricia Nelson, 10
Lincoln National Forest, 23
Lindbergh, Charles, 90
Lobo Week, 171, 185, 188–89
loggerhead sea turtles, 2, 173
Los Alamos Boys School, 151
Los Alamos National Laboratories (LANL), 2, 10, 59, 64, 67, 77, 85, 115–16
Los Alamos Scientific Laboratory, 102
Loving, Oliver, 30
Luhan, Mabel Dodge, 11
Lujan, Manual, 189–90
Lynch, Kevin, 12, 206n16

Madrigal, Jorge Mario Rojas, 108–9
Magee, John, 63
Magoffinsville, 26
malignant catarrhal fever, 139
Malpais Spring virus, 139
Manhattan Engineer District (MED), 20, 55, 58, 60, 63, 66, 82
Manhattan Project, 52–53, 56, 58–62, 64, 67, 80, 151
Marshall Islands, 56
Martin, Bob, 33
Masco, Joseph, 11
Matador guided missiles, 102
Matthias, Franklin "Fritz," 151
McBride, Roy T., 179, 184
McCarran, Patrick, 42
McCarran Senate Committee on Public Lands and Surveys, 42

McCarthy, Cormac: *Cities of the Plain*, 51

McCollum, Charles S., 70

McDonald, Dave, 45, 144–45, *145*, 161, 164, 166, 168, 170

McDonald, George, 55

McDonald, Mary, 144–46, 161, 166

McDonald, Ross, 45

McGregor Range, 20, 47, 50–51, 102, 160–61, 165, 167, 169

McIlhaney, William E., 188

McKeen, Hugh, 195–96

McKinley, E. D., 40

Mech, L. David: *The Wolf*, 181

Mechem, Edwin, 54, 74–75

MED. *See* Manhattan Engineer District (MED)

Meiklejohn, Doug, 189

Meinzer, O. E., 31

Merrill, Karen, 18

Mescalero Apaches, 18, 24–26, 193–94

Mescalero Apache Tribal Government, 194

Mescalero Office of Environmental Protection, 193

mesquite, 19, 22, 32, 34, 36, 134

Mexican-American Political Association, 105

Mexican-American War, 17–19, 25, 84, 105

Mexican Border Patrol, 105

Mexican Nuclear Agency, 110

Mexican Revolution, 106

Mexican Wolf Coalition, 189

Mexican Wolf Recovery Plan, 180, 189–90

Mexico, errant missiles into, 83–84, 104, 105–13

Miles, John E., 40

militarized landscapes, definition of, 3

Military Conservation Partner Award (2007), 1, 201

Military Construction Act (1973), 155

Military Construction and Reserve Forces Facilities Authorization Acts (1973), 155

Military Construction Appropriation Act (1980), 156

Mine Impact, 115–16

Morrow, Patrick, 140–42, 199

Movimiento Estudiantil Chicano de Aztlán, 105

mule deer, 23, 122, 135, 138–39, 142, 178, 183–84, 193–94, 197

Nalda, Louis, 65–66

Nash, Gerald D., 37

National Aeronautics and Space Administration (NASA), 5, 86, 96, 110

National Audubon Society, 189

National Cattlemen's Association, 148

National Council on Radiation Protection and Measurements, 62

National Environmental Policy Act (1969), 2, 124–25, 127, 140, 174–76, 195–96

National Historical Preservation Act (1966), 78

National Park Service (NPS), 54–56, 70, 72–78, 84, 101, 126, 138, 174, 191

National Register of Historic Places, 79

National Weather Service, 96

natural security state, definition of, 175–76

Navajos, 26

Naval Air Weapons Station at China Lake, 119

Naval Research Laboratory (NRL), 86, 92–93, 99, 101

NEPA. *See* National Environmental
  Policy Act (1969)
Ness, Erik, 188
Neumann, John von, 59
Nevada Test Site, 2, 10, 58, 85
Newell, Homer, 101
New Mexico Cattle Growers Asso-
  ciation, 35, 40, 48–49, 145, 153,
  169–71, 186, 188, 195–96
New Mexico Department of Game
  and Fish, 23, 117–18, 123, 127–36,
  140–43, 171, 185–86, 201
Nichols, John, 11
Nieland, John B., 103
Nike rocket series, 91
nilgai antelope, 123
1985 Minor Scale event, 114
Nobel, Alfred, 92
Non-indigenous Aquatic Nuisance Pre-
  vention and Control Act (1990), 124
NPS. *See* National Park Service (NPS)
NRL. *See* Naval Research Laboratory
  (NRL)
Nuclear Effects Laboratory, 5
nuclear landscapes, 2–3, 54, 57–58
nuclear tourism, 57–58, 70. *See also*
  tourism
nuclear weapons testing, 6, 20, 52–53,
  58–70, 60, 61, 73, 80
Nye, David, 96, 201

Oak Ridge TN, 59, 151
Odum, Eugene, 56
Odum, Howard, 56
Office of the Chief of Ordnance,
  Research and Development, 42
O'Keefe, Georgia, 11
Oliver, G. B., 161, 164
Olsen, Harold, 185
Operation Great Sand, 112

Operation Wetback, 105
Oppenheimer, J. Robert, 59, 80
ORDCIT (Ordnance–California Institute of Technology), 42, 45, 90
Organ Mountains, 21–22, 27, 29, 186
Ortiz, Priscilla, 167
oryx, *120*, *129*; adaptation and survival
  strategies of, 131–36; competition
  of, with domestic livestock, 135;
  competition of, with feral horses
  and native ungulates, 200; and
  decline in mule deer population,
  194; as disease carriers, 135–36,
  138–39; establishment of, 123–31;
  introduction of, 118–23; irruption
  of, 136–43, 224n6; as prey for reintroduced wolves, 183
Oscura Mountains, 5, 21–22, 29, 59,
  134, 182, 194
Otero County Board of Commissioners, 186–87, 192
Owens, Joe, 185

Padilla, Thora Walsh, 193
Patraw, P. P., 76
Patterson, Robert, 71
Peace Aware, 115
Pearson, Paul, 73–74
Peck, William G., 26
Peralta, 26
Pershing, John J., 106
Pershing missiles, 86, 102, 106–10,
  107, 113, 115–16
plutonium, 7, 10, 55, 58–59, 68–69, 77,
  85, 151
Porter, Charles, III, 73
Powell, W. Carlos, 31
Prather, John, 50–51
Predatory Animal and Rodent Control,
  177

Prescott, Heidi, 199
Price, V. B., 11
Private A Rocket, 90
Private F Rocket, 90
Project Bumper, 92
Project Paperclip, 89
Project Plowshare, 10, 85, 110
pronghorn, 23, 135–36, 138–39, 178, 183
property rights, individual, 13, 49, 148, 152, 160, 170, 192, 196
Public Land Order 833, 44–45, 151
Public Law 100-383, 166

Quatro Amigos Cattle Company, 154–55

rada cows, 65, 65
radioactivity: and depleted uranium, 14, 114–16; and desert ecosystem, 66–68; effect of, on domestic animals, 65–66; effect of, on humans, 64–65; effect of, on plants, 67–68; effect of, on wildlife, 66–67; in errant Athena missile, 109–11; public knowledge of, 70; safe exposure levels of, 62–64; at Trinity test site, 53, 56–74, 76–77, 80–82, 213n13; weather's impact on, 68–69
ranchers: myth of rural West as rightful domain of, 12–13; opposition of, to military seizure of land, 15–17, 40–42, 46–52; opposition of, to wolf reintroduction, 173–76, 186–89, 192, 195–97; and White Sands Missile Range Ranchers, 149–50, 153–59, 162, 186, 200. See also lease and suspension agreements; property rights, individual; range wars
Range Improvement Task Force, 164–65

range wars: background of, 144–50; and imagined economies, 161–70; and Taylor Grazing Act, 156–61; and White Sands Missile Range Ranchers, 150–56
Reagan, Ronald, 147, 156, 162
Real Estate Directive 4279, 42
Red Canyon Sheep Company, 45, 65
red wolf, 2, 173
Richardson, Bill, 159, 169
Robbins, William, 149, 228n9
Rocky Mountain Arsenal, 119
Roosevelt, Franklin Delano, 37, 150
Russell, Edmund, 3, 202
Russell, Keith, 186

Sacramento Cattle Company, 30
Sacramento Mountains, 21–22, 26, 30, 33, 43, 177
Sagebrush Rebellion, 13, 148, 162, 174
Saiz, Richard, 131, 134–37
Salt Target, 115–16
San Andres National Wildlife Refuge, 139, 141, 193
San Andres Mountains, 21–22, 25, 27, 39, 43, 59, 134, 182, 194
San Augustine Ranch, 167
San Augustín Mountains, 21
San Augustín Pass, 26–27, 201
A Sand County Almanac (Leopold), 181
Sanders, P. F., 159
Sandia National Laboratories, 10
Schiff, Steve, 159, 169
Schmitt, Harrison, 146, 159, 163
Scoyen, E. T., 72
Second War Powers Act, 37
Seth, J. O., 49–50
Sevilleta National Wildlife Refuge, 141
Shikar Safari Club, 128
Sierra Club, 175, 189

Sierra County Commission, 192
sika deer, 123
Silva, Filipe, 111
Site 65, 116
Skeen, Joseph, 146, 150, 153, 159, 162–
    63, 166–67, 169, 187–88
Smith, E. R., 48
Soil Conservation Service, 50, 53
Sonnichsen, C. L.: *Tularosa*, 21
Southern Pacific Railroad, 27–29
Spear, Michael, 185, 189
Staley, C. G., 31
Stenlund, Milton H.: "A Field Study of
    the Wolf in the Superior National
    Forest," 181
Stevens, Ted, 148
Stimson, Henry, 38, 40
Stringer, Bruce, 127
Subcommittee on Public Lands and
    Reserved Water, 165
Sweeney, Arthur H., 134
Szasz, Ferenc, 55, 82

tarbush, 32
Taylor Grazing Act (1934), 17, 19, 35–
    36, 40, 46, 150–53, 156–61, 165–66
Teller, Edward, 59
Tepeyac Cemetery, 83
Terminal Effects Research and Analy-
    sis Group, 115
Territorial Bounty Act (1893), 177
Thomas, Homer D., 76
Tillotson, M. R., 74
Toftoy, Holger N. "Ludy," 89–91
Tolson, Hillory A., 54
Tonopah Bombing Range, 41–42
tourism, 11, 13; accessibility of, 101;
    economic benefits of, 8, 57–58;
    exotic game and, 121, 124, 128,
    137; nuclear, 57, 70; shaping of, by

science, 200; and Trinity test site,
    53–58, 82, 213n9
Trinitite, 53, 55, 69, 72–75, 77, 81
Trinity Atomic National Monument,
    69–82
Trinity National Historic Landmark, 80
Trinity test site, 60, 61; commemora-
    tive monument for, 69–75; and
    fiftieth anniversary observation,
    80–81; as National Historic Land-
    mark District, 76–77; on National
    Register of Historic Places, 79;
    obelisk monument at, 75–82, 79;
    radioactive fallout at, 53, 56–74, 76–
    77, 80–82, 213n13; reclamation plan
    for, 53–58; as tourist attraction,
    54; White Sands Proving Ground
    control of, 76
Truman, Harry, 72
Tularosa (Sonnichsen), 21
Tularosa Basin, 15–52; annual precipi-
    tation in, 21–22; cattle ranching in,
    29–36; climate of, 21–22; drought
    in, 33–35; flora and fauna of, 22–23,
    32–36; history and geography of,
    21–36; indigenous peoples of, 23–
    26; militarization of, during and
    after World War II, 25–27, 36–52;
    militarization of, pre–World War
    II, 15–20; mining in, 29; railroads
    through, 27–29, 28; Spanish
    exploration of, 24–25; surveying of,
    26–27; water resources in, 30–32
Tularosa NM, 26
Turner, Harold R., 91
Turner, Ted, 142
Tyndall Air Force Base, 173

U-235, 59, 114
U-238, 115

Ulam, Stanislaw, 59
undocumented aliens, 105–6
Unexploded Ordnance Hazards and
    Munitions Management Team, 114
United States Biological Survey, 177
United States–Mexico Joint Commit-
    tee on Wildlife Conservation, 180
uranium, 10, 14, 57, 59, 85, 114–16, 151
U.S. Border Patrol, 105
U.S. Fish and Wildlife Service, 2, 171,
    174, 179–81, 184–86, 189–92, 194–
    95, 201
U.S. Highway 70, 5, 43, 46–47
U.S. Weather Bureau, 96, 99
utopianism, 11, 87, 95, 99, 117

"V-2 Rocket-Eye View from 60 Miles
    Up," 88, 89, 94–99, 218n7, 218n11
V-2 rockets, 44, 83, 86–101, 88,
    218nn6–8, 218n11, 220n30
V-2 Upper Atmosphere (Rocket)
    Panel, 92
Valverde, 26
Vanderbilt, Tom, 16, 84
Vargas, Narcisco, 83
Vasquez, Inocente, 111
Viking rocket, 91
Villa, Pancho, 106
Virilio, Paul, 97
von Braun, Wernher, 86, 89–90

WAC-Corporal rocket, 90, 92
Waddell, Tom, 142, 227n53
Walker, A. J., 34
Walker, R. G., 15–16
Walters, Ann, 45
Walters, William, 45
Warren, Louis, 228n9
Warren, Stafford, 60, 64, 66–67
water resources, 30–32, 182–83

Wendover Bombing Range, 41
Westbrook, Corry, 1–2
The Western Family, 148
Whipple, Fred Lawrence, 92
White, Richard, 10, 175, 203
White, Ronald, 132–34
White Sands Bombing Range, 48–49
White Sands Missile Range (WSMR),
    4, 28, 104, 202; description of,
    5–6; and Earth photos, 86–100,
    88, 218nn6–8, 218n11, 220n30;
    economic benefits of, 51–52;
    encroachment of, on WSNM, 100–
    101; environmental lessons learned
    from, 203–4; and errant missiles,
    87, 100–13; fiftieth anniversary
    observation of, 200; history of,
    6–7; original name of, 42; renaming
    of, 44
White Sands Missile Range Ranchers,
    149–50, 153–59, 162, 186, 200
White Sands National Monument
    (WSNM): agreements to add land
    to, 45; encroachment on, by WSMR,
    100–101; evacuation of, during
    tests, 44; location of, 6, 22, 27; and
    management of oryx, 119, 141;
    and Trinity test site, 54, 70, 77;
    V-2 rocket crash at, 101; and wolf
    reintroduction, 193
White Sands Proving Ground:
    economic benefits of, 51–52;
    establishment of, 6, 19–20, 43;
    expanding mission of, 82; expan-
    sion of, 76; and mission challenges,
    84–86; as natural security state,
    171–98; non-nuclear high explosive
    tests at, 114; opposition to, 50,
    212n77; and Trinity test site, 76;
    and V-2 rocket tests, 91–92

White Sands pupfish, 1

White Sands Ranchers of New Mexico v. United States, 159–61, 165, 168, 231n37

White Sands Wolf Recovery Area, 193

Wilderness Society, 175, 189

Wild Free-Roaming Horses and Burros Act (1971), 199

Williams, Edward, 185

Wise Use movement, 13, 17, 148, 162, 174–75

The Wolf (Mech), 181

Wolf Action Group, 189–90

Wolf Action Group et al. v. the United States, 189–91

wolf reintroduction to WSMR, 171–98; adverse environmental factors of, 194–95, 197; cancellation of, 193–96; and extirpation of wolves, 176–80; opposition to, by community, 192; opposition to, by military, 185–86, 192; opposition to, by Native Americans, 192–93, 235n43; opposition to, by ranchers, 173–76, 186–89, 192, 195–97; overview of, 171–76; planning for, 181–85, 192–96; support for, 189–92; and water resources, 182–83

Wood, John, 132–34

Woodward, Larry, 180

World War II, 6–13, 15–20, 36, 43, 52, 57, 76, 97, 100, 105

Worster, Donald, 56

WSMR. *See* White Sands Missile Range (WSMR)

WSNM. *See* White Sands National Monument (WSNM)

Young, Thomas, 49

Yucca Mountain nuclear waste site, 10

CPSIA information can be obtained at www.ICGtesting.com
Printed in the USA
BVOW03s1256040514

352333BV00001B/1/P